D1349554

THE LOST KINGDOMS
OF AFRICA

THE LOST KINGDOMS OF AFRICA

GUS CASELY-HAYFORD

BANTAM PRESS

LONDON • TORONTO • SYDNEY • AUCKLAND • JOHANNESBURG

TRANSWORLD PUBLISHERS
61–63 Uxbridge Road, London W5 5SA
A Random House Group Company
www.transworldbooks.co.uk

First published in Great Britain
in 2012 by Bantam Press
an imprint of Transworld Publishers

A CIP catalogue record for this book
is available from the British Library.

ISBNs 9780593068137 (cased)
9780593068144 (tpb)

Addresses for Random House Group Ltd companies outside the UK
can be found at: www.randomhouse.co.uk
The Random House Group Ltd Reg. No. 954009

The Random House Group Limited supports the Forest Stewardship Council (FSC®),
the leading international forest-certification organization. Our books carrying the
FSC label are printed on FSC®-certified paper. FSC is the only forest-certification
scheme endorsed by the leading environmental organizations, including Greenpeace.
Our paper procurement policy can be found at
www.randomhouse.co.uk/environment.

Typeset in 12/14pt Bembo by
Falcon Oast Graphic Art Ltd.
Printed and bound in Great Britain by
CPI Group (UK) Ltd, Croydon, CR0 4YY

2 4 6 8 10 9 7 5 3 1

For my dear Sascha, Sarah and Mother

AFRICA - LOCATION OF THE EIGHT KINGDOMS

MOROCCO

Mediterranean Sea

Almoravid and Almohad

Sahara Desert

Nubia

Jenné-jeno ○ MALI

Dogon

SUDAN

Ethiopia

Asante *Benin*

SOUTH
SUDAN

GHANA   TOGO

UGANDA *Bunyoro*
Buganda

INDIAN

OCEAN

○ Kilwa Kisiwani

Swahili Coast

ATLANTIC

OCEAN

ZIMBABWE

Zulu Kingdom

SWAZILAND

LESOTHO

SOUTH
AFRICA

Contents

Under the veranda of the Oba's Palace:
detail of Benin Bronze. (Drawn by Gus Casely-Hayford)

Introduction

THERE IS A WOODEN BENCH IN THE BASEMENT OF THE BRITISH Museum. It is not a particularly comfortable spot to spend any length of time. The seat is low and hard so joints have to adopt awkward angles to compensate. But I somehow find myself returning there, to sit, to reflect, to be; but mostly just to look. I return to the spot to be among the Benin Bronzes and the Ife heads, a room's worth of mysterious and controversial figurative brass plaques and busts that have intrigued and troubled generations of Western historians, anthropologists and ethnographers. Over the years I have felt a growing closeness and familiarity with these pieces. Like so many other African objects in Western museum collections, they exude a confident beauty. But there are aspects of their histories, their original use and context, that are frustratingly and enduringly obscure.

Mystery can be an important component of beauty, but ancient African history is an area of cultural studies with a suffocating surfeit of unknowns. A lack of knowledge, a dearth of evidence, of corroboration, have choked the subject, in some areas threatening the integrity of meaningful study. Beyond the unquestionable aesthetic merit of the Ife heads, there is plainly a great deal more to these objects; layers of narrative and context that have for the most part been lost. And while sitting on a bench filling the void with romantic interpretation can be thrilling, frustration at being left with both profound and basic questions about such iconic objects remains.

So I return to this bench to replay a mute discussion with the bronzes and Ife heads. I ask the same questions on every visit, questions posed by generations of historians to so much African material culture: why, when, how, and who? Over the years I have felt those big ambitious queries slipping to the status of moot rhetorical incantation. But perhaps things have begun to change. I believe that we have reached a defining moment in our understanding of African history. There are burgeoning innovations in thinking that will allow different histories to be constructed. New technologies and perspectives are being brought to bear in pursuit of a more profound, perhaps more sensitive understanding of the early history and ancient civilizations of Africa.

I began my relationship with the Benin Bronzes and Ife heads during the summer of 1976. I was still at school but I had already developed a voracious appetite for African culture and colonial history. It was a period when a pioneering generation of post-colonial historians, academics who sought to redefine history free from the lens of imperialism, were still the intellectual custodians of the subject. They wrote for the most part, with profound disappointment, of the shattered dreams and unfulfilled promise of a broken continent. But beyond new theories of history, Africa's material culture was different. Artefacts from ancient artistic traditions stood out as tantalizing glimpses into the past. I can remember reading about the Ife heads as glorious enigmatic objects of such beguiling, startling beauty that they could almost overcome the contextual void that surrounds them by speaking to us directly. So I set out to the British Museum to see them.

It was a gloriously hot summer and I felt every degree of that heat as I squirmed back down the steps beneath the portico of the British Museum following a short and unsuccessful visit. I had been told at the information desk that Africa, Asia and other material culture of the former colonies was not held at the Great Russell Street site; objects like the bronzes were housed in the Museum of Mankind. When I asked why the bronzes were not side by side with the other great cultures, I was informed that in a dedicated building there was more space to explore their particular complexity. Even at twelve I was not convinced – why was Egypt then exhibited in the British Museum just as part of the Western canon?

As I wandered around the Africa collection at the Museum of Mankind and eventually found the bronzes, I began to understand for the first time the role of a curator and a historian. The story of mute objects could be profoundly important to the living. In the absence of evidence, interpretations of these ancient things could become corrupted and contentious. Mystery, while romantic, could also offer cover to tainted perspectives and bad history. How could we sort the truth from the monstrous black hole of unknowns that threatened to engulf the subject?

Standing among the bronzes, I became overwhelmed by a feeling of cultural disorientation. I had come in search of a story in which I could see something familiar, but I was left with a range of questions. It felt personal. I was reminded of the emotional confusion I'd felt while going through my father's belongings after his death. On the top of a wardrobe I'd found an old suitcase; inside was a small box and two old rolls of cloth that smelt of petroleum jelly, paraffin and palm oil. I opened the box, and inside were dozens of letters and photographs of people unknown to me. I looked at each picture, each one an enigma. I tried to read each image as an artefact, as a piece of archaeology. Each tear and wallet-crease, the smell, the traces of termite and foxing, and an inscription on the back were all potential clues, but like the figures in the bronzes, they seemed to say very little. Strangely, rather than making me feel closer to anything or anyone, I felt distanced. In the same way, my physical closeness to the bronzes only made more stark the distance and barriers that obscure these objects. Up close you could sense that someone had laboured to make them, finessed and refined the metal to tell a particular story, but why, when, how, and who? I wanted to give back to the objects something of their story, their context, their due respect. While I felt frustrated, I also felt an unwarranted emotional connection to these things. We had both lost histories.

Two years later, as soon as I was able, I made my first trip to Africa, to Cape Coast in Ghana, to the home of my father's family. I wanted to visit the house where my father grew up. I wanted to begin to understand my history, my own archaeology, to really feel part of the culture of a place. I was surprised how easy it was to start such a journey. After just twenty-four hours of travel I arrived in fading light at the side door of a crumbling house set a few streets back from the frothing, fluorescing 20-foot breakers on the Atlantic Ocean.

It was not what I'd expected. As I approached the house, a spider's web stretched and collapsed over my face, and bits of shattered stucco crunched underfoot. My pupils tried to suck in the last vestiges of light, but the day was gone. Daunted but excited, I made my way inside. I could hear my great uncle running his hand around the doorframe, feeling for the light-switch. Even in the pitch-black I could sense it was a small room with a low ceiling. Camouflaged under the heavy tang of paraffin was a subtle secondary odour – palm oil and petroleum jelly. In different proportions I knew that particular combination of smells. I'd first breathed in that distinctive mixture when my Ghanaian aunts came to visit my family in South London. They would arrive with cases full of cloth and yam. They would lay out a length of *keta* or a fragment of one-hundred-year-old silk kente and tell us its life story. Roll after roll of cloth would be un-ravelled, each with its own biography, and then each length of material would be carefully packed away, leaving the house smelling of paraffin, palm oil and petroleum jelly. Standing in the darkness, I thought what a sad and unpleasant smell it was.

In the next few moments a number of things began to come clear to me for the first time. Firstly, history is not a singular thing. There are many kinds of history. Yes, history could be a list of corroborative dates and facts, but it could also be the ebb and flow of narrative between the dates and facts, the shadow thrown by an object on to the culture that created it, the ripples of ancient tradition still present in modern thinking. Yes, we could bring new technologies to bear in our pursuit of chronological histories, but there had also to be an empathy and understanding to build connection and story. We sometimes needed to allow ourselves to walk into the collapsed web of subtle possibilities of what history could be.

I already knew something of that kind of history. For my family, like many from Ghana, objects have always been part of our shared narrative. Growing up, cloth was a fluid medium that carried our changing story. The narrative that cloth wove around us was not a series of individual stories, it wasn't simply shared sentiment or nostalgia, it had a kind of objectivity. It gave us a frame for our communal history. They were more than records. What they gave us was a form of corroborative testimony. Scraps of magenta-dyed hand-spun silk created a framework for particular oral histories; as our story changed so too could the cloth be altered.

For many West Africans even ephemeral cloth could be the perfect vessel to carry a community's conjoined consciousness. The very fragility and portability of fabric served as a physical metaphor for the frailty and ever-changing nature of the family narrative. Cloth could and still can be incomparably important; in the right hands, each mark and tear can be read as an indication of some defining communal incident. A piece of *kpokpo* funeral cloth, its weft-face faded from lying on a dozen family coffins, was more than an archaeological remnant of a family's mourning processes; one could smell in its fibre a meal cooked in palm oil a generation ago, see on its surface where pearly globules of candle wax had spilt when the cloth was new, trapping the intensity of fresh cobalt blue for ever. The cloth had written into its fabric the collected forensic evidence of family life. It reminded us of our part-Nigerian ancestry; its fabric gave focus and coherence to the lives of people united by blood but separated by geography and death. And thinking back to the day when I looked through my father's things, I could now understand how objects could grow to become impotent, how neglect and isolation could destroy meaning.

I heard my great-uncle say something under his breath, then

the room filled with a flickering violet neon light. What happened next made me want to become an historian. He walked over to an old dresser, knelt down, opened a drawer and carefully pulled out a bundle of deep indigo-coloured cloth. He shook the fabric and let it unravel over his knees. Appliquéd to the surface was a multi-breasted figure suckling several silhouettes of soldiers, beneath a monochrome Union Jack. The material was old, the appliqué was wrinkled and worn. It was an Asafo flag. Then he began to speak.

Two centuries before Daguerre and Fox Talbot pioneered photography these objects held the record of the lives of thousands of people who lived on the coast of Ghana. Asafo flags were once used to mark out companies within armies on the battlefield and so their history was deeply tied into many of the complex political machinations along the coast. Part-traditional African military machine, part-European army, the Asafo company system was identified by its powerful flag-making conventions; traditions that had been learned from the European military, and adapted to fulfil local needs. Although the flags could be classified as weaponry, they were – powerfully, struttingly – objects of art. It was only through combining and distilling myths, layering history into folktales, and humour into personal testimony, that the correct image could be chosen. Like football chants that are created to exclude, to privilege an elite few with clever puns and clandestine codes, these flags are considered a dynamic form of people's art.

At the core of Asafo ideology is a philosophy of continuity. The Asafo rely upon a central notion of an enduring genealogical and cultural continuity. Not only do Asafo companies pass on their history through oral testimony, they also create material metaphors for the passage of time. As a family, which is at heart an army unit, they are never allowed to forget the ephemerality of life. And so most Asafo communities have become extremely active in putting down physical markers that can more readily defy the corrosive power of time.

These markers are not time slices, they are not created to

preserve in temporal aspic what they depict or the epoch of their creation, they are constantly open to re-negotiation; their meaning is constantly in flux. A flag designed to represent a particular moment in history could grow to represent periods of great duration. A flag that depicts a particular victory might become, through use, a flag of a victorious people. And the fact that the vessel for this narrative is so fragile, so ubiquitous and so portable makes it all the more powerful. And so flag-making has become a very important, highly guarded skill that is passed down within families and veiled from the broader community with great secrecy.

The Asafo flags showed one way in which material culture could bind and anchor a community; how it could become the basis for its history, its jurisprudence, its myths and morality was a revelation. But almost the only substantial things that can withstand the constant assault of the African environment are objects made from stone and metal – objects such as the bronzes in the British Museum. And the ancient history of African stone and metal is for the most part the story of an elite. Most ancient organically constituted material culture and bio-degradable archaeology has disintegrated, taking with it these stories of ordinary people and leaving historians fighting to resist the temptation to overstate the importance of what is left behind. Even while my great-uncle spoke I began to ponder how we might give back to pre-colonial African history some of this kind of contextualization. How could we build some of this subtle, beautiful complexity back into Africa's early history? Might it be possible to reconstruct some of the texture and tone around the surviving material culture, or begin to profoundly reconsider the archaeology and re-imagine ancient sites?

The Asafo flags tell the story of the colonial period, but were there equivalents for the truly ancient sites? There are a few places, such as the confluence of the Limpopo and Shashe rivers that divide Botswana and Zimbabwe, where a constellation of archaeological sites tell the stories of both the humble hunting communities and the powerful trading aristocrats. In such places we can do that rare thing: mine the ancient archaeology and the fragile remnants of a current anthropology to help us build a picture of a region in ancient times. This is not just the story of the powerful, the people who built this region of southern Africa a thousand years ago, it is also about the diverse social ecologies these sites supported in the surrounding countryside. But this is a rare thing. My big question was this: how could we extend that kind of connection to build complex, rich histories and augment our understanding of the Lost Kingdoms of Africa?

In the years since my first visit to Africa the disciplines of African history and archaeology have significantly changed. New technologies and theoretical approaches have emerged to fulfil the intellectual demands of post-colonial, post-Cold War, post-apartheid and post-modern generations. Each monumental change in Africa's fortunes has thrown up a new cohort of ambitious academics, and across the African continent a number of universities and research institutes have emerged, offering their own specialist historians and archaeologists the opportunity to write new histories undaunted by long-accepted constraints. In many instances local knowledge and empathy have informed their work, the customs and practices of contemporary Africa helping to reveal the ancient history more clearly than ever before.

This book is a record of a series of journeys I made across the continent looking for Africa's ancient past in the archaeology, the material culture and the lives of contemporary Africans. It was a trip that offered me the chance to reconsider what I knew about some of the most well-known ancient African civilizations and to test and corroborate some of the most innovative current archaeological thinking. I spoke to the brightest and sometimes the most radical specialist academics, visited sites, consulted the custodians of the traditional histories and engaged in traditional practices. I travelled on the ancient trade routes and walked the paths of pilgrims to find my way back to what remains of great civilizations. The culmination of each journey was a drawing together of new and ancient knowledge, I hope helping to move us a little closer to the Lost Kingdoms of Africa.

The particular challenges of considering a whole continent's archaeology can be testing. The logistics of travel on a continent that makes up a quarter of the world's landmass but which is in many areas sparsely populated and under extreme ecological stress did on occasion make me baulk. Climate change and migration mean that the archaeology of many of the ancient civilizations is now scattered in some extremely remote locations where the lack of physical infrastructure can make research and excavation very tough. But the rewards were many: the relationships I built, the awe-inspiring natural beauty I encountered, the variety and quality of the living traditions I saw, and, of course, the astounding history. And this is history on a monumental scale. The length of the timeline to be considered and the richness of the evidence are daunting: five millennia of archaeology – the oldest human remains, the earliest pottery, the most ancient rock paintings. It often felt as if history was bursting up through the earth everywhere, virgin archaeology in an almost unique abundance. The variety and quality of finds make Africa the rival of any other continent.

Over the course of two years I travelled the equivalent of two circuits of the globe on Africa's roads, working with dedicated crews in each of the countries, men and women who know the continent's history better than anyone else. Even so, together we barely grazed the surface of this vast, beautiful continent's history. But I am proud of this handful of histories. They offer a vivid sense of the sophistication, complexity and diversity of pre-colonial and ancient Africa, and the contemporary echoes of that past.

I began my journey in Sudan. Although I did not go to Egypt, I took time on the next leg of the trip to look at ancient Egypt from the perspective of their southern neighbours, partners, conquerors and slaves, the Nubians. Travelling through Sudan prior to South Sudan's secession in July 2011, I unravelled an enthralling story charting the rise and fall of one of the great African farming empires, set against some of the most spectacular landscapes on earth.

Ethiopia, the location of my second quest, is a place that claims to be the home of Christianity, where some of the earliest Christian traditions originated. Spread across this huge and glorious country, and still very much in use, are churches and temples that seem to corroborate claimed links to King Solomon, the Queen of Sheba and the Ark of the Covenant. This is a country that invites one to enquire into that ancient past, to tease out where history becomes myth and religion.

And then I travelled on down through the Great Lakes of Uganda, researching the devastating rivalry of the once struttingly confident Buganda and Bunyoro kingdoms and discovering the spell-binding story of how the maintenance of tradition ultimately led to bitter division.

In Tanzania I retraced the pre-colonial gold trade routes down across Mozambique from Africa's oldest ports into South Africa and finally to Great Zimbabwe, at each stage trying to tease out how they both influenced and were changed by their trading partners. In Great Zimbabwe I tried to unpick the enigma of that great civilization. In South Africa I went in search of the legendary Shaka, king of the Zulu. To some he is the 'Black Napoleon', a skilled and innovative military leader who through sheer determination and courage succeeded in uniting disparate southern African peoples into one of the most powerful kingdoms the continent has ever seen. To others he is a brutal tyrant whose rule terrorized the people and led to a catastrophic refugee crisis and chronic chaos across southern Africa.

I then travelled right across Africa to Benin City in Nigeria to discover a beautiful story of a people who, in a highly competitive and unstable environment, were driven to craft their identity through material culture. The by-product of their striving to tell their story on their own terms is some of the most expressive metalwork ever made. And then I moved on to Ghana, the land of my ancestors, to trace the origins of one of West Africa's most famous ethnic groups, the Asante, who came to prominence by defeating a number of their rivals and constructing a single overarching regional history. But before this campaign, who were they, and where did they come from?

I ended my travels in Morocco with the Almoravid and Almohad, Berber dynasties driven by rival interpretations of Islam that rose to dominate much of North-west African and Mediterranean trade.

It was a series of exhilarating journeys that took me from mountains to coastal fishing communities, from the most success-ful farming societies to the most isolated religious brotherhoods, across deserts following trade routes, through tropical forests, to the ancient slave ports. Travelling gave me lots of time to think about how we are served by the available history. Africa's ancient empires exist on an epic geographical and temporal scale and we need big history to appreciate them. Working intensively over a relatively short period of time in such a variety of contrasting places reinforced my impression of the continuity and longevity of many African cultural phenomena. I am completely convinced that vast trade and idea networks connected ancient Africa over extended periods of time. Some networks driven by trade may have been controlled by specific empires, others defined by ideas were more subtle and ineffable, but their effects could be every bit as profound. My feeling is that there is a paucity of macro-history that considers Africa or its regions as the ancient traders or nomads did, as a series of interconnected communities. It is fairly apparent that there was never a time in recorded history when this continent was not at the epicentre of intercontinental trade routes and systems of cultural exchange. But it is also time to acknow-ledge both the uniquely African elements of African cultures and the range and depth of contributions Africans have made to inter-regional cultural activity. If there are two stories that demonstrate that subtle complexity it's the history of the Buganda and the Swahili coasts: one an African state that traded and exchanged cultural ideas with almost every nation that has an Indian Ocean coastline, the other a still thriving African culture that can demon-strate a direct cultural link to ancient times, both bound by a Bantu lineage and the drive to create. Observing these large regional and continental stories over extended historical periods can reveal the cultural complexity and ambition of the African peoples in unique ways. I have tried to offer space to histories that both illustrate those big panoramic narratives and reveal something about a particular place or community.

To many, Africa remains the Dark Continent, backward and primitive, a landmass that for many thousands of years remained isolated from the rest of the world. But such a view of Africa is not just hopelessly out of date, it should never have held any currency. If there is a single conclusion to be drawn from my travels it is that Africa was a major global player long before colonization, and through that contact became fundamental to how the rest of the world developed. Africa determined our destiny. The continent is part of our story. Without it, the world would be a very different place.

Perhaps we are at a high-water mark; certainly a number of factors seem to have come together to make this an important moment for African archaeology. Years of international isolation and local neglect have allowed a shocking number of sites to be looted and destroyed, but that neglect has simultaneously saved much of Africa's more subtle and inaccessible archaeology from attention. The growing international realization and acceptance of Africa's deep untapped archaeological well is changing attitudes. And as new research technologies come of age there is a co-incidental strengthening of indigenous governmental support for African archaeology and a growing influence of a variety of centres of excellence on the African continent. It is a very interesting time to be looking at Africa's ancient past. Jaw-dropping finds that rewrite history seem to emerge from the ground with amazing regularity, and it still feels as though we are just getting started.

Meanwhile, tourism is growing across Africa, many people ironically attracted by the hope of experiencing some sort of authenticity and escaping the tourist-focused over-commercialization of many world heritage sites. While the income generated is often desperately needed, the growth of archaeology-tourism in Africa might well be the slow-slaughter of the golden goose. But perhaps that is a contradictory balance that only really unsettles the very international tourists who would be keen to visit. I am a proud member of that club, confused about what I think is best for the sites and for the people who live amid the archaeology, wanting both to shout from the rooftops about Africa's ancient past and to keep it a well-guarded secret.

I can live with those contradictory impulses, comforted by something I carried with me over thousands of miles on African roads and while meeting people in dozens of African communities – my great-uncle's thoughts: 'Africa's material history may be somewhat fragile, but thankfully there is a powerful history that exists both within and beyond buildings and objects, in oral traditions and a myriad of cultural practices still celebrated in Africa today.' It is a form of history that has shown impressive resilience in the face of colonialism, globalization, wars, migration and disease, and continues to underpin many communities. It is a spark that can bring the material culture to life; it is the particular poetic richness and beauty that distinguish African history from almost any other. It might occasionally be mysterious, but it is the kind of mystery that enhances knowledge.

This is a form of history to which it is easy to get emotionally attached. It is the stories that reach out from treasured objects to bring the past to life. It is the continuity of tradition that can still manifest itself in a variety of thrilling ways. I have been inspired by so much of what I encountered while writing *The Lost Kingdoms of Africa*. I hope that you draw some of that same energy from what follows.

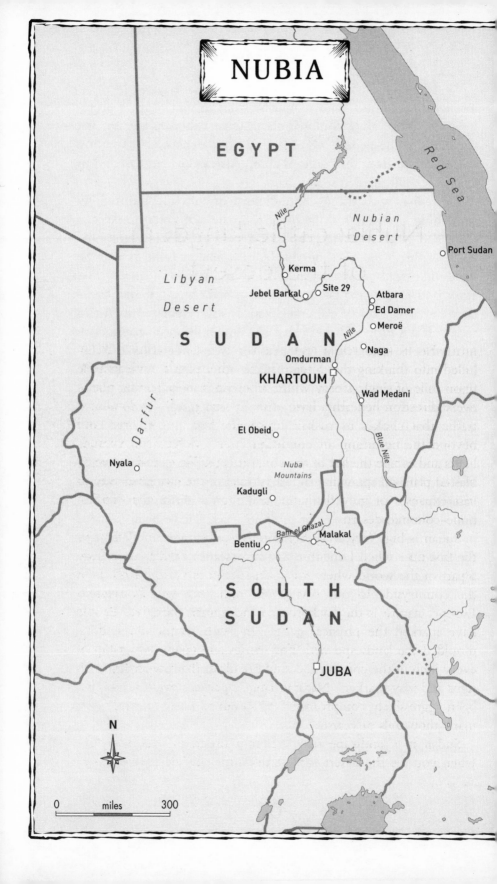

Nubia: cattle kingdom
of the desert

ARRIVING IN KHARTOUM FOR THE FIRST TIME, IT IS EASY TO BE lulled into thinking that Sudan is like other places, with its mile upon mile of single-storey white suburban houses fanning out in every direction beneath a haze of sandy smog, and the demented traffic that chokes its rush-hour streets. But as you drive out beyond the humming air conditioners and violet neon veranda lights and escape the last of the concrete bungalows and the sand-blasted plant on sprawling industrial estates, the city gives way to vast expanses of grey flat sand, and then a seemingly limitless bone-coloured desert.

Sudan is big, very, very big. I only really understood that for the first time when I encountered its deserts by car. I come from a part of the world where we mapped and broke the land, bent the countryside to our own ends, millennia ago. In western Europe, nature is the backdrop to the human narrative. People have marked the physical geography with fences and hedges, moulded the landscape with boundaries and taken ownership of every inch of the countryside, and broadcast that ownership with signs and way markers. Natural danger, perhaps even beauty, has been aggressively compromised by sustained human assault over many thousands of years.

Sudan is a landscape of a different order, as becomes plain when you see the desert for the first time. Before partition, this country was almost the size of western Europe, but with a smaller population than Spain. Even its post-partition borders demarcate enormous expanses of geography. Here the Western pre-occupation with controlling and containing land seems strange; here the landscape contains, encompasses, its people. This place never allows you to forget the smallness of human presence and the fragility of the biological negotiation that is the basis of so much Sudanese life.

Over millennia, the desert has aggressively devoured the human imprint, voraciously consumed everything with life in it, then preserved and mummified the archaeology in a shroud of sand. Leaving Khartoum, you immediately begin to understand that process as you are drawn down into the desert as if being pulled beneath waves by the wake of a whale. The irresistible gravitational pull of this country's environment and the sheer scale of time and geography that is evident in every vista simply rise up and overwhelm you.

This landscape is a buffer to the outside world, a desiccant that has turned parts of Sudan into a time capsule. It is said that millennia ago much of what is now desert was green, and that gradually since then humans have retreated as the desert ate up arable land, towns and cities, consumed cultures whole and left the north of Sudan a bleached, white, faceless wilderness, a space that holds the ancient history of this country in an impregnable sandy grip. For under the desert in the rocky outcrops where only the nomadic camel herders and industrial pioneers remain are abandoned towns and frozen material culture of the distant forefathers of the farmers and cattle communities that now live in the lush and fertile south. At least that is the theory.

Trying to put a historical narrative together, to build a coherent sense of ancient Sudan, is a complex, perhaps impossible task, but one that I will nevertheless attempt on this journey. It is not quite as nebulous an ambition as it seems, but very nearly. I'm looking for the legendary kingdom of Nubia – the traditional name for the northern part of Sudan, near the Egyptian border. For thousands of years a civilization dominated the area here, in what is now the

Eastern Sahara. Nubia was first mentioned by the ancient Egyptians, as a primitive and exotic outpost, a source of slaves and treasure, dancing girls and wrestlers; to the Romans it was a barbarian wasteland. Yet these people were sophisticated, conquerors in their own right, ultimately defeated not by their rivals but by this environment. Nubia has left in the desert some of the most spectacular monuments not only in Africa but the whole world. This was a major civilization, but its history is barely remembered.

I hire a white 4×4 with a driver and we drive from Khartoum north beyond the suburbs into the desert. But the scale of my task quickly begins to sink in. The areas that constitute Sudan combine to make an unfathomably huge area. I have only been on the road for a few hours when I ask my driver to pull over. Perched on the edge of the desert in my hire car I realize that this vehicle will not be up to the task I have set myself, to discover what Nubia was actually like, how powerful it was, and what happened to it in the end. I decide, like so many who have gone before me, to retreat to Khartoum.

Two days later, having learned to take this place more seriously, I take off from Khartoum airport in a chartered ex-Soviet Sikorsky helicopter, with a guide from the Sudanese Museum Service: Mahmoud Bashir, one of the country's most respected archaeologists. While a vast improvement on a car, this is not a luxurious helicopter but a huge, hollow, shuddering ex-military beast with a riveted metal internal frame and low, hard metal benches. It takes off in an explosion of dust and noise and carries us out low and fast above the Khartoum rooftops, across the northern suburbs towards the open desert, every rotation of the blades sending ear-splitting juddering pulses through our bodies, rendering us silent and eventually lulling us all to sleep. We have begun a journey not just through space but time, going back nearly ten thousand years to a time when humans first began to plant crops and keep domestic animals.

When I wake up we are still flying north, following the line of the Nile, hugging the thin strip of vegetation that surrounds the river and cuts through the endless grey sand. From above it is starkly apparent that if it were not for the Nile and its irrigation the whole of this landscape would be desert. And from the air it is easy to see just how narrow the strip of cultivation is, how fragile is the basis upon which human life rests. It is reassuring to have that gorgeous green corridor beneath us, but after 100 miles we leave the banks of the Nile and forge out into the desert proper.

The desert seems to throb hypnotically with heat, mirroring the vibration of the grinding blades. Each mile feeling hard fought, we fly on more than 250 miles into the heart of the Nubian desert – 15,000 square miles of arid sandstone without a single oasis. This is one of the toughest places on earth: the temperature in the Nubian desert is often pushing towards 50°C (120°F). But even from up here, hundreds of metres above the desert floor, it is obvious that there are still people working in what looks like a crucible of crackling burning sulphur. This, for reasons I am beginning to question, is where I have planned to start my journey, in the back of beyond.

It's dusk as the helicopter flies off over our heads, leaving Mahmoud and me at one of the most remote B&Bs on earth, with the reality of what we have taken on beginning to sink in. The hotel consists of a small stove protected from the desert wind by sheets of corrugated iron; the guests are allocated beds in an al fresco dormitory. We eat a small meal of mutton and bread and retire for the night. I lie back on my bed, my ears still throbbing out the rhythm of the rotating helicopter blades, and look up at the stars, wondering what the journey will bring.

From here we are planning to drive across the sands in search of Nubia. The name Nubia is said to come from the Noba people who settled along the banks of the Nile in the fourth century, when this region of Africa was green. It was a civilization that lasted more than a thousand years and only collapsed with the fall of Meroë, one of the most spectacular of the ancient African kingdoms. Tonight in the desert, lying under a burgundy sky laden with stars, it seems impossibly distant. The sense of silence, space and isolation is daunting. Dawn cannot come quickly enough.

We are woken just before sunrise by the sound of a car horn. I have no idea how, but after two days of near continuous driving my original driver has found me in the desert. He looks completely shattered, his eyes are bloodshot, but he is keen to get going. I respect his local knowledge, so I gather my things and within minutes we are on our way. I sit in the back of the car with the spectacular amount of equipment that is needed for this kind of trip. Every eventuality and contingency seems to have been thought of, but most of the space is taken by bottles of water. In front, Mahmoud and the driver scour maps and talk animatedly in Arabic. Mahmoud is young for the position he holds, but everything he seems to say crackles with authority and imagination. Trusting your fellow travellers in the desert is vital. We are completely on our own and we are on our way to a place that does not even have a name and is not marked on any map; archaeologists call it Site 29, and it is somewhere out here in a rocky outcrop. I have no idea what to expect, but Mahmoud tells me that anyone who is interested in the early history of this region must begin with Site 29.

We drive into the shade of a rocky outcrop, and the GPS flashes twice – we have arrived at our destination. At first glance there is nothing to mark this place as special; perhaps the sand is a little ruddier, but maybe that is my imagination. It is a valley surrounded on three sides by low, craggy sandstone hills, but other than that it looks like more featureless desert.

It is almost noon. Stepping out of the car, we are assaulted by a dry ferocious heat that almost instantly becomes intolerable. Without asking the question Mahmoud answers, 'Actually this is a very important place and here is where our story will begin.'

We climb up between rocks. I stop for a moment on top of a large boulder and scour the scene, looking for any signs of human activity or life. There is nothing. The only piece of geography that could have survived in recognizable form from ancient times is the line of rocks we are standing on, so what brought archaeologists here? And what did they find that was so important?

I climb between some rocks to catch up with Mahmoud. He is kneeling in the shadow of a double-bed-sized slither of rock perched precariously at an angle across our path. In Mahmoud's hand is a large stone. Very calmly he lifts his palm over the slither of rock and brings the stone down on its craggy surface. A gorgeous, true, deep bell-like tone rings out, amplified by the natural rocky auditorium.

'Is it a bell?' I ask.

'No, it's not a bell. It's what we call a rock gong.'

I know these objects. I sit next to Mahmoud in the shade with a stone in my hand and we try to beat out a staccato tune together. The surface of the gong has been shaped so that different tones are produced by different areas, rather like a convex version of a modern steel drum. Once we begin to understand the sound geometry a rudimentary rhythm forms, a galloping set of beats that are joined by their echoes bouncing off the rocks 200 metres away, filling the valley. It is instantly obvious how these drums could have been used.

For thousands of years a nexus of communication systems have carried news of political change, philosophical ideas and techno-logical development across the African continent. Stories have always been traded across Africa and beyond, slipping along the trade routes or flowing through the dedicated transcontinental communication infrastructure. The most important tools for dis-tributing information were drums, bells and gongs.

Many of the first Europeans to visit Africa marvelled at the continent's communication systems. During the colonial period the miracle of the tam-tam was well known. Experiencing 'talk-ing' percussive instruments would have been high on the list of any European traveller's itinerary. The famous eighteenth-century travel writer Mungo Park was mystified by speech surrogacy systems. Like so many of his contemporaries, he wrote about drum communication as one of the many unfathomable mysteries of a deeply inscrutable continent. Half a century after Park, the Victorian explorer Captain Henry Trotter described how people on the banks of the Niger 'could communicate . . . at a very great distance by the war drum which is kept in every village . . . so that there is an intimation of danger long before the enemy can attack them'. By then the view of Africa was changing: communication systems had begun to be seen as strategic weapons, as potential instruments to maximize localized control. In 1881, R. E. Dennet wrote, 'we in Landana heard of the wreck of the mail steamer, *Ethiopia*, sixty or seventy miles away one or two hours after its actual occurrence in Luango, by drum message . . . The drum language, so called, is not limited to a few sentences but, given a good operator, and a good listener, comprehends all a man can say.'

British explorers had already begun to utilize one of Africa's great advantages for their own ends. But almost simultaneously, as some drum messages were being used alongside the telegraph as part of the colonial communication infrastructure, percussive instruments became a way of subverting colonial intrusion, a method of spreading African news for Africans only. News of the fall of the British at Khartoum was said to have been celebrated by the people of Sierra Leone on the very day of the siege. That might be more folklore than history, but these communication systems really did work.

But what Mahmoud and I are looking at here is different. This is not a rock gong from the colonial period; this slice of rock was placed here more than seven thousand years ago. The sound is the natural result of the consistency of the rock but it has been fashioned and worn smooth by the actions of people playing it over and over again. Long before the Romans, long before the pharaohs, this is a sign of human civilization right in the middle of what is today desert. In the last few years archaeologists have found hundreds of rock gongs in the Nubian desert – possible evidence of a sizeable population. They think that the people here used the rock gong to communicate across the valleys, and that this was the beginning of Nubian culture. And what a spectacular voice from the past it is – an authentic sound of ancient Africa still resonating.

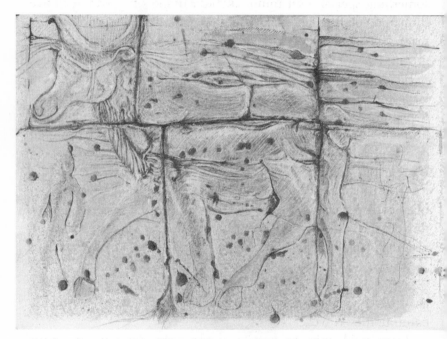

Cattle wall relief, Meroë. (Gus Casely-Hayford)

But as spectacular as the gong is, it is not what we are here for. Mahmoud has something else to show me. It's a bit of a secret, known only to a handful within the international and Sudanese archaeology world. That is until now . . .

As we clamber on over the rocks I can hear Mahmoud continuing to hum our tune, but then he stops and says quietly, 'Now I will show you a very special thing.'

Beaten into the surface of a large flat vertical rock is indeed something special – an unmistakable carving of a cow. It is five thousand, perhaps six thousand years old and we are only the second group of people to see it since this valley ceased to be green.

Rock art is the oldest form of pictorial representation known. Research has shown that the pictures are unlikely to be just depictions of everyday life; instead they concentrate on subjects of immense significance to the people who made them. This region could not have been desert when these images were made. Recent research has shown that some seven thousand years ago most of the Sahara was green. From above you can see the outlines of dry valleys, or wadis, which were once big rivers that flowed into the Nile. And between them stretched grassland savannahs of the kind you have to travel much further south to see today.

I ask Mahmoud, 'So this area here once upon a time would have had grass on it and supported cattle, and probably complex communities as well?'

'Even wild animals, based on the rock drawings we have around here,' he responds. 'We have lions, we have elephants, we have giraffes.'

Indeed with a stretch of the imagination you can see the cattle here, the river meandering its way across the floor of the valley, and someone at some point picking up one of these stones and making this art. It took thousands of years for the desert to dry out completely, so the cattle-herding – or pastoralist – society that created the rock art was able to develop into a more complex community.

The heat is too great to bear for long. We are soon back in the air-conditioned car, drinking water and driving back across the desert, marvelling at what we have seen. It may be monstrously hot and arid now, but all of this was once lush and fertile and covered in cattle and herdsmen. We spend the long drive north animatedly discussing it.

We are heading some 700 miles north of Khartoum, and less than 200 from the Egyptian border. Our destination is the small town of Kerma that sits by the Nile. Kerma was once the capital of a kingdom that the Egyptians knew as Kush, and which is today called Doukki Gel or 'the red hill'. This was the very heart of Nubia.

People have lived at this site, just above the third cataract of the Nile, for more than ten thousand years. Its strategic position is protected by shallow, unnavigable stretches of river to the north and the impenetrable desert, while the rich soils that bounded the Nile made it a relative paradise. Over the last few decades archaeologists have uncovered the remains of an impressive city here dating from around 2000 BC. And they believe this city was created by the descendants of the people who made the rock art in places like Site 29.

Founded on a fertile plain irrigated by the Nile, this city grew wealthy on trade and agriculture. The archaeology suggests that at its height Kerma consisted of a central city surrounded by a series of defensive walls and moats that contained a palace, a religious sanctuary and about two hundred houses. At the heart of this city was the huge mud-brick Deffufa, a large solid brick platform which when complete stood about 20 metres high and measured about 50 by 25 metres. It's the oldest known mud-brick building in Africa, and one of the largest. But it has no rooms. It's a solid block of masonry, a piece of man-made geography. In this place where the environment governs the landscape, this building has stood as a defiant piece of architecture against the corrosive power of time and nature.

As we park our car in the shadow of the Deffufa, Mahmoud tells me, 'We believe it is something to do with rituals. For sure it is a temple or something like this.' The truth is that archaeologists do not really know who the god or gods were that these people worshipped; archaeological exploration at Kerma is still in its youth. But according to Mahmoud it was the temple on top of the Deffufa which was the main focus, and which attracted royal attention.

We get out of the car, and it is only when I stand beneath the Deffufa that the scale, the bulk of the building really begins to dawn on me. This is ancient architecture on an Egyptian scale. The earth of the wall is deep brown and baked smooth. It lies there almost animate, as if it could roll over. I follow Mahmoud over a small hump on to the back of the sleeping Deffufa. 'You can see that surrounding the Deffufa is the administrative city of Kerma,' Mahmoud observes, and indeed on each side are the outline remains of a nexus of ordered buildings that surround the central colossus that is the Deffufa. Judging by the buildings the archaeologists have uncovered in the last ten years, Kerma was not so much a residential city as a place where people would come from miles around for ceremonies. Then, of course, it would have looked very different.

There is a small museum in Kerma that contains a number of finds from excavations of the Deffufa and the surrounding buildings. They give a flavour of Nubian culture. Even in cases with the artefacts numbered off and catalogued you can see how dramatic and distinctive the material culture of Kerma is: beautifully delicate earthenware bowls coated with black clips and glazes, flat-bottomed, black-rimmed polished red beakers, vases with covers that resemble small houses – exquisite in quality and variety. People started to make pottery extremely early in this part of Africa, even earlier than ancient Egypt, and at Kerma they specialized in it. The polished surfaces and black rims imitate the forms of polished drinking gourds I've seen used elsewhere in Africa. They are extremely finely made, and done entirely by hand. They were not using a potter's wheel to construct these pots, which makes them all the more miraculous. And the extraordinary thing is, this technique can still be found in modern Sudan four thousand years on.

We are soon back in the cool comfort of the car. Suddenly

everywhere I look along the roadside I see wide-necked, round-bottomed water-jars just like the ones dug up in the shadow of the Deffufa. Even today they aren't mass-produced in a factory; they are made as they ever were by women in small towns and villages. Just outside Kerma is a village famed for its pottery production driven by a collective of women and led by a senior potter. I ask Mahmoud if we can visit it to gain a sense of how some of those ancient pots may have been made.

The senior potter holds my hands. I can see from the look on her face that she does not think much of my soft palms, but she is prepared to give me a chance. She sends me out into the court-yard to pick up goat excrement – not a punishment but a vital stage in creating these pots. The pots are not made on wheels or coiled, they are simply crafted with slices of flat clay and a huge amount of experience. I have done some pottery in my time, but even though the potter crafts the pot before my eyes, how the material supports itself remains a beautiful mystery to me. In its own way it is as sophisticated as the mud-brick architecture of the Deffufa. This technique may be ancient, but it's perfectly adapted to conditions here. The clay is deliberately designed to be porous, so that evaporation keeps the contents cold, and the consistency of the aerated clay aids effective insulation in this violently hot climate. It is ingenious technology.

I do attempt several times to make a pot, but the meringue lightness of the clay simply will not support itself in my hands. I know clay, but this material is very different in consistency. Accepting that millennia of experience will not be imparted to me in a morning, I leave the women carrying their perfect finished pots out into the yard to dry.

Soon we are back on the road. What a day it has been. To think these are a people who have never developed writing. These con-tinuities of tradition and practice are perhaps an even more important insight into the culture of ancient Nubia and maybe they carry vital components of historical narrative for these people. Perhaps as I continue this quest I should treat material culture and archaeology with even more respect.

Before we head back out into the open desert we find a final dramatic reason to respect the people of Kerma. Archaeology has revealed some astonishing insights into this ancient city, but none more intriguing than the Eastern cemetery. Visually it is a flat, barren, wind-swept plain with only a brick-built fort to mark it as anything remarkable. But even from a distance the arid, deserted valley does give off an eerie feeling. It is where the Nubians of Kerma buried their dead. We are at the edge of what was once an enormous funeral mound, nearly 100 metres in diameter.

For a few minutes we sit in the car and simply look. It is a place with an other-worldly feel, a subtly undulating valley cemetery of grey sand that seems to suck the light out of the sky. The necropolis was first excavated by an American-led team in 1913. What they uncovered told an astonishing story.

Even from its edge, through the swirling dust devils, it is possible to see that the centre is marked by a white rock set in the middle of a smooth avenue that bisects the space. It is a huge area that was once the burial mound of a king. But he wasn't buried alone.

We climb out of the car. It is late afternoon, but it feels like dusk. A veil of parchment-coloured sand has completely filled the air. It is like moving through a snow globe. As we get closer, it is possible to make out the outlines of dozens of low tumuli.

Once you understand what you are looking at, the cemetery is in many ways more impressive than the Deffufa. Here the scale and influence of the Kerma empire are at their most vivid. When this cemetery was in use, the Kerma empire was vast. Its northern reaches are only now being assessed, possibly as far as Aswan in southern Egypt, and stretching to the south beyond Kurgus to the fifth cataract, more than 300 kilometres away. This was a mighty and impressive kingdom that more than three thousand years ago bartered goods from the Sahara to the Red Sea, from sub-Saharan Africa right up into Egypt.

This cemetery and the Deffufa would have sent a message to the citizens and trading partners of Kerma about the power of this Nubian kingdom. And they cemented that reputation in the most dramatic way. The archaeologists think that men, women and children were sacrificed to provide servants and retainers for their master in the life beyond. In all, thirty thousand bodies have been discovered in this cemetery, many of them apparently having died as a result of what would appear to be ritual sacrifice.

And among the human remains, clothes, hide bags, receptacles and chests, archaeologists have found something that ties Kerma directly to the people of the rock art: cattle. The grave goods are made up of substantial amounts of tanned sheepskins and leather goods – these people were deeply reliant on their livestock. And around the edges of the mound five thousand bucrania, or cattle skulls, have been unearthed. As the wind erodes the topsoil, the tips of more cow horns continue to reveal themselves. Looking out across the valley it is possible to make out row upon row of horns, the dark hollows of eye-sockets and the bleached bucrania – an alarming carpet for this strange place. It is more than apparent that wealth in Kerma was measured in terms of slaves and cattle.

I turn to Mahmoud, astounded. 'If that many cattle, that many people, were being sacrificed for one person, it suggests that this ruling dynasty was incredibly powerful. There must have been an enormous cattle culture out here and probably a big population that supported it. That really does get me thinking in a different way about Kerma. This was an enormous civilization.'

His response is simple and emphatic: 'It's a real kingdom.'

We stand among the graves as the sun sets and the sky turns burgundy. This is a strange but impressive place. The scale and relative sophistication of the Nubian civilization here in Kerma led Western archaeologists in colonial Sudan to assume that this culture must have been imported from Egypt or elsewhere. But thankfully now it is accepted that this was an indigenous development, a civilization created by the descendants of the people who created the rock art at Site 29. What they shared, beyond their tenacity to turn this environment to their advantage, was their love and respect of cattle. The horn silhouette I saw at Site 29 is identical to the haunting bucrania sticking out of the graves here in Kerma; indeed across this region you still see everywhere the same breeds of cow being led to pasture and to drink along the narrow strip of fertile land that skirts the Nile. Powerful continuities that crackle across the millennia. This ghostly ancient place is still a part of contemporary Sudanese life. Indeed, on special occasions local people continue to gather in the shadow of the Deffufa simply to be close to its history in this magical city.

All great empires eventually come to an end. And although four millennia ago this kingdom was thriving, it was dependent on an increasingly scarce and contested local commodity – water. Access to water was key to the success of the Nubian kingdom. It maintained the lushness of the land on which their cattle-herding society was based and was crucial to the empire's wealth. But it was a different story for Nubia's northern neighbours, the Egyptians. Their lack of pastoral land had led to the development of irrigation technology, but even with this it was a lot harder for them to transform parched desert soil into the sort of rich greenery Nubia had in abundance, thanks to the rivers and tributaries that ran through it. Nubia was a tempting target for the ambitious Egyptian pharaohs and there were frequent raids and retaliations. Around 1500 BC the Egyptians invaded with a mind to colonize Nubia, building fortresses to deny any chance of a local insurgency, and to secure trade and redirect supply routes, sucking valuable and vital goods northward. The Egyptians also aggressively imposed their gods on Nubia, constructing temples to Amun, originally a Theban cult but now a symbol of the new, confident Egypt.

Mahmoud and I are soon back on the road, following the ancient Egyptians' invasion route. The Egyptians' goal was not just to capture Kerma; they continued another 180 miles up the Nile to where the river bends at a sacred place called Jebel Barkal, a small flat-topped mountain that towers over fertile fields that stretch out either side of the river. Our objective is the same as the ancient pharaohs': to continue our quest for ancient Nubia at the symbolic mountain.

After days of tough off-road driving, the journey along the

tarred Nile roads to Jebel Barkal is smooth and easy. It is the end of Ramadan and people are going home to be with their families. We arrive at the town just as the Eid moon is rising and Jebel Barkal is coming to life with calls to prayer. It is one of those crystal clear evenings when the moon rises ice white. The city streets are overflowing with local men and women gathering to celebrate with food, drink and prayer. The only place we can find to stay is a dusty courtyard full of chicken coops, but we are tired and just grateful to be off the road. Beyond the walls of our court-yard dormitory the whole city ferments with music, smells of warming food, incense and perfume as dozens of Sufis compete to praise God on distorted speakers at the tops of roofs and minarets. We light a small fire, cook a meal and listen to the evening. Tonight the whole Muslim world feels close.

After our meal we wander out on to the busy streets to mingle with the celebrating people of Jebel Barkal and are invited to join a small group of Muslim Sufis who honour the traditions of a local sheikh who is buried in a shrine at the foot of the holy mountain. Sufi mystics were instrumental in the conversion of Sudan to Islam in the late Middle Ages. In the process they adapted and made use of local cultural traditions. So although this ceremony is clearly Islamic it may be that it contains glimpses of far more ancient religious observances from this area.

Jebel Barkal is one of Sudan's most important archaeological complexes. It is the site of the Napata, an ancient city that remains largely unexcavated. Before it was rediscovered by Victorian archaeologists, Jebel Barkal was the semi-mythological home of the Queen of Meroë, which had been attacked by a Roman legion in 24 BC. But by the late nineteenth century, when serious archaeology began here, there was a realization that this was a site of real significance. The earliest inhabitants of this region were Neolithic and there are pre-Egyptian graves, but the site became best known for a complex of temples dedicated to Amun.

The next morning we are up before dawn. Mahmoud wants to show me the Amun Temple in the early light, an ancient place of worship that is carved into the foot of Jebel Barkal mountain. As we get close to the mountain, Mahmoud asks the driver to pull the car over. From where we are parked the thick, squat mountain is bathed in a pink light. It is monolithically solid in form, but one side has been eroded to create a separate tall stack of rock.

Mahmoud wants to show me something. He points up at the thin column of rock standing proud from the side of the mountain. 'You can see there is a feature on the mountain itself like a very interesting pinnacle. You can just see, at the top, a kind of crown on the head of a cobra.'

I look at the stack and struggle to understand what he is saying.

'You can see if you look at the pinnacle,' he perseveres. 'On the top is a crown. And beneath the sides you can see the mouth of a cobra. And if you concentrate you can see part of the eye.'

It is then that it strikes me. The tall column of rock is the eroded remains of what was once a 50-metre natural feature embellished with the carving of a hooded cobra, its neck arched and ready to strike. I had seen the Deffufa, the graveyard, the cow carving above the gong. This was their match. The Nubians were masters of making marks on this landscape; this was the Egyptians demonstrating to the Nubians that they could be just as ambitious.

Around 1500 BC the Egyptian pharaoh Thumose III invaded this region. To the conquering ancient Egyptians the rearing cobra was a symbol of kingship. And here was a natural feature that signalled to them that within the mountain dwelt Amun, king of the Egyptian gods. The records tell us they felt that justified their conquest of Nubia. So they built an enormous temple to Amun at the foot of the mountain. 'At that time Nubia was completely controlled by the Egyptians,' Mahmoud informs me. It does seem unnervingly like colonialism. Egyptian images at the time of the conquest are explicit about the subjection of the Nubian people. They clearly regarded them as inferior. 'At that time for the Egyptians they are just looking at the Nubian as a barbaric savage . . . they used to call Nubia during that time "The Miserable Nubia".' The images also make it clear that the Egyptians made the most of Nubia's abundant natural resources and demanded riches as well as respect. After all I have seen of this deeply impressive culture, it is shocking to see the Nubians, who ruled this landscape with such style and confidence, laid so low.

And the Egyptians rubbed their neighbours' noses in their subservient role. There are many propagandizing images of Nubians taking tribute to the Egyptians: gold and ivory, of course, along with wild animals, monkeys and leopard skins – and of course cattle are prominent. The Egyptians even seem to have imported Nubian wrestlers to entertain them in the manner of gladiators, and preserved their sporting prowess in carvings and paintings. The people who had built Kerma's magnificent buildings had, it seemed, been reduced to the status of slaves – or certainly that's what the Egyptians wanted everyone to think. There's a suggestion that even the name by which we know them is pejorative: in one local dialect the word Nuba means 'slave'.

After coming all this way I am keen to get a little closer to Jebel Barkal. So, while it is still cool, Mahmoud and I set out to climb the mountain. The sides of the Jebel Barkal are steep and precipitous, but at one end thousands of years of erosion have built a ramp of loose rocks, sand and stones. We begin our ascent here. The rubble makes climbing quick and easy and within a surprisingly short period of time we are at the top. We sit silently looking at the views – the bend of the Nile, the temple below, the sun climbing over the horizon. What a couple of days it has been! We have seen glorious evidence of the Nubian civilization rising up and then being humbled. I am struck by the continuities that nevertheless seem to persist. History is piled upon history here; the gong that began my journey, hearing those Sufis chanting repetitive ancient prayers and incantations – all of it reflecting back over the generations, over millennia, telling the story of ineffable Nubia.

Surrounded by all these impressive imperial Egyptian remains, it is hard to believe that the Nubians were able to turn the tables on their conquerors. The Nubians may have been brutally colonized, but the Egyptians ruled Nubia only for a few centuries. The hard evidence of that reversal of fortunes is buried behind huge locked doors at the foot of the cobra in a temple built by a Nubian ruler called Taharka in around 700 BC. Mahmoud's position at the Museum Service really pays dividends at times like this: he has managed to negotiate rare access to this hidden tomb.

We weave our way into the belly of the mountain, into an excavated space in the rock, carrying torches that cast strange shadows which add to the eerie atmosphere. We round a passage and are soon in a series of hot, claustrophobic rooms. Even in the limited light the lifesize relief wall carvings are exquisitely precise. And one of the things I instantly recognize is the profile of the Jebel Barkal mountain in Egyptian times when the cobra had been freshly carved. It must have been an awe-inspiring sight, a towering gilded cobra carved on a mountain at the apex of a bend in the Nile, visible from up and down the river and across the fertile, highly populated valleys.

Mahmoud gives names to the row of carved figures depicted on the wall, stopping to point out Taharka making an offering to Amun. It seems that King Taharka represents the people. But these images show that Taharka was not just ruler of Nubia, he had also become a pharaoh of Egypt; as Mahmoud explains, 'Taharka is wearing the crown with two cobras which means he is the king of the two lands.' The subjugated Nubians had become the conquerors of all of Egypt.

Taharka was one of a dynasty of Nubian pharaohs who ruled over the entire Nile valley under the auspices of Amun, the Egyptian god of the mountain of Jebel Barkal. He was the greatest of the Kushite pharaohs and in his twenty-six years on the throne he transformed the region. He had come from a humble lineage within the royal household, but from a young age he demonstrated a zealous ambition. Working his way up through the ranks of the army, winning campaigns in the eastern and western deserts, he developed a formidable reputation. Egypt expanded under his leadership into the lands of the Phoenician port cities and into the Western Oases.

As we wander through the chambers, our torches highlighting details of the hieroglyphs, we pick out how Taharka celebrated his joint Nubian/Egyptian kingdom in the sanctuary of his temple. On one side he depicted the Nubian gods, with Egyptian deities on the other. This black African civilization held sway from the Upper Nile all the way to the Lebanon for over a century. These statues, discovered only a few years ago, give us a portrait of the Nubian pharaohs in all their self-confidence.

And though they were unable to keep hold of Egypt, the Nubian kingdom survived for centuries afterwards. But now they had acquired some Egyptian habits. From this time on Nubian rulers were buried in pyramids like the pharaohs of old. There are more pyramids in northern Sudan than in Egypt. But this wasn't simple imitation. It had been centuries since Egyptian rulers used pyramids, and Nubian pyramids are a very different shape. This was the Nubians celebrating their own glory.

But the Nubians had a greater enemy than the Egyptians: the environment. At the time of Taharka, temperatures were still climbing. The archaeological records show that the desert was steadily encroaching on the lives of Nubians living in this region. Although Jebel Barkal remained a key religious centre, the heartland of the Nubian kingdom moved 350 miles further south along the Nile, around a place called Meroë.

It is time for Mahmoud and me to leave. We have another long drive ahead of us, back out into the desert.

The desert is not a uniform bland environment as I imagined when I began this trip. In some places it is flat, it shimmers and luminesces silver; in other places it is rugged and mountainous and scattered with dramatic boulders and rocky outcrops. On the road to Meroë the desert turns a deep orange, the sand becomes fine and light and the vistas are often broken by the remains of pyramids and temples. The society that constructed these buildings flourished between 700 BC and AD 400 at the time of the emergence of an independent Nubian kingdom at Meroë. It's possible that the encroaching desert was their friend as well as their enemy, protecting them from another invasion from the north. It's certainly a period marked by the creation of countless new palaces and temples in what was then a fertile, rich environment ripe for some of the most ambitious Nubian building. The Egyptians may have left their mark on Nubian culture, but the Nubians were obviously a proud people. There is evidence of confident indigenous Nubian beliefs in these bold new architectural developments. This was a renewed dynasty sending a message to Nubia, Egypt and the world beyond that here was a civilization that would not easily be cowed.

On the road to Meroë we stop at countless temples and pore over carvings and hieroglyphs, but it is the Lion Temple at Naga that really reiterates just how the Nubians felt about their Egyptian neighbours. A line of relief carvings made in 200 BC shows the Egyptian god Horus being demoted to the back of the line. Here the great Amun of Jebel Barkal plays second fiddle to a completely non-Egyptian Nubian war god, the lion-headed Apedemak.

Meroë is the ultimate target of this journey, the culmination of the Nubian architectural campaign – the royal cemetery itself, where the Nubian kings of this period were buried in their distinctive pyramids. Between 800 and 290 BC, when Jebel Barkal ceased to be viable arable land, it was from this region that the Nubians forged new trade links and built a powerful and influential empire. Today the Meroë complex is one of the most impressive sites on the African continent, a group of almost two hundred steep-sided beautifully preserved pyramids that sit in a number of discrete complexes on a bed of golden sand. It is easy to see the Egyptian influence in the shape of the Meroë temples, but the relief sculptures on the walls express a decidedly unEgyptian, pro-Nubia world-view. Once again there's evidence of a return to their traditional way of life, where one thing was of utmost importance: cattle.

We spend an afternoon wandering in and out of the tombs, revelling in the magnificent carvings of a people at their confident height. There are signs of cows everywhere, but carved into the walls in the entrance of one of the last chambers we enter is something spectacular: row upon row of cattle lined up not as beasts of burden, not as milking machines, not as animals for slaughter, but

A Naga relief of Horus and Apedemak.

as supernatural symbols of the continuity of Nubian culture. Seven hundred years after they were subjected to Egyptian domination, the Nubians of Meroë were still a distinct people looking back on their traditional cattle culture with an aggressive confidence – a heritage that still connects them to African cultures today.

After our time at the old Meroë, even as beautiful as it is, I find it a relief to be back in the air-conditioned car. I am keen to see modern Meroë city; it is where Mahmoud carries out his main research.

Modern Meroë is something of a disappointment after the majesty of the ancient sites, but just surviving in this environment is something of an achievement. What remains fascinating is the network of ironsmiths. Mahmoud's speciality is the history of the iron trade, and many of the old techniques survive unchanged. The Nubians are thought to have developed the earliest iron industry in Africa. The first iron technology appeared here during the first millennium BC – around the same time as the European Iron Age. The archaeology shows us that Meroë became a relatively large industrial centre, producing vast amounts of iron. For a thousand years after the loss of the Egyptian kingdom, the Nubians at Meroë flourished. By the second century BC they had even developed writing; archaeologists long ago decoded the sounds of the alphabet, but no one has yet cracked the language itself. This was a confident, independent civilization far from the barbarian wilderness described by the ancient writers, justly famed for its architecture, its ironwork, its wrestlers and its cattle.

Nubia is a remarkable society that seems to have acculturated and come to terms with the aggressive, inexorable advance of the desert. The desert had long ago destroyed their civilization at Kerma, now too the Nubians of Meroë began to see their grazing lands disappearing. With the desert came one of the few animals to thrive in arid conditions: the camel. It was first domesticated in Arabia around 1000 BC and took some time to reach Nubia. They eventually brought a nomadic way of life to the Eastern Sahara, and everything changed.

As we leave Meroë, we see something very strange rippling through the heat haze ahead on the road. It looks as if the desert has melted, liquefied. It then becomes clear that we are facing an enormous camel train. Hundreds of them are being herded across the desert by a handful of men, following the ancient camel drives that link the southern Sudan with Egypt.

By the end of the fourth century AD the nomadic camel herders around Meroë controlled the trade routes, which began to undermine the Meroitic state. It may have been the loss of trade routes to camel-riding nomads that ultimately destroyed the Nubian kingdom at Meroë; certainly the archaeology suggests that by AD 400 the ancient kingdom of Nubia was in terminal decline. The Nubian cattle-based way of life had become impossible. There were new kings of the desert.

Camels have no fear, as we discover when we climb out of the car. They completely surround us, their massive bulks shambling past, pushing and brushing against the car and nudging us out of their paths. The smell of the mud on the camels' hides and the sound of their breathing and their hoofs in the sand are overwhelming. In the midst of the enormous herd are a handful of herders. These men have travelled all the way from Darfur, near the border with Chad. They've covered more than 700 miles and have several hundred more to go. This is the way of life that now dominates the desert where once the Nubians ruled. The herders spend their days guiding their camels from well to well, oasis to oasis. But they don't seem to think it is any hardship. The driving of this camel train will take another forty days, travelling 10 kilometres a day and resting when the sun is highest in the sky. They completely fill the valley, then they are gone, vanishing back into the haze.

I am left wanting to know more about these ghost-like men who come and go across the desert. I know from our helicopter trip that there are still small settled communities out here in the desert, people who eke a living out of this harsh land. They too are dependent on the camel. At the next water hole we find one of these small communities. They seem a humble group, with a handful of possessions. Are these people surviving descendants of the original mighty Nubians? But their ancestors lived their lives out on lush grazing land; these people cluster around small wells. It strikes me as both desperate and deeply admirable. We are miles from anything I would understand as civilization, but there are men, women and children out here seemingly thriving with their camels.

Mahmoud and I sit with them for a while drinking camels' milk and eating a crunchy sand-encrusted bread cooked on the ground beneath the embers of their fire. This is a culture perfectly honed to the desert. But it isn't really Nubian. To see if there are any traces of the old Nubian civilization I'm going to have to head out of these desert zones and travel further south. Here I also part company with Mahmoud, as he is heading back home. We have been through a great deal together, a lot of it astounding, but we have also grown close simply through talking on the long journeys about the unrelenting tenacity of the Nubian people, who never stopped remaking their societies in order to take advantage of the limited resources nature offered them.

I drive south on the longest leg of the trip, 700 miles to an area that still enjoys regular rainfall and is highly sought after by pastoral communities. After several days in the car, gradually but unmistakably the desert begins to give way to greenery. Suddenly there are more people, more traffic, more towns. This dangerous frontier region between desert and greenery continues to be a source of conflict, just as it was for the Egyptians and Nubians three and a half thousand years ago. We stop at a level crossing and watch mile-long trains full of food, medicines and UN vehicles wending their way towards Darfur. Scarcity of resources – the same issues are still driving the politics of this region today. A key component of the recent fighting in Darfur in western Sudan was a dispute over fertile, well-watered land. The same issues were a factor in the deadly civil war that engulfed southern Sudan for over twenty years, and the long-discussed partition.

After days in the desert I can understand why well-watered arable land is, and always has been, so contested here, but I am keen to complete my journey, to see if I can find descendant communities of the ancient Nubians, the people who first made this journey south. After everything I have encountered, I want a happy ending.

I'm exhausted when I arrive at Kadugli. Slurries of thick mud, for the first time on the trip, make the last few miles to my destination in the enclosing darkness long, tough and precarious. Everyone travelling with me is tired as well, so much so that none of us complains about our al fresco lodgings beneath the porch of a local school. Even the first rainfall of my trip and the tropical buzz of insects are not going to keep me from a coma-deep sleep. Just before I close my eyes lightning allows me silhouetted glimpses of the Nuba hills. I have made it to Nuba. It is said that these people believe they are descended from the ancient kingdom of Nubia. What will dawn prove?

For most of this trip the vistas have been limited to a very narrow spectrum of the colour palette – greys, and every possible variation of sand – but we wake to a scene of violently deep rich verdant hues that vary from almost blue to acidic lime; even the sodden ground sings out in a violent orange. The colours seem to jostle and shout after the muted tones of the desert. This is the Eden that generations of people have fled to.

I've come to meet Shaza Rahhal, a member of a traditional ruling family here. Her uncle, the leader of the village community, remembers the family traditions well and has passed down the history to her generation. Shaza lives in London, but her history is vital to her identity. She believes, like everyone else in this idyllic valley, that they originally came from an area near the ancient Nubian city of Meroë, more than 500 miles away. I ask her if the connection is credible. Shaza is emphatic: 'Between the Nuba people of this region and ancient Nubia they are all the same people. They just separated. There are some that stayed in Egypt. Some came to Sudan. The rest stayed in Meroë. The only difference between here and there you will see is the colour of the skin. But the language is the same. The traditions are the same.'

The extraordinary thing is that although we are miles from ancient Nubian lands, there do seem to be echoes of those far-off times. Young men still compete in what has become their most famous sport – wrestling. When the German filmmaker Leni Riefenstahl spent sixteen weeks in these hills in 1975 while composing *The Last of the Nuba* she tried to redefine this part of Africa, in a period of devastating drought and famine, as a place of strength, dignity and beauty. For more than a decade she had been living in the Sudan and knew the Nuba as well as any outsider. Perhaps her most beautiful images were of Nuba wrestlers, their massive muscular torsos and shaven heads dusted with white chalk. Those images evoked the work of the great George Rodger, who had photographed these wrestlers a generation before. Both captured their strength, poise and elegance. Riefenstahl remarked at the time how 'young children, not yet able to walk properly, begin to imitate the dancing and wrestling positions of their elders. From his earliest youth every healthy boy will prepare himself to become a wrestler. The children hold wrestling fetes among themselves and decorate themselves in a similar way to their older brothers and sisters. The best of them rise to higher and higher grades. Their heart's desire is to be selected for "initiation" by being the winner of the ceremonial wrestling matches, and then to be accepted into the highest grade of the strongest wrestlers.'

Now I have the chance to see some Nuba wrestling for myself. The village I'm in is tiny, but everyone has gathered to see the wrestling. Two young men skirt the edge of a small circle, sizing each other up. The smaller of the two jumps on to the balls of his toes, then trips backwards into the crowd and is promptly pushed back into the ring. His bigger opponent smiles – he has already won the psychological pre-fight battle. They are bare-chested and lean but surprisingly small. They are not the giants of Riefenstahl's images, these are ordinary young farmers, but they mean business.

The bigger fighter, sensing fear, lunges forward and tries to pull his opponent's left foot out from beneath him, but he slips in the

Nuba wrestlers, captured by George Rodger in 1949.

dust. Some of the women in the crowd laugh, he retreats, the smaller wrestler smiles. Then they throw themselves at each other, locking arms, their cheeks pressed together, legs tense and braced, arms taut, fingers tight, clinching in a momentary stalemate, each waiting for the other to flinch or weaken. Then, slowly, a leg wraps around a torso, a head is forced back by an elbow and they begin to writhe and twist in an attempt to rock their opponent to the ground. The wrestling is just as depicted in the paintings and carvings from Nubia's ancient past – the same stance, the same grips even. The crowd scream and ululate, then both wrestlers crash to the ground with an uncomfortable thud.

To me, an outsider, it is difficult to know who has won. Both fighters look shattered, glistening with sweat, their abdomens contracting and expanding in unison to try to catch their breath. But the referee is in no doubt. The smaller of the two wrestlers screams and punches the air before being lifted on to shoulders as the new champion.

But there's a price to pay for a revelation like this. Someone behind me in the crowd pushes me hard in the small of the back and I stumble into the ring. Everyone cheers. They want me to fight, and the newly crowned champion wants to wrestle me. I turn and try to back away but the wall of bodies is not parting. I am now a wrestler.

I throw down my hat in the sand and face my challenger. He is panting and his body is still covered in sweat, but there's a steely determination etched across his face. He wants to teach the visitor a lesson. I cast my mind back to the Egyptian wall reliefs of Nubian fighters for some tips.

Go in low and hard.

I lunge forward, but he swerves back out of my reach. I try again, even more forcefully, and inadvertently tread on his foot, my huge size ten boots crushing down on his bare toes. He recoils, his face wincing in pain, but I am off balance and he knows it. Within a fraction of a second he pushes my heavy torso back and I am bracing myself, preparing to fall, but I somehow grab hold of his upper arm and pull myself upright. He is much smaller than me but also much stronger so my weight is constantly cancelled out by his strength.

The referee takes mercy, stepping forward to proclaim my opponent the winner. The fight has only been minutes long but my body aches – and I know I have to perform one final act. I lift the winner on to my shoulders and present him to the applauding crowd.

It somehow feels so ancient, so right. But of course the similarities in style between this wrestling and the wrestling of old Nubia may be a coincidence. I know, as any historian would, that if there really is an inheritance from old Nubia it should show up in more fundamental features of the Nuba way of life.

In the crowd I spot Shaza who seems to sense that I am not convinced. She wants to introduce me to someone, Abdu, a cattle-drover, a man who certainly believes that the way of farming cattle has not changed in a long time. Shaza argues that this way of being with cattle 'has gone through tradition, through history, through family. From an early age everyone is allocated a certain number of cows. So if they can raise them, they can feed from them. They can use the milk from them to grow the children. They build on those. So obviously the more cows you have the more wealth you have.' Once again it is clear that cattle are absolutely integral to politics, to culture, to weaving the whole of this community together. There are cattle cultures like this one right across Africa, from the hills of Sudan down to KwaZulu in South Africa. And so many of them are connected to kingship.

Then, the crowd that had cheered the wrestling begin to clap rhythmically and a group of drummers start playing. It is the beginning of the Kambala, the Nuba's most venerated dance. It's possible that many of the stories played out in these dances may have begun in old Nubia, right the way back to the rock art people and Kerma. The Kambala's origins are in ceremonies which initiate young men as full members of Nuba society. Rows of dancers take turns to dance down through a column of people, but what makes it fascinating is that the headdresses are made out of cattle skulls. In this gorgeous hubbub, who could fail to be convinced? It is the ancient Kerma culture brought to life. The cattle masks, the women singing about the cattle, the men reliving ancient traditions through drumming and dance . . . so much of what I have seen along the journey made alive in dance.

But are these people really the descendants of that ancient kingdom? There certainly seems to be an inheritance but it's difficult to be certain of the links between the people of Nuba and those of old Nubia. Still, such a connection would only be the icing on the cake. The most important thing is the weight of evidence we now have for the existence of Nubia as a remarkable, long-lasting and indigenous kingdom, one that equalled, even conquered Egypt, leaving a profound material culture legacy that points to Nubia at its peak being Egypt's rival in more than just military might. Yet, sadly, we know so little about it. Nubia wasn't a barbarian wasteland on the fringes of civilization, as the Egyptians and Romans would have us believe. It may have sat out on the edge of a great desert, but it was a significant power that developed independently with a distinctive way of life. In the end it fell victim to climate change, but I think Nubian ideas of power, wealth and kingship continue to resonate in modern Africa. As archaeology reveals more of this great kingdom, I believe its cultural sophistication will continue to amaze us, and to challenge our ideas.

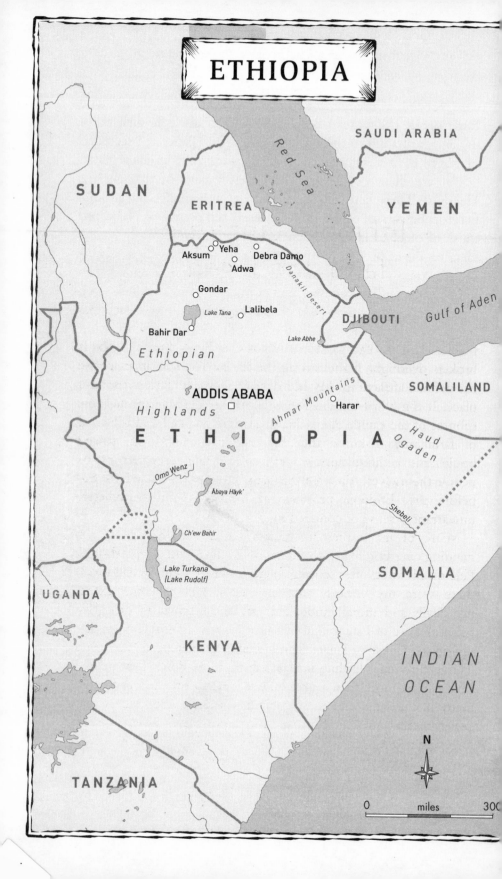

Ethiopia: empire of faith and legend

I AM NOT A GREAT COFFEE DRINKER, BUT AT THE END OF A broken overnight flight, strong, black, stewed Ethiopian coffee has definite attractions. My taxi driver tells me he knows the very place. It is my first time in Ethiopia, but as we drive through the suburbs of the capital Addis Ababa I am overcome with a feeling of familiarity. I know the city, not just the broad straight boulevards or the distinctive earthy odour, but something of the people themselves. It is a feeling many Western travellers have had before me. Ethiopia prompts an immediate and completely unwarranted sense of connection.

Many of my earliest memories are television related. Ali standing over Foreman's crumpled body, the World Cup debutant Pelé on his knees after scoring, Neil Armstrong's one small step – these were my wizards and fairy tales, and to some extent my devils and moral guide. But my most powerful early TV memories are of Ethiopia in 1973, of Jonathan Dimbleby reporting on the *Unknown Famine* standing among emaciated Wollo and Tigray children, pleading for something to be done. It pre-dated Live Aid by more than a decade, but it was a situation driven by many of the same endemic problems: drought, crop failure and governmental inertia. But the most powerful, poignant and lingering image was the people, who in their desperation somehow managed to maintain a resolute dignity. I remember watching and thinking that one day I would find a way to get there.

The international aid response only heaped further pressure on an already weakened leadership. Haile Selassie, descendant of King Solomon and the Queen of Sheba – more than a head of state – could not claim ignorance of the situation, nor could he admit to having ignored it. The once loved, once seemingly omnipotent emperor looked vulnerable, weak even. More than the logistical chaos that surrounded the last days of his regime, it was this frailty and procrastination in the face of impending disaster that seemed to affect hearts and minds. It made the previously inconceivable seem reasonable, perhaps inevitable. Within months Selassie, the personification of the state, a living deity, was deposed and placed under house arrest and the military government declared an end to the Solomonic dynasty. Within a year Selassie was dead, some say smothered by his enemies, others that like his empire his body simply buckled and gave way beneath him. It felt as if a time of legend had come to a close; a culture in which epic historical narratives had flowed seamlessly through current affairs was at an end. It was the climax of a cascade of seismic events over the course of a handful of months that finally snuffed out one of the world's oldest living dynasties.

At its height, Ethiopia was more than a kingdom, more than an empire. For much of the colonial era it was a symbol of African pride and independence, a political philosophy in a culture, in a way of thinking, in a people. In 1911 my grandfather, who lived thousands of miles away in West Africa, penned one of the earliest pieces of Pan-African fiction and called it *Ethiopia Unbound*. For many of his generation the very word Ethiopia was synonymous with a continental African history and black resistance. The colours of the Ethiopian flag had become the colours of Pan-Africanism; red for the blood spilt in fighting for freedom, gold for the mineral wealth of the continent, and green for the fertility of its lands. Ethiopia is, and always has been, special. While so many other African territories fell to a frenzy of European colonial expansion, Ethiopia stood like a beacon of resistance and pride. But for many Pan-Africanists the moment in modern history that encapsulated what a properly marshalled and focused Ethiopia was capable of was the battle of Adwa.

In 1889, after centuries of fractious inter-regional relations, Menelik II, Emperor of the Shewa, with the support of the Italians, defeated his neighbours, the Tigray and the Amhara, and consolidated his empire, creating a contiguous Ethiopian landmass from the Red Sea coast to the border with Sudan. But this was not a time for celebration. The alliance with the Italians that had delivered the emperor victory began almost immediately to unravel. What the Ethiopians had seen as a strategic partnership the Italians saw as an opportunity to institute a protectorate, control Ethiopia and open up lucrative trade routes from the coast into the African interior. War seemed inevitable. Italy felt under huge political pressure to give itself a stake in the economic and strategic benefits of colonial engagement in Africa. They looked across Africa at the French, the British and the Germans who had managed with relatively small but well-armed and well-organized forces to defeat and maintain control of vast African territories, and they felt confident.

In late 1896, armed with light firearms, a small advance Italian unit marched deep into Ethiopian territory to test the water. What happened next surprised everyone – everyone except the Ethiopians, who had spent years building stockpiles of weapons and ammunition and training troops. They saw a strong army as a key constituent in the cementing of an equitable relationship with their Italian allies; they never intended to be junior partners. And they demonstrated that in the most vivid way possible. The Italians suffered an almost unimaginable defeat, simply overwhelmed by a huge Ethiopian force. What remained of the unit limped back and rejoined the main Italian force, surprised, shaken, but smarting for revenge.

The Italians had learned a lesson: this was an army that needed to be respected. Perhaps it was arrogance, maybe it had some basis in fact, but despite the defeat the Italians still thought there was something they as Europeans had in their favour: the relative tightness and superior training of their forces. The loss of the

Menelik II and troops rally before the battle of Adwa.

advance unit had been costly in one sense, but the foray had provided valuable intelligence. The Italians now knew that the Ethiopian army was a diverse group of a hundred thousand men mostly living off the land, a core force of trained fighters expanded by additional numbers of itinerant followers and casual supporters. This torrent of people seemed to be quickly depleting already scant local supplies. With this new information the Italians drew some confidence from surmising that once food supplies had begun to dwindle, substantial numbers of the Ethiopian force might begin to drift away from their ranks and return to their families.

In increasingly desperate messages home the Italians asked and then begged for more time. But their government made it clear that for domestic political reasons time was not a luxury the Italian forces could be afforded. The government was under pressure; it wanted results, and quickly. And so, against almost impossible odds, three Italian brigades were sent to engage the Ethiopian army in the hilly area around Adwa, a rough region where huge rock formations and boulders fracture the landscape, making navigation tough and travel difficult, even perilous. But perhaps they could use the landscape to their advantage and surprise the Ethiopians.

Tragically, when they needed it, their training and organizational tightness was found wanting. As they marched through the night on difficult terrain the three brigades became separated. As dawn approached any thoughts of the Italians using surprise or geography to their advantage had already been dashed. The Italian forces were spread out and isolated over miles of rugged stony ground; bad maps and broken supply lines made things worse.

What happened next is part of Ethiopian legend. Some say the Ethiopians were already preparing to retreat to replenish supplies, others that Menelik the master-tactician had risen early in a state of preparedness. Whatever the truth, as the sun rose the Ethiopians were ready, dressed, armed and waiting. The fighting was over by noon, the Italians broken, beaten and humiliated. Seven thousand had lost their lives, five thousand were wounded, and the surviving stragglers limped back towards the coast having left behind for a jubilant Ethiopian army an arsenal of their most valuable weapons. Although Italian forces eventually returned and took control of Ethiopia, the population never completely capitulated and the country and the battle of Adwa remained for people across the continent and beyond a shining symbol of African resistance and pride in the face of colonial encroachment.

The battle of Adwa is one of many glorious chapters in a long and romantic Ethiopian history of sage and brave emperors, besieged castles, ferocious battles and ancient churches. Some of that history, like Adwa, can be corroborated by contemporary accounts, records and paintings, but the fabric of much of pre-medieval Ethiopian history is only evidenced through oral histories, mythologies and a fragile trail of surviving material culture. On this journey I want to try to tease out the history of Ethiopia's monarchy, to unearth the story of the oldest continuous Christian narrative and to see if there is any basis for their assertion that this is the home of the most important Christian artefact: the Ark of the Covenant.

Without doubt the most important source of those ancient Ethiopian histories is the thirteenth-century manuscript the *Kebra Nagast* ('The Glory of the Kings'), written in Ge'ez, a South Semitic language which like Latin is long dead but is still used in some religious ceremonies. It tells the story of the emperors of Ethiopia and does it in a form that seems part record and part scripture. The 117 chapters are obviously written by a number of hands, but they combine to form a fascinating insight into the complex machinations of a dynasty over millennia. Where they are overtly partial or fantastical they give us a sense of the internal thinking and sensitivities within the empire. But a significant amount of the history is clearly supported by other verifiable sources. It is a unique document in which the accounts of figures such as Solomon and Sheba straddle both sides of the line between legend and known history.

The *Kebra Nagast* makes some interesting claims about the Ethiopian empire's royal line. The kingdom, it states, was founded in 950 BC. Menelik, the first emperor, was a man with illustrious parents, King Solomon and Queen Makeda, better known as the legendary Queen of Sheba. Sheba was the monarch of a kingdom that was believed to have been located in Yemen, Ethiopia, or perhaps ranged across both. According to the Book of Kings in the Bible, she heard of the wisdom of King Solomon of Israel and paid a visit, carrying many of the goods that Ethiopia is famous for: spices, gold and rare woods. Solomon, beguiled by her, reciprocated, offering her 'everything she desired'. The genealogical link between the royal family and the Old Testament was important: it conferred on every subsequent emperor of Ethiopia a divine, cultural and historical legitimacy.

Some observers have said that the weaving of the royal genealogy deep into the Old Testament was done consciously and systematically at state level over millennia. This may have been because these were genuine links and the ancient Ethiopian emperors were justly proud; it may have been done because there was only tenuous evidence and the royal family wanted to strengthen their weak connections to the narrative of the Bible. But it also has to be considered that the links between the Ethiopian royal family and the Old Testament were fabricated to lend legitimacy to a new dynasty. Trying to deconstruct the past, or to draw out the substantive history from fabricated and embroidered myth, is difficult; perhaps I may have to accept it is now impossible. But there remain clues in the buildings and living traditions, in the material culture and the landscape, that may help us to answer some questions about the truth behind the connections between Ethiopia's emperors and the Bible, perhaps even to uncover the links between Solomon and Sheba and the ancient kingdom of Ethiopia.

The best way to begin to answer such questions, to blow a little of the fog from ancient Ethiopian history, is to speak to those who hold the official history. Today, the accepted primary custodian of the state history is the Abuna, a living conduit to God – Father Paulos, the Metropolitan Bishop and head of the Ethiopian Church. In the absence of an Ethiopian emperor the Abuna is the

Haile Selassie I, Conquering Lion of the Tribe of Judah, King of Kings,
Emperor of Ethiopia, Elect of God.

most important spiritual figure in the state. Historically the Abuna was appointed by the Pope of Alexandria, the Patriarch of All African Christians and head of the Coptic Church, but after the Second World War a politically ascendant Haile Selassie came to an agreement with the Coptic Church that all subsequent heads of the Ethiopian Church would be Patriarchs in their own right, direct conduits to God.

The Abuna has a palace in the centre of Addis Ababa. As one might expect, getting access isn't easy. But once I've been granted permission to meet him I am welcomed by palace staff with great warmth. The palace is not just the Abuna's home, it is also a glorious warren of stately municipal buildings of varying ages in which every area of Church management is coordinated. Round every corner, in every doorway gather groups of chattering, willowy priests and novices wrapped in their brilliant white cassocks and hats. It is far from being dry and dusty like many ancient state institutions. The palace feels vibrant and loved, its halls and stairwells full of gossip, discussion and life.

After weaving through crowds of priests, I make my way up an imposing staircase to the first floor and push my way through several layers of thick curtains into a large, cool, quiet room with deep red carpets and comfortable chairs – an ante-chamber where the Abuna receives his guests. It is not a room designed to intimidate, although waiting there to see a man who is considered by many of his followers to be a living god does make me feel uneasy. But the smiling grey-bearded man who enters is far less formal than I'd imagined, though every bit as imposing and impressive. He is dressed in layers of white, and around his neck hangs a buttery gold cross studded with cherry-coloured stones; in his right hand he softly holds a gold cross pattée. This man is the Patriarch of the Ethiopian Church, the embodiment of the state, religion and history. He makes it very clear that he wants me to feel at ease, but I find that difficult.

In a quiet voice that makes you sit forward in your seat and listen hard, Abuna Paulos explains how a thousand years before Christianity Ethiopians had already officially accepted the Old

Testament order and adopted its tenets. This was a state that accepted Judaism before it adopted Christianity. For the Abuna, that conversion from Judaism to Christianity was not a profound philosophical change but an incremental cultural development, building new Christian thinking upon the good foundations of Judaism. And so the Ethiopian Church, a single institution with one belief system, is today three thousand years old, dating from the very beginning of the Ethiopian kingdom. Faith and the dynasty of emperors were born together. The foundation of this belief lies in a fascinating but somewhat astonishing claim: that the very basis of Judaism lies in Ethiopia and that 'the Ark of the Covenant, containing the Ten Commandments, was brought here from Jerusalem in 950 BC by Menelik I, the son of King Solomon'.

I leave the Abuna's palace a little more confused than when I'd arrived. The Patriarch of the Ethiopian Church, a man his followers claim is a living god, had not only said that the Ark of the Covenant was in his Church's possession, but that Ethiopia is the fount of the Judaeo-Christian tradition, which ties the kingdom directly to the world of the Old Testament, the world of Solomon and Sheba. He had ostensibly answered many of the questions that had drawn me to Ethiopia, but he could offer me no real empirical proof. As an outsider I would never be allowed access to the Ark; it is deemed so holy that only a limited few are allowed to see it. And despite what the *Kebra Nagast* says, there is no historical evidence that Menelik was really the son of Solomon and Sheba. I respect the kind of faith that makes these seemingly untenable facts the basis of a culture and widely followed belief system, but I am keen to discover more, to find something concrete that I can touch, feel, read, use for corroboration.

Can there be any surviving evidence to support the Abuna's beliefs? And where shall I start looking for it? I have a theory. I want to try to track back across millennia of Ethiopian history, to look for clues at a point where recorded history begins to fold into the time of *Kebra Nagast*, the time of legend.

I drive out of Addis eastwards about 500 kilometres, up on to the eastern extension of the highlands, close to the border with Eritrea, to the ancient walled city of Harar. It has been said that Harar is Ethiopia at its most magical, unruly and complex. It is the city that attracted the romantic rebels Arthur Rimbaud and Richard Burton, a melting pot of multiple worlds that collide and collapse into Ethiopian culture. Attracted by coffee and the possibilities of the dynamic trading hub, Burton and then Rimbaud were some of the first Europeans to visit the city.

For centuries this old Muslim city was the trading gateway between Ethiopia, the Horn of Africa and the Arabian Peninsula beyond. It has acted as a conduit for goods and ideas that have entered and left Ethiopia for hundreds of years. It was founded between the seventh and eleventh centuries and emerged as a centre not just of trade but also of Islam, boasting dozens of mosques, shrines and important Sufis. Traditionally one of Ethiopia's most fertile and productive regions, supplying and exporting huge quantities of grain, it thrived in good years and was the last place to suffer in lean times. It is said that more crop species can be found in this area than anywhere else on the continent – staple crops, but also luxurious goods such as frankincense.

For Rimbaud, a poet and a merchant who spent time here towards the end of the nineteenth century, Harar was a place that was made for him, full of exotic goods, intellectual hybridity and liberal thinking. As Rimbaud described it, Harar was a romantic walled city of twenty thousand people where almost anything was tolerated. It seemed a frontier for many things, cultural and conceptual. While that did indeed make it romantic, it also made it wild. In Rimbaud's day the sanitary system consisted of throwing refuse, including corpses, over the city walls to the waiting hyenas. And when Rimbaud grew bored of coffee he turned, in this semi-feral town, to gunrunning for King Menelik II of Shewa, helping him to conquer Harar.

It turns out to be a great place to begin an Ethiopian journey. Wandering around the old market below the crenulated city walls; feeding offal off-cuts to semi-tame hawks and hyenas; sampling frankincense and the local stimulant khat on the market stalls; getting lost in the labyrinth of backstreets; getting high on the repeated khat-suffused rhythms of sleepy Sufi songs – you can easily get a sense of the chaotic entrepreneurial dynamism that made Ethiopia.

While this city introduced and integrated new goods and thinking from wide and far, the Muslim population played a remarkable role maintaining Ethiopia's independence and shoring up the relationship between Ethiopian Christianity and royal legitimacy. In the seventeenth century, Ethiopian Muslims allied with Ethiopian Christians in a deal brokered by an emperor named Fasiladas.

Fasiladas, whose name means 'to whom the world bows', was born at the turn of the seventeenth century and was proclaimed emperor in 1632; he therefore straddles the gap between the modern period of corroborative dates and the ancient time of the biblical dynasty. He came to the throne after a period of instability and war and wanted to make his mark. His first act was to restore the full status of the Ethiopian Orthodox Church, requesting the appointment of a new Abuna from the Patriarch of Alexandria. Fasiladas was ambitious, he wanted to restore the glory of the Ethiopian empire, but there were complex challenges. In the years before he had taken the throne Portuguese traders had arrived with two purposes in mind. One was to take over the lucrative Muslim trade routes. To the east, the other was to find a mythical African Christian ruler by the name of Prester John. The idea of a Christian Patriarch, a descendant of one of the Magi, who would lead a definitive crusade had been popular in Europe from the late Middle Ages. Over the centuries the legend of Prester John was embellished and the idea that he was African was increasingly accepted.

The Portuguese did not find Prester John, but in Fasiladas they found a real Ethiopian Christian king who seemed every bit as powerful, well connected and ambitious as the mythic figure they had sought. The only problems, as the Portuguese saw it, was that Fasiladas was not Catholic and the trade routes were controlled by Muslims and protected by the emperor.

Initially the Portuguese enjoyed success building new trade routes linking Ethiopia with Europe and their other Indian Ocean trading outposts in India and beyond, but their attempts to convert the local population to Catholicism drew attention and angered the emperor and his Muslim allies. The emperor was growing in confidence and ambition and unlike his predecessors saw no reason to exercise diplomatic caution. The Portuguese promotion of Catholicism, an alien version of Christianity, united Ethiopian Christian and Muslim under the banner of Emperor Fasiladas in a bid to expel them and their Jesuit priests. Fasiladas confiscated Portuguese-owned land and began to put pressure on the Portuguese merchants in an attempt to force them to leave. The Portuguese resisted his efforts: Ethiopia was logistically and economically vital to their Indian Ocean supply chains. When he later heard that the Portuguese had tried to invade Mombasa further down the coast, Fasiladas felt fully justified in banishing the remaining Portuguese from his land.

These things are running through my head as I leave Harar for Lake Tana to catch a boat to Gondar, the hilltop capital built by Emperor Fasiladas. Here you really get a sense of the man in the city he conceived. Dominated by an impressive castle, Gondar is a fairy-tale place. The towers and crenulations of the central castle complex might well have been constructed for defensive reasons, but Fasiladas was also keen to build a visually fitting capital for his empire. This was the administrative hub of the region and many of the most lucrative trade routes came over the mountains to Gondar. The most precious goods and most important people would have come here to trade and to be in the city of the great emperor. It became known as the 'Camelot of Africa'. Gondar was also a place of ideas. Sadly, the rooms of the castle no longer contain the furniture, paintings, cloth and papers that once adorned the interiors. But thankfully there remain architectural features and iconography that attest to the complex range of intellectual influences that made the city.

In the main hall of the castle is a restored ceiling that I have come to see. Fasiladas may have embraced Muslim traders and foreign trade goods, but he was fiercely patriotic and protective of Ethiopian history. Architectural features such as the ceiling carvings are telling clues that Fasiladas wasn't just displaying his power with this building, he was also asserting his legitimacy by reminding people of the link to King Solomon. The ceiling is studded not just in painted relief carved crosses, but also in other symbols that tie the Ethiopian royal family to the Old Testament, most obviously the Star of David. The building is a confident statement about the modern Ethiopian state – outward looking, but with a potent connection to the most ancient and venerable Ethiopian history. This was not just the centre of intra-regional modern trade it was also the fountainhead of Judaeo-Christian thinking.

Once you get your eye, you can begin to decode the castle. It is a curious building that freely informs on the world of Fasiladas in almost every room. It is quite apparent that Fasiladas was more influenced by outsiders than he would have cared to admit: the battlements look Portuguese, and the domes look eastward, perhaps towards India. But there is an unusual architectural motif that is used in various areas of the building, a highly curious technique of placing wooden beams across apertures over doorways in the stone building. The lintels are unnecessarily long for their function and unlike anything I have seen elsewhere. My intuition is that while there are few documents or material culture clues about the past here in Gondar, this feature may help me in my quest. The beams may be a throwback to an earlier time, almost like an architectural quotation from an earlier period in Ethiopian history. Fasiladas was a deeply proud and patriotic leader and while there were some outside influences on the kingdom, it is obvious that local heritage and traditions were fundamental. In the absence of traditional records, perhaps we can track some of these idiosyncratic, uniquely Ethiopian features across time and see where they lead.

Just as in western Europe, many of the oldest buildings still standing in Ethiopia are churches. And I feel sure these religious buildings can tell me a little more about the relationship between the emperors, their faith and their history. On the edge of Gondar

Late afternoon sunlight illuminates the decorative lintel of a Lalibela altar. (Gus Casely-Hayford)

sits Debra Berhan Selassie, a church built by Emperor Iyasu, a close successor of Fasiladas, in the seventeenth century. The exterior is modest, just like a plethora of sandy-coloured stone churches in the area. A solid, squat building with a short bell-tower and a traditional tiled roof – it gives no hint as to what lies within. While only the ceiling at Gondar castle is studded in a handful of relief carvings, the walls of Debra Berhan Selassie are covered in large, brilliantly painted panels and the ceiling is an explosion of angelic faces that stare down at you. Everywhere, distinctively Ethiopian almond-shaped eyes painted with an astounding line economy peer at you through the taper light. In this semi-light they twinkle like constellations. But as you begin to get accustomed to the light, familiar Bible scenes loom out of the darkness, each with an Ethiopian particularity. The paintings were completed on cloth that was glued to the mud-plaster walls. The church gives a clue not just to what Gondar castle might once have been like, but how the Ethiopian royal family had wrapped their own family history deep in the narrative of the Bible. Faith was, and for the historian obviously still is, vital to understanding the Ethiopian imperial family. They were desperate not just to celebrate their Christianity but also to enfold their own history and culture tightly in biblical traditions.

On my way out of Gondar the next morning, weaving through small groups dressed in Sunday white, I notice a line of people following a meandering track that leads away from the road across the rocky landscape and up towards one of the highest, most precipitous hilltops on the edge of the town. The Ethiopians have a tradition of building in some inaccessible places, but these people are not wending their way towards a building. Several hundred metres above our heads the line of people seems to disappear into the mountainside itself. I find myself following a young woman through the thick grass on the edge of the road and we begin to climb the steep pebbly path that hugs the edge of the hillside. Climbing at that altitude quickly leaves me light-headed and clammy and my eyes struggle to focus against the sand-coloured rock and the dazzling white gowns in the dawn light.

But I walk on. An hour later, panting and sweating, we reach a point where the hill levels off in front of a cave entrance.

It is immediately apparent what I am looking at. The Ethiopians assert that theirs is the most ancient and original form of Christianity and there are places, like these cave churches, where that claim feels credible. Cut into the rock face are some of the architectural features of an Ethiopian church, but they do not disguise the fact that this is the entrance to a cave. From the sound of chanting and tinkling of sistrums within, it is obvious that the service has already started. But this is not a sit-down formal service; people are gathered outside in groups praying, and wandering freely in and out of the two doors. Then a deep drumming begins within the cave, the sort of resonating boom you feel in your gut as much as hear.

Negotiating several layers of velvet curtain, I push myself between the worshippers inside the cave. Once the curtains have closed behind me I have to stand still for a few moments. After the brightness of an Ethiopian morning it feels like being plunged into a pool of swirling ink. It isn't just dark; the cave church is full of the smoke of spent waxy tapers. As my eyes grow accustomed to the darkness it is possible to make out a series of low interconnected rooms full of chanting people. In the centre of the biggest space I can see the silk vestments of a priest stooped over a large book from which he is reading in Ge'ez, the ancient language of the Ethiopian kingdom (said to be related to Arabic, and also significantly to Hebrew, the language of the Old Testament and King Solomon himself). Behind and to either side of him are gold cross-bearing novices and sistrum-twisting young boys. To the left, two men play textile-bound kettle drums that set the pace for a low, beautiful incantation that the whole congregation sings. It is a magical scene, and not just for me. All around me people weep openly. Perhaps it's the climb, or the heat, perhaps it's the unnerving beauty of the chanting, but a big wave of tearful relief overwhelms me too.

Perhaps sensing my confusion, a novice moves through the congregation towards me and gestures to the wall above the door through which I have just stepped. This is not the wall painting of Debra Berhan Selassie, but something even more thrilling in this setting: a living, thriving, seething beehive. From honey, the Ethiopians make a kind of mead that they use as communion wine, representing the blood of Christ. It is said that no one brought the bees to the church, the bees built the hive here as the church was founded, simply knowing it was a holy place. For Ethiopians it conferred a double blessing on this place, for honey is not just holy, it is royal. As descendants of King Solomon, Ethiopian emperors claim to be part of the same extended family as Jesus Christ. So the honey wine of communion also represents the blood of the royal family.

The rhythm of the drumming alters and the congregation push past me out into the fresh air. I follow and find myself watching a priest treat a leper, rubbing honey still full of bee larvae deep into the stump of his ruptured nose. All around ailing children and old people clamour, stretching out their arms and thrusting their hands into the broken comb and gushing honey that seeps across a stone font. This is a strain of Christianity that needs no evangelizing. In both form and function it seems to work today as effectively as it has ever done. It is not just that it means something spiritual to the congregation, it is also the cultural and social glue that binds them.

The smell of burnt tapers and the slow rhythm of Sunday sistrums is still with me when I get back into my car and begin the long, slow ascent on the old mountain road to Lalibela, the next stage in my quest. The Chinese have invested billions of dollars in a network of roads that connect Africa's great industrial and agricultural centres with the coast. This old pilgrims' road that for centuries carried trade goods curling up and around the mountains to and from the remote imperial Shangri-La, Lalibela, is now slowly being turned into a highway. Almost its entire length is a dusty aggregate-covered building site that is suddenly opening up once isolated communities to roaring pantechnicons full of new technologies. But in one sense this is an old story.

Towards the end of the twelfth century the saintly King

Lalibela came up this road to found a glorious new holy city at what was then the remote village of Roha. Lalibela was a special emperor, and the city that he founded, and which was named after him, is a spectacularly fitting epitaph. It was said that at his birth he was surrounded by a swarm of bees, which his mother read as a sign that he would be a future emperor. The prophecy came true, but Lalibela wasn't satisfied with being emperor; he wanted to change Ethiopia, not just through trade but through ideas. He wanted to open up places to influences from far and wide and simultaneously to promote the sophistication of Ethiopian culture.

In his new city Lalibela planned to create a new centre of Christendom, a New Jerusalem. He chose to do this in the most dramatic of ways, by building thirteen churches. Though 'build' is not an adequate word for the Lalibela churches. They were not constructed in the traditional fashion through a process of material accretion, they were carved, hewn, excavated from the solid crimson sandstone mountain. Part geography, part sculpture, their very ambition and seeming impossibility inspire awe. It is a breathtaking display of the emperor's power, to be able to command his people to excavate thousands of tons of rock without any form of mechanization – it is almost beyond imagination. They are so well designed that they suffer from none of the dankness of most troglodytic environments. The soft red sandstone almost glows and feels plaster-like cool rather than damp to the touch. The more you wander around and over the churches, the more questions they raise.

Understandably, a number of legends grew over the centuries about this miracle site, including the belief that the buildings were completed at superhuman speed. It is easy to understand Lalibela inspiring such stories; it is still difficult to comprehend how or even why they were built. Ethiopian tradition says that Lalibela visited Jerusalem as a young man, lamented its loss to the Muslims and vowed to build a new city that would be a worthy true centre of Christian thinking and worship.

According to the *Kebra Nagast*, which was written more than a century after the churches were built, Emperor Lalibela was an interloper, a member of a rival royal dynasty that could not claim Solomonic descent. While Lalibela did not have the blood of Solomon running through his veins, he claimed he had the support of a higher authority: God himself had commanded him to build these churches. And in doing so he attempted to claim legitimacy as emperor, because he was doing God's work. It is an interesting distinction, because it defines the Ethiopian Church, even the Christianity of the emperor, as being founded upon faith, not genealogy.

Despite the *Kebra Nagast* account, if you give it more than the most superficial thought, Lalibela is something of an enigma. Modern archaeology is beginning to furnish us with clearer insights into the history of the city and the man. And as so often, the material culture has a way of undermining accepted histories. It may well be that Lalibela began or contributed to the construction of the thirteen churches, but recent research by a team of French archaeologists led by François-Xavier Fauvelle suggests that there were a number of periods of development over two or three centuries to the fifteenth century. For some Ethiopians the very idea that Emperor Lalibela might not have built this city is troubling. Not just because it challenges the veracity of the miraculous nature of the city's foundation, but by extension it contradicts the holy book, the *Kebra Nagast*.

Whenever it was built, there is one thing that is beyond question: Lalibela was conceived and developed as a new centre of Christian thinking right in the heart of Ethiopia. Perhaps the most powerful surviving evidence of this is what at first glance appears to be one of the most modest of the thirteen rock churches, Beta Maryam. Its painted interior is one of the best preserved of any of the Lalibela churches. The ceiling is a collage of symbolic influences from all over Christendom and beyond: the two-headed eagle from Constantinople, a star of David, Greek icons, and of course a plethora of different styles of crosses. Lalibela has a scale and quality of architecture on a par with many of the achievements of medieval Europe. And it's fascinating to see evidence of cosmopolitanism in a place medieval Europeans would have considered the extreme fringe of Christendom, if indeed they were aware of it at all. It is intellectually enthralling, and simultaneously its sheer visual quality sends a frisson of exhilaration through my body. This is what churches should do.

Beta Maryam is a visual metaphor for how Emperor Lalibela saw Ethiopia as the epicentre not just of intellectual endeavour but also of Christendom. As in Gondar, Lalibela may well look beyond Ethiopia for many of its influences, but there are also strong architectural features that puzzle. Around many of the windows are distinctively styled square blocks, and lintels that seem to have no role in a building carved out of rock. They obviously point to an architectural tradition that pre-dates Lalibela and which was important to the people of Ethiopia. Everything Emperor Lalibela did was to secure credibility and legitimacy. If, as history suggests, Lalibela was not descended from Solomon, perhaps in copying this particular architectural style he was emphasizing his claim to be the heir of earlier emperors. Maybe encoded in this architecture lies Lalibela's claim to royal legitimacy, to biblical descent, and to Fasiladas's Gondar and greatness.

I'd gone up to Lalibela looking for answers, but I leave with more questions. The best I can say is, at least my questions have been honed by what I learned in the castles of Gondar and the churches of Lalibela. I do not know how old the buildings that inspired Lalibela are, or whether they will lead me to discover a connection between the kingdom and Solomon and Sheba, but I feel that these intriguing architectural features are somehow pulling me even further into Ethiopia's past.

As I drive away from Lalibela I am reminded that Ethiopia is one of the oldest inhabited places in the world. Archaeologists and palaeontologists have discovered signs of early human development here, from over four million years ago. Unlike many other places in Africa, the human presence in Ethiopia has been consistent; so many of the contemporary indigenous traditions, from religion to art to farming, can be traced back over many generations. Even things that appear recent are ancient: the mile upon mile of crop terraces that hug the mountains of Tigray province – our backdrop for hours of driving – are believed to have been first ploughed three thousand years ago. In pre-colonial times, Ethiopia was the only sub-Saharan country to use the ox-drawn plough – a crucial step away from the pastoralist culture of the rest of the continent further south.

I put my car in a low gear and begin the long, slow haul up to Debra Damo, one of the most important religious sites in Ethiopia.

Eventually even the tenacity of the Tigray farmers is tested beyond its limit and the terraces give way to huge craggy barren landscapes and then dramatic golden-coloured peaks. Debra Damo is one of the oldest buildings in Ethiopia, dating back to the sixth century, and it sits on top of a kilometre-long table mountain. It is a strict monastery, and its famed isolation is justified. It was built thanks to another Ethiopian emperor, Gabra Masqal. He ordered the construction of a colossal ramp to help get building materials on to the plateau. It is said that the monks then decided that the ramp made access too easy so after completion of the main buildings they destroyed the only means of gaining the plateau without difficulty. That left a sheer-sided mountaintop with a monastery on top. Today, the only way to get to Debra Damo is by climbing a rope made of goatskin. No women are allowed up on to the mountain, not even female livestock.

By the time I get to the foot of Debra Damo it is late afternoon and the shadows of the mountain are edging down into the valley. The climb wouldn't be that terrifying almost anywhere else, but at more than 2,000 metres above sea level the air feels very thin for someone who lives in London, and the 70-metre climb looks like Everest. All around me young and old men skip up the rock face without safety harnesses. It does not make me feel more confident. I pull down on the goatskin rope and sense a troubling amount of give in its old sinewy length, but this is the only way up, the only way to answer my questions.

When I pull myself up off the ground, the leathery rope slips through my sweaty palms almost as quickly as I can lift myself. It is only when I lean back and brace my legs against the vertical rock surface that I start to make progress; but within a few metres my back, my arms and my legs are aching. In the absence of any technique or experience I know only strength will get me up the mountain, so I dig deep, grit my teeth, close my eyes and climb.

About 30 metres up – too far up to contemplate giving up – I have to stop to draw breath. By now my whole body is pounding with fear and oxygen deprivation. I look up. The top looks no closer. I dare not look down. I climb on, and by the time a group of young monks pull my exhausted frame over the lip of the mountain on to its level surface I am sweating, gasping, shaking, dizzy and shattered. I lie on a sandstone carved bench, my lungs screaming for oxygen, the sun setting, as the novices continue to pull themselves effortlessly on to the plateau and glide past my prone body to attend evensong in one of Ethiopia's holiest churches.

By the time I have regained my legs it is dusk and the monks and novices have disappeared. But in the distance I can hear singing coming from what I can make out as a squat rock-built church planted on the centre of the plateau. When the monastery was first established, it's believed that up to a thousand monks lived there. Today there are around three hundred on Debra Damo. I find a bed for the night on a floor of cobbles in the disused hay-covered dormitory. As I drift off to sleep listening to the sounds of lowing bulls at the far end of the building, I cannot help thinking about the hundreds of previous inhabitants of the dormitory, all those monks who must have lived, slept, prayed and died under that roof. Debra Damo claims to have been permanently occupied for longer than any other religious site in the world. It's at least five hundred years older than Lalibela. The fact that Debra Damo has been so completely cut off for so long may be useful in my search for evidence of how this kingdom's traditions echoed through the ages. I wonder what the morning light will reveal.

Despite tiredness, my excitement wakes me before dawn, and the sounds of chanting pull me out of bed. The Debra Damo church is exciting and puzzling in equal measure. From the outside it is unlike other Christian religious buildings, certainly not built to visually impress. It looks like a mountain chalet, a very square two-storey building made from different kinds of stone. As I get closer details begin to strike me. I can pick out a number of architectural features that reflect some of the decoration I saw earlier in my trip, the square-ended long beams I saw on the corners of the windows in Lalibela's rock churches. The rising sun window design is there too. But there is a profound difference: the designs of the beams and the windows in Debra Damo are structurally integral.

As I stand in front of the church, it hits me like a wave. This is what the architects of Gondar and Lalibela were echoing. The last time I saw the distinctive, long wooden beams in the castle at Gondar the architecture struck me as being from an older local tradition. And here they are in a sixth-century church made from small, uneven stones.

Another feature literally stands out – more wooden and different-shaped beams that extend beyond the walls. I know about these, or at least have read about them, but I have never seen them before. They're called monkey-heads. They sit like dumb-bells buried within walls, their round ends poking out of each side, bracing the downward pressure of the substantial building. It is simple, beautiful, very effective engineering. Here is a distinct continuity of architectural styles that almost certainly developed indigenously over nearly two thousand years.

The interior of the church and the morning service are as moving as anything I have ever seen. I sit behind a blind choir-master with long matted locks of bluish grey hair as he rocks gently back and forth, setting the rhythm for the chanting of the liturgy by the young novices and old monks – living tradition as it has been practised for a thousand years, in the same taper-smoke-stained vault. Standing in the half-light, hypnotized by the singing and the sistrums, it is hard not to believe that this continuity stretches back even further, to pre-Christian times; to feel that perhaps there is evidence somewhere of the connection to King Solomon and the Queen of Sheba.

Debra Damo deliberately cut itself off from the world. By contrast, my next destination was once the busiest and most important city in Africa. I know from reading the *Periplus of the Erythraean Sea*, a first-century travel guide that describes the city of Aksum as a thriving, bustling city, that at the time Debra Damo was at its most influential, Aksum ranked alongside Rome, Persia and China as one of the four great world powers. Given its significance, I think it's remarkable we know so little about its history. Aksum, according to Ethiopians and their Orthodox Church, was where the son of the Queen of Sheba and King Solomon actually brought the Ark of the Covenant three thousand years ago.

Unlike Debra Damo, Aksum has changed profoundly since its heyday. Today, busy roads, telephone masts and some quite unspectacular post-war architecture surround the ancient heart of the city. Nevertheless, Ethiopian Christians believe that beyond the cathedral walls, lying in a small chapel, is one of the foundations of the Judaeo-Christian tradition: the Ark containing the Ten Commandments. Until 1974 that Ark was the cornerstone of the legitimacy of the Ethiopian empire itself. Its existence would go a long way to prove that the Ethiopian dynasty of emperors was founded by King Solomon and the Queen of Sheba. It would confirm legends that have been around for centuries and perhaps answer the questions that inspired me to make this trip. But the Ark is deemed so holy that no one is allowed anywhere near it. So I stand for some time with my feet touching an invisible line beyond which no unauthorized person is allowed to go, thinking about what might lie inside the modest church that is so near yet so far from me.

But the Ark is not the only potential evidence of this kingdom's ancient heritage. I have actually come to see a site right next to the Ark's purpose-built resting place, a building said to have been constructed in the fourth century by King Ezana.

Archaeologists believe that Ezana was responsible for Ethiopia's first Christian church. He was certainly the first Ethiopian emperor to convert to Christianity. Here the material culture sings out loud and clear from the past. Archaeologists know about

Ezana's Christianity with a rare level of certainty because coins minted during his rule show almost the moment of Ezana's conversion. The site has given up late Ezana period coins that have Christian crosses, while earlier coinage shows the pre-Christian religious symbols of a crescent moon and the sun. This is hugely significant. It means that there was a continuity in terms of rulers before and after Ethiopia became a Christian country. The Judaeo-Christian tradition here does seem to be unbroken. And the coins confirm another fact: by the fourth century this was a significant, well-established kingdom. This is the only place in sub-Saharan Africa known to have issued currency at that time.

Aksum is a place rich in archaeology; but the coins aren't the only objects that point to the power this city had at the beginning of the Christian era. In the centre of old Aksum, on what today feels like a municipal roundabout, stand a row of long, elegant grave-markers, giant stelae that are some of the most important monuments in Ethiopia. The stelae are made from solid granite and the earliest date back to the first and second centuries. They are thought to be the largest pieces of stone ever to come out of a quarry in the ancient world. The tallest stands at over 30 metres and weighs around 500 tons. They are as impressive as any monument in Athens or Rome.

Yirgalem Fisseha, a local tour guide, walks me around the site and helps me to decode the exquisitely precise relief carvings that adorn the surface of the stelae, still clear almost two millennia after they were made. They depict the facades of great buildings it was believed the emperors would inhabit in the afterlife – storey upon storey of beautifully carved buildings, tall skyscrapers to immortality. Yirgalem points out the long carved wooden beams, the monkey-heads, the windows on each tapering floor that ascend into the sky. I have seen all of these features before. It's the architecture used at Debra Damo around half a century later. And over a thousand years later it appears to have inspired the stonework of the churches at Lalibela. It is the long-beam visual vocabulary of Gondar.

I am near the end of a long journey, tired but feeling more

Stele at Aksum.

inspired than ever. Yirgalem's words seem to unlock a quiet moment of epiphany; for the first time my journey really begins to make sense. The Aksum stelae hold many of the elements I have seen on my journey, configured in a way that gives them a kind of contextual sense, offering a continuous narrative which I suppose is the history of Ethiopia. The features on these stelae, marking the ancient burial places of Ethiopian emperors two thousand years ago, have been consciously echoed down the years by the emperors who followed them. What I am witnessing at Aksum are continuous traditions taking the story of the Ethiopian kingdom back to the very beginning of Christianity.

This answers part of the question that lured me to Ethiopia, but I still want to find evidence that the kingdom goes back even further, to the days of Solomon and Sheba.

Yirgalem has one more ancient artefact to show me. A short walk from the stelae in the centre of old Aksum, by an overgrown track we stop at a small hut. Inside is an almond-coloured carved stone that in its own way is as important as the Rosetta Stone. It was inscribed at the time of Ezana with simple details of his military victories and political power. It is a proclamation, a kind of tourist information sign, informing visitors to Aksum about the might of the emperor, especially in his battles against his neighbours. It describes a series of battles with red- and black-skinned adversaries, but particularly the Nuba, and in each they seem to vanquish their enemies. The content of the message is possibly less informative than the languages it is written in: the inscription is in the local Ge'ez language still used in Ethiopia's churches, in the international language of the day, ancient Greek, and also in Sabaean.

After everything I have been through during this trip and the questions the material culture has thrown back at me, this is deeply rewarding. The one thing I know about Sabaean is that it was spoken for only a brief time, and only in this part of Africa and southern Arabia. Historians think it died out around the eighth century, but it first appeared around 1000 BC. And it's the language of Saba, the part of Yemen where the Queen of Sheba is said to have come from. This stone is from the fourth century AD, some 1,400 years after the Queen of Sheba was supposed to have lived, so it's hardly conclusive evidence, but it does indicate a link – and nudges me deeper into the past in my search for the kingdom's origins.

Just 20 miles from Aksum is Yeha, said to hold some important connections to the Old Testament world of the kind I have been looking for. There were worshippers here when the Old Testament prophets were writing. In this ancient town is a mysterious pre-Christian Judaic temple that archaeologists believe is the oldest surviving building in Ethiopia. It pre-dates everything I have seen so far. The quality of the perfectly laid brickwork belies the fact that the temple hails from 500 BC – contemporary with the Parthenon in Greece, and centuries older than Rome's Colosseum.

Although little is known about it, archaeologists claim that the pit to the side of the altar is where the blood from sacrifices would have collected – just as would have happened as part of Old Testament Judaism, in which offerings were made to God in the form of slaughtered sheep and goats. It echoes what Patriarch Abuna Paulos told me at the start of my journey: the faith of the Ethiopian Orthodox Church is based on traditions adopted here a thousand years before Christ. But the most exciting thing about this temple is a collection of artefacts found on the site by archaeologists that are now kept nearby in a small Christian church. They offer a final clue about Solomon, the Queen of Sheba, and the ancient kingdom of Ethiopia.

Upstairs in a dusty chamber I find a strange assortment of Ethiopian crosses, ancient vestments, disintegrating religious paraphernalia and old scriptures spanning many years of this country's Christianity. Among it all there is an incense burner that doesn't belong in any church. It is carved with the pre-Christian symbol of the crescent moon and sun, and archaeologists think it dates from the fifth century BC. In the same glass case, from the same era, are stone tablets, again inscribed in the language of the Queen of Sheba, Sabaean. These are almost certainly objects from the time of the Old Testament, and they speak of an ancient link between Ethiopia and Saba, the home of the Queen of Sheba. It is substantial pre-Christian evidence of the Queen of Sheba's language in the heart of ancient Ethiopia. It means it's just possible that the legend of her son founding Ethiopia's kingdom is based in fact.

I came to Ethiopia wanting to find out whether there was any truth in the legend of this kingdom being founded by the son of King Solomon and the Queen of Sheba. My journey led me from the Abuna's palace in Addis Ababa to the tenth-century walled city of Harar and up to the castles of Gondar, tracing the Christian narrative back into the early Middle Ages. In Lalibela, Debra Damo and Aksum it was possible to chart that narrative back to the earliest times. I found at each stage of my journey that separating legend from fact in Ethiopia is difficult. But in that small building in Yeha was evidence of what I sought. The stones in the church inscribed with Sabaean characters are estimated to be two and a half thousand years old. Not quite the three thousand years the Church claims for its connection to the Bible, but not far off. There may not be proof of a blood connection to Solomon, but there is a striking cultural connection to the world of the Old Testament. It is also interesting that faith in this legend has lasted for centuries, closely tied to the unique traditions of the Ethiopian Church. I think it has endured because of the country's determination to resist the influence of outsiders and remain independent. Ethiopia's emperors may have died out, but its kingdom survives in the material culture, buildings, languages and traditions of the people. It is an extraordinary history, one that deserves to be better known.

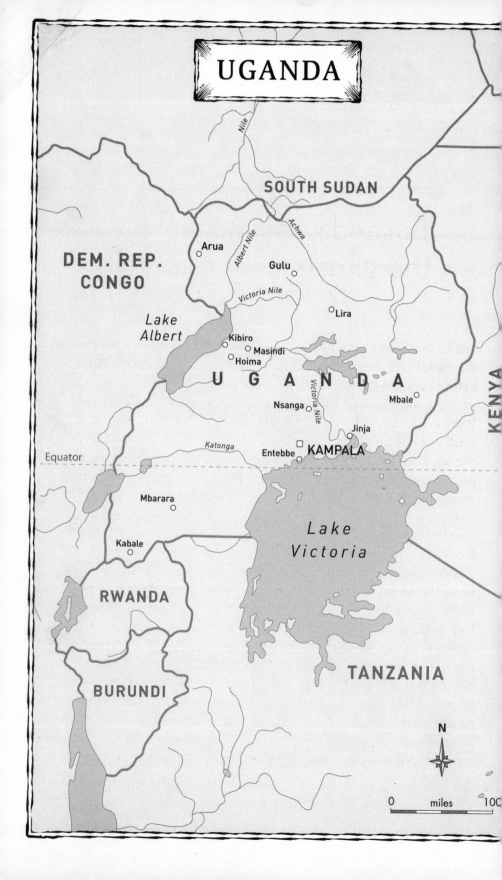

Buganda and Bunyoro:
the ghosts of the lakes

THERE WERE AT LEAST HALF A DOZEN SMALL GROUPS OF MEN ON the dark street corner behind Kiev's Republican Stadium. Even before I crossed the road towards them I could feel one man's eyes studying me. He must have known I was not Ukrainian, nor even Russian. It was risky, but I approached nevertheless. And in a small pool of lamplight I was slipped one of the last few tickets to the big Dynamo Kiev–Leningrad football match. When I tried to push a handful of roubles into the tout's hand, the painfully skinny young man closed his palm into a tight fist and refused to take my money; when I insisted, he simply stepped back and evaporated into the crowd. That touching and surprising gesture was the perfect end to what had been a gruelling journey.

Travelling in the pre-perestroika Soviet Union, driving down from the snowy north and sheltering in the great Russian cities before descending across the plains into the Caucasian Mountains, had been fascinating and frustrating in what it revealed of a country trying to contain burgeoning change. As a Western traveller I had been given the kind of access to the country's culture that few natives ever were. I got up close to the scagliola in the Hermitage, spoke to the conservationists who were painstakingly remaking the wooden stained-glass screens in the most remote mountain churches, sampled the finest caviar and something the locals called red champagne on the banks of the

Caspian, but for all that I was allowed little contact with the people. So on my very last afternoon, as the crowds flooded into Kiev, I had given my guide the slip and gone in search of match tickets. I remember very little of the game, but to be able to sit among ordinary people, to share their excitement, to feel the crowd's conjoined agony at missed chances, and to witness the stadium shudder as fifty thousand men gasped in ecstatic unison, was thrilling. I came away thinking, it's easy to gain a sense of a country when you travel yet so hard to come to know its people. It's in the stadiums of great cities where ordinary people gather to watch their heroes that I have often felt closest to places, briefly gaining a sense not just of ambient hopes but also some of the spectres from which communities hide.

So on my last day in Uganda with a few hours to spare I found myself following the crowds to watch the national team take on Guinea Bissau. The Kampala Stadium has a capacity of just over forty thousand, but that hot afternoon at least fifty thousand gathered to cheer on the 'Mighty Cranes'. Even with a ticket I had been advised to arrive at least two hours before the match to be guaranteed a seat. And it was good advice. By the time I had negotiated the crowds and found my seat the stadium was filled to capacity and the pre-match formalities had begun.

A government minister with a huge entourage briefly made a circuit of the stadium, followed by a cascade of bottles, seat-cushions, cans, insults and boos from the crowd. He bravely waved back at the baying people, but the abuse was unrelenting. He did not run, but he did leave as quickly as his dignity would allow. The crowd's vitriol was quickly replaced by laughter when a clown followed the minister on to the pitch. Like all the best clowns, while being very funny, he was also somewhat terrifying. The smiling middle-aged man, wearing sunglasses, a peaked cap and a white military uniform bedecked with outsized medals and epaulettes, waved extravagantly to the fans. The jacket was junior-sized, drawn tight around his ample wobbling belly with a wide belt. He walked with an exaggerated Mussolini strut, his chest out, his chin up, every now and then stopping and gesturing, appealing to the crowd, who responded by rising up out of their seats, erupting with laughter. As he made his way up and down the pitch he was followed at each shoulder by two men dressed as skeletons. He was a comedy composite of every military dictator, but he also said something very particular about Uganda. As waves of belly laughs echoed around the stadium, so did a palpable shared understanding of something else.

In 1970, it was in an earlier manifestation of the Kampala Stadium that Uganda's second president Milton Obote had tried to appeal to his people, to calm nerves after surviving an assassination attempt. But just as Obote began waving to the crowds, an entourage led by a large soldier dressed in military fatigues and a red beret had entered the stadium, immediately sucking all the attention and credibility away from an almost visibly shrinking president. The soldier was Idi Amin, commander of the Ugandan army. Less than a year later, while Obote was abroad (having left orders for the dangerous Amin to be arrested), the president was deposed in a coup. And so Idi Amin became Uganda's third president and Obote was forced to sit seething in exile in Tanzania.

During his period as head of state Obote had gained a reputation as barbaric and despotic, but Amin, a soldier who had worked his way up the ranks in one of the toughest armies in Africa and who had fought the Mau Mau and the Somali Shifta rebels, understood how to impress and intimidate in a way the previous regime had not dared nor dreamed. Amin created a State Research Bureau backed by a Public Safety Unit to coordinate a campaign of intelligence gathering, torture and murder. In fewer than eight years at least a hundred thousand Ugandans were killed, some say up to five times as many. He laid waste to the commercial sector, expelling seventy thousand Ugandan Asians, nationalizing industries and cutting diplomatic ties with Britain. Today there is barely a family in Uganda not still affected by the repercussions of that period. The spectres of that time cast long dark shadows, not just over politics but over ordinary people's lives too. If the conjoined consciousness of the crowd in the

Kampala Stadium that day revealed anything, it was the shared lament of a people putting their best foot forward, but not forgetting or forgiving the past – a phenomenon I recognized from my journey through the country as an often-repeated pattern.

I quietly watched the crowd. They had earned the right to laugh, but I could not quite laugh with them. And as I watched the match I reflected on the fact that, although I do not believe in ghosts, I had over the weeks of my journey come to believe that this landscape is haunted. I had enjoyed my time in Uganda, but I was left shaken by these spectres that stalk its history. The people of this region lived in an awkward relationship with their past beyond Amin too. Yet, despite everything, it remains a romantic and arresting region that maintains an enduring, almost super-natural power to attract us.

Even by the standards of the African continent, the Great Lakes region has had a tumultuous history. The area where Uganda, Rwanda, the Democratic Republic of Congo and Tanzania meet in a tangled nexus of overlapping cultures and contested lands is a beautiful place featuring massive bodies of fresh water, forested hills, misty mountains, fertile lush valleys and the source of the Nile. It is an area that has witnessed violent colonial regimes, terrible post-colonial turmoil, crazed and corrupt leaders, and more recently ethnic and religious genocide; before the arrival of Europeans and colonialism it was a place of conflict, power struggles and bitter rivalries. Sitting on the southern fringe of the Nilotic language groups where they meet the Bantu speakers, it has long been a place of demographic flux and instability. Some of that turmoil was driven by competition for resources, by struggles for control of the lakes, by intermittent campaigns waged over the region's fertile lands, its abundant crops and good grazing. At least in part, beyond commercial and strategic advantage, this place was fought over because, as was the case with the early Europeans, for the indigenous population it has always simply been seen as inher-ently special.

The archaeological residue of kingdoms that have risen and fallen here offers an insight into a rich and complex history. There is an overwhelming gravitational force of material evidence and oral history that draws one towards the people of Bunyoro and their regional rivals, Buganda. This region was once a patchwork of several kingdoms, but from the sixteenth century until the arrival of Europeans in the nineteenth century its history revolved around Bunyoro and Buganda. On this trip I wanted to follow regional histories from the earliest times right up into the period of British intervention, to gain some sense of what this magical part of the continent was like before the scramble for Africa began, to gauge what effect European encroachment and then colonialism had on the local political balance.

Even before I began my journey I knew this regional history was dominated by competition, rivalry, warfare and opportunism as a small group of lakeside clans consolidated into the Buganda kingdom, turning the tables on their rival Bunyoro, who had long been the most powerful force in the area. I wanted to track how over two hundred years Bunyoro and Buganda jostled for position, competing for valuable resources and using their contested histories and mythologies to claim connection to the land. I was keen to see how by the mid nineteenth century, when Europeans first entered the region, Buganda had come to control the area (it dominates the culture of Uganda to this day). Yet just two hundred years earlier it barely existed and it was Bunyoro that was all-powerful. I wanted to unravel how each kingdom claimed its authority, which flowed from ancient ghost-like cultures and monarchs whose very existence remains contested.

I had begun my quest some weeks earlier at the Uganda Museum in Kampala. I had started to think that to understand why Bunyoro fell from its position of dominance it would be vital to understand its early history, to map out the nature of the state and its origins. And I knew that there were objects at the museum that reputedly gave an insight into the kingdom of Bunyoro's glory days, and the foundations of its power.

The very first national museum in South-east Africa, founded in 1908, is a fitting place to make a start. Despite many of the cases and displays looking as old as the building, it remains a well-visited and well-loved institution. Its collection was reconsidered during the period of post-colonial confidence to accommodate new thinking. It seems to hold on to its relevance through a clever curatorial narrative that tells the story of a new but confident nation united by its passion for its histories and not cowed by differences or divisive events from the past.

I have an appointment to see Jackline Nyiracyiza, the senior history officer. I am hoping not to be given the standard tour, but to visit the museum's basement stores. I have been told that is where a unique collection of artefacts is held that shows how the people of Bunyoro trace their culture back to the ancient Kitara, and to the mysterious Chwezi, in a period of history that seems to dissolve into myth.

Thankfully Jackline is as excited by my quest as I had hoped and within minutes of meeting we have slipped through a door at the back of the museum and in near pitch darkness negotiated a long flight of stairs down to the basement. Boyhood dreams of days like this are what inspired me to become a historian; you can almost smell history in the dust disturbed by our footsteps. The Uganda Museum is a repository of the country's distant past, from fossils showing evidence of early human occupation through to the advent of British colonization. History is important to Ugandans; it seems always to have been important to the people of this region. The kingdom of Bunyoro reached its height during the course of the sixteenth and seventeenth centuries, and it was able to do so in part because of one crucial factor: knowing the importance of history, and being able to claim that its history went back further than anyone else's.

As I descend the stairway I begin to wonder if some of the surviving material that may shed light on early Bunyoro history really is hidden here in this basement. Ahead of me I can hear Jackline unpadlocking a huge metal door, and with some effort she eases it open and presses a light switch. The basement is bathed in a pulsing yellow neon light revealing hundreds of buff-coloured cardboard boxes full of archaeological finds. The air, unbreathed for a considerable time, is heavy with clay-dust, rendering the atmosphere more like a tomb than the sort of museum store I am familiar with. Almost all the boxes are marked with the word *Ntusi*, the name of a late Iron Age site in western Uganda which is said to have been occupied by the Chwezi, the dynasty that ruled over a region called Kitara between the tenth and fourteenth centuries. Today the Ntusi region sits within Bunyoro territory, but in the tenth century, along with most of Uganda, it is thought to have belonged to Kitara. The Bunyoro claim they and the Chwezi are one and the same people; they even often call themselves Bunyoro Kitara.

The link between the Chwezi and the Bunyoro has been hard to prove. There were obvious benefits to claiming descent from an ancient powerful dynasty, but some historians and rival ethnic groups have contested Bunyoro's claims. The Chwezi sit on the far edge of what can be historically corroborated; indeed they are said by many to have been mythological, perhaps part of a deliberately elaborated recent narrative. The basement I am in is full of little-studied material from a number of sites at Ntusi that have been excavated over the last three decades, and it may hold some answers.

Most of the boxes contain carefully packed bags of finds, each telling a story of a layer of archaeology excavated from a particular place. The finds are all individually wrapped in transparent plastic but even in the limited light they reveal enough to excite: knapped flint axe-heads, shards of thousand-year-old pottery, small pottery amulets, pieces of jewellery. These objects are material testimony to the fact that there was indeed a settlement in the area occupied by the Bunyoro kingdom for many hundreds of years.

There are hundreds of artefacts, but is there any proof that Kitara and the Chwezi really existed? When I pose the question, Jackline's eyes twinkle; scholars are divided on this, and have been for years. Kitara might have existed, but it might simply be myth and legend. It is frustrating. Exciting the finds may be, but there is legitimate concern over what they reveal about Bunyoro. Historians have argued that just because ancient indigenous archaeological finds have been discovered in the region, that may not mean a connection to the modern Bunyoro. Bunyoro's claim to the ancient history evidenced by these finds gave them the authority and inspired the sense of belonging necessary in order for them to expand and organize a kingdom. The political capital gained from the idea that Bunyoro was descended from the ancient kingdom of Kitara was significant. Especially as Kitara was reputed to have been vast and powerful.

I am disappointed that despite the volume of material there is no hard proof of a connection between Bunyoro and the ancient Chwezi. But there is something down here – evidence of a sig-nificant and sophisticated early civilization. Jackline shows me a tray of partially reconstructed pots. In the centre is an almost com-plete bowl. From its shape and decoration it is possible to deduce that it must have been used for food storage or transportation, and it's about 1,200 years old. Time has not eroded its tactile attractions. Jackline seems to intuit my thoughts and through the soup of swirling clay-dust invites me with a gesture to touch it.

I pick the bowl up. It is a lovely thing, comfortable between my hands, just as it probably felt when it was made. The curve of its bulbous base sits perfectly in a cupped palm. This may be a period of history that is shrouded in mystery and disintegrates into myth, but this brittle piece of ceramic is real and allows a personal connection with someone from our distant past. It is beautiful; every aspect of it has been considered and crafted with obvious care. Sitting inside it is a shattered water vessel, the light airy clay mixed by an experienced hand – the perfect insulation material for keeping cold water cool. Just from looking at these two pots we know that these people stored and probably traded food. Their exterior profiles are decorated by impressing a rolled piece of papyrus while the clay is still wet to create a ring of rouletting textile-like ripples across the surface. This was not done just for aesthetic reasons; the rouletted ring made for better grip and more condensation on the outer surface, promoting cooling. I may have

Ugandan herder and traditional long-horned cattle.

been denied a tangible, concrete connection, but I feel like I am gazing back through a portal, making an immediate sensory link with history.

As we're replacing objects and preparing to leave, Jackline finds something at the back of a shelf. She brings down a small bag. Within it are a variety of tiny Ntusi finds: two bullhorn amulets, iron arrowheads, beads carved from horn, all of which date from at least a thousand years ago. Each is small but has been worked with great finesse. As Jackline locks the door in the darkness, I reflect that this must have been a complex society in which people developed sophisticated aesthetic traditions (which suggests wealth and leisure) and water storage technologies, and they were obviously trading with local, and perhaps distant, neighbours. Aspects of the society's history may remain a mystery, but what is clear is that there was a significant culture at Ntusi.

The next morning I get on the road travelling west from Kampala to the centre of the country, to the great grasslands of Bwera. The road to Ntusi cuts through some of Uganda's most beautiful landscapes, lush green vistas of thick bush interrupted by ancient trees that stand like knowing tors. It is a place that has changed little over centuries. Uganda is one of the most rural countries in Africa. Its countryside remains a patchwork of small subsistence farms and drovers herding from pasture to pasture flocks of cattle with magnificently long and elegant horns and waxy antelope-like skins.

In mid afternoon I arrive at Ntusi. Blue-green hills undulate out towards the horizon. This is the landscape where the finds in the Uganda Museum basement were discovered. It is a quiet, isolated place today, but it was once at the heart of a series of large conurbations, perhaps cities. Most of the Ntusi finds were retrieved from two large midden mounds. The site may be shrouded in mystery, but these knolls continue to be known by local people as the 'female' and 'male'. The almost humble-looking mounds may not take the breath away, but they remain the most significant surviving repositories of evidence of the early Bunyoro kingdom.

Nubia The earliest Egyptian references to Nubia described it as a place of exotic goods, of gold, of amazing athletes, of dancing girls and slaves. These Egyptian wall paintings show Nubian traders bearing skins, precious metals and fruit.

Top left: As the wind erosion slowly reveals more and more of the site, the scale of the Nubian necropolis in Kerma is becoming apparent. There may be as many as thirty thousand people buried on these plains, and among the grave goods are thousands of sacrificed cattle. These sites may date back more than nine thousand years, and be among the oldest cemeteries in Africa.

Top right: The wall reliefs at Meroë are a glorious celebration of Nubian cattle culture. Here, carved into the sandstone, are symbols that celebrate the Nubian way of life, with its central focus on livestock. Cows were not just agricultural assets, they were a mechanism through which Nubians mapped their continuity.

Above: The Kambala, the cattle masquerade, is the Nuba's most loved dance – it introduces young men to Nuba society. At its heart it is an acknowledgement that to be a part of this society is to strive towards an individual strength, a group loyalty and a communal dignity. Perhaps in these dances is the residue of traditions that link the contemporary Nuba to the

Welcome to my al-fresco bedroom and en-suite bathroom in the desert. And as I discovered later, it is a hotel with the most glorious views of the Milky Way.

Meroë is one of the largest complexes of pyramids in Africa. Here some of the highest-ranking Kushites were buried, leaving a vivid record of their lives carved into the sandstone walls.

Looking down from the top of Jebel Barkal, it is still possible to see the top of a tall discrete stack of rock that was once a carved hooded head of a gigantic cobra that gazed down, poised to strike, over the Nile. It is not just a beautiful spot: the promontory on a bend in the Nile offers obvious strategic benefits in long views up and down the river.

Ethiopia

Above and above right: It is late afternoon, the sun is already low, and so there cannot be any delay in checking the last knots as I prepare to climb up the final cliff-face to Debra Damo. The cowhide rope and the sheer climb do not fill me with confidence. The altitude, more than 2,000 metres above sea level, makes the climbing tough.

Middle right: The monastery is constructed from limestone, and uses wooden monkey-heads, or large dowels, to support the walls. Its ancient Axumite structural features gives us a sense of what this region's buildings might have looked like in the pre-Christian era.

Right: The congregation gather from miles around, many parishioners walking for hours to get to the Honey Church for the Sunday service. The last mile is up a steep incline, but young, old and infirm make the climb.

On the summit, the monks are gathering for the early evening service. After the physical exertion of the climb, Debra Damo is serene. The whole site shimmers in the light of the setting sun.

Above: A honey-based mead is used as the communion wine in these traditional Ethiopian church services, and honey taken from the beehive that sits above the altar is used as a curative.

Above left: Priests chant psalms from illuminated manuscripts in the taper light. Outside (*left*), people gather to receive the sacrament and the honey, among them a young man who is suffering from leprosy.

Right: The church of Debra Berhan Selassie was one of Emperor Iyasu's great accomplishments. The ceiling is the most stunning feature of the church – row upon row of radiant angels.

Below: The quality of the architecture at Yeha belies its age – this temple was constructed around 500 BC, before the Parthenon in Greece or Rome's Colosseum.

Bottom: The church of St George is the most stunning of the twelfth-century rock-carved Lalibela churches. Its perfect 25-square-metre sides are carved with exquisite precision in the solid rock – it was said to have been created to the express designs of King Lalibela after its form appeared to him in a vision.

Right: The atmosphere inside the church inspires silence, and as your eyes adjust to the candlelight you might notice a meditating priest by the altar – a man who has dedicated his life to the church of St George.

Far right: The cloth-covered tabots are processed by the site where the Ark of the Covenant lies to the cathedral at Axum.

Main picture: The largest of the Axum Stelae is 33 metres high and displays architectural iconography that has inspired Ethiopian architects and builders over thousands of years. Its fascia is made up of decorative lintels and monkey-heads surrounding windows and doors.

Top right: The late-twelfth-century Lalibela windows are surrounded by decorative lintels that seem to replicate the fascia of the stelae at Axum. They offer no structural support, but tie this site back into the earliest Ethiopian history.

Middle right: At the sixth-century Debra Damo we see architectural features that were decorative in Axum and Lalibela still being used structurally. The tops of four monkey-heads are clearly evident protruding from the wall, offering a vivid window on to pre-Christian Ethiopian architecture.

Bottom right: The internal mechanics of the monkey-head technology is simple and effective. Dumb-bell-shaped lengths of wood help to hold the wall upright against the downward pressure placed upon it by the upper storeys.

The female mound sits above the hollow of a heavily farmed valley. Uganda is known for its rich soils, but the fertility of the land may well have been enhanced a millennium ago when generations of earlier residents used this as a place to deposit their rubbish. Today, the female mound is overgrown; banana trees grow right up to her very edge. But as you get close, even in the thick undergrowth you can feel the slope steepen to the summit of the mound. It is hard going, but I am inspired by the thought that this 4-metre-deep midden may tell the story of how early Bunyoro rose from the embers of the fading Kitara. Perhaps here, myth and legend can be given some flesh. When these mounds were first excavated in the mid 1930s, archaeologists could barely believe what they were seeing. The evidence they were unearthing pointed to an ancient organized society dating back as far as AD 1000.

Dismas Ongwen, an archaeologist who knows the site well, has agreed to meet me here. For Dismas, Kitara is not the stuff of legend, it is very real. As we climb through the bush he tells me about how, as Kitara went into decline, the huge kingdom that stretched from Uganda to northern Tanzania and from the eastern Congo to Rwanda and Burundi fractured into smaller kingdoms, and that Bunyoro may have grown from one of its regions. Bunyoro may be able to justifiably claim an indirect link to ancient Kitara, through the continuity of genealogical lineages and cultural heritage. This site was many hundreds of acres in size, stretching as far as the eye can see, and probably supporting many thousands of inhabitants. The people who lived here left a vivid record of their trade and cultural relations. As the topsoil erodes, archaeology percolates up through the layers, leaving the hilltop scattered with layers of ancient ceramic and bone.

From the top of the mound we spot a bank of ominous clouds folding over and pouring sheets of rain into the adjacent valley. If we are to make it to the second mound before the area becomes a slurry of mud we will need to hurry. As we walk along the unpaved road on our way to the male mound, Dismas picks up handfuls of fragments of pot from its surface – a fat shard of an eight-hundred-year-old water pot here, a slither of storage vessel there. A small boy stops to watch us. I open my hand to show him a piece of pot and he says 'Chwezi' and disappears into the undergrowth. I am reminded again that in some people's minds the Chwezi are ghost-like spectres who are celebrated as part of local mythology, in others' they are a very real part of local history, the original inhabitants of this place and the forefathers of present-day Bunyoro.

I follow Dismas into the undergrowth and we are soon climbing again. The male mound sits beside a small-holding. Outside the front door of the house, rain and constant use have worn the topsoil away and a layer of archaeology has come to the surface. Cow bones and pots sit partially exposed on the surface; in their garden a tethered pig forages in a muddy mix of dark soil and splinters of ceramic. Archaeologists have found what appear to be long-horned Ankole cattle enclosures on this site; this combined with the relative youth of the slaughtered animals suggests the presence of large herds and sophisticated herd management strategies.

We scramble up a steep bank on to the apex of the male mound. The views are spectacular. Dismas suggests that for the early communities these mounds were a sign of prestige, a mark of their accreted history. These cattle-based communities would judge their wealth by the size of their dung mounds; the huge volume of cattle bones suggests that there were plenty of them, providing meat and profits to a substantial population. Perhaps the detritus of their lives told their story in a way that was meaningful to them. Perhaps like us they enjoyed the idea of being able to see the passage of time, to record history in a tangible form.

The rich grasslands were ideal for a pastoral society. There were plentiful resources for whoever lived here. They were also growing grain and carving wood – activities that require an advance in technology that would have given them an edge over their competitors. In addition, these lands were rich in iron ore deposits, and it was the ability of these people to mould and craft this resource that gave them a power that may well have laid the foundations for the success of Bunyoro.

A fork of lightning and a rumble of thunder in rapid succession send us scurrying back down the path in search of shelter. We run and fall through rivulets of muddy rainwater that throw up even more archaeology. But time has run out – the heavens have opened.

As we get into the car, I ask Dismas, 'Do we have any idea who these people were?'

'Well,' he replies, 'the date of this site coincides with accounts in oral history that talk about the Chwezi people, reputed to be the royal dynasty of Kitara. It is possible, but we cannot say much more than that.'

The Chwezi people may have created these mounds a millennium ago; whatever the case, they throw up enlightening historical data about the empire of Kitara. But perhaps it is in the stories that have been passed down through the generations and which endure to this day that we will find the key to this kingdom.

According to oral history, the people of Bunyoro attributed the huge mound that we have just stumbled down to the first Chwezi king; the other was said to belong to his queen. The belief that these mounds were connected to Chwezi royalty, and that the Chwezi were here at Ntusi, deep in Bunyoro territory, was and remains hugely significant. It did not simply link them to Kitara, it gave the people of Bunyoro a sense that they were part of this landscape, and had been for centuries. The legend rooted Bunyoro in this place. It gave the kingdom of Bunyoro its legitimacy. As we drive away, passing children gazing out from beneath sodden thatched-roofed houses, I am left pondering the nature of historical truth. It is however clear that the story of the Chwezi endures and is vitally important to people from miles around.

The next morning the storm has passed and the air feels fresh. I join a convoy of buses carrying pilgrims to Mubende Hill, to a shrine dedicated to the first Chwezi king, Ndahura. In the oral history, Ndahura is the progenitor of the Bunyoro kingdom. He may well be a real historical figure. For all the people around me on the bus he exists in some shape or form, perhaps as a living god, maybe as a great king who in death took on metaphysical form.

The site is focused around a large silk cotton tree. It is not the biggest I have ever seen, but it possesses a stately presence that only these great ancient cotton trees can achieve. Dr Ephraim Kamuhangire has been writing about the history of Bunyoro for more than three decades and is the perfect person to walk me around the site. He was involved in the late twentieth-century dig here that aimed to sort myth from history. If anyone can give me some clarity on early Bunyoro, Ephraim is the one.

It is a day of worship and people are arriving from all over Bunyoro, Buganda and even the Democratic Republic of Congo and Rwanda. It is an unusual place. Even though it's a fairly obscure site, it retains the power to draw people as it always has. There is a presidential residence on the hill that sits adjacent to a house once built by a colonial administrator. Over millennia people have gathered here; whether they fully understood its religious power or not, they certainly knew of its ability to affect others. Today, this place that once defined Bunyoro is a place of spiritual pilgrimage. Just as at Ntusi, the Chwezi, who are said to have founded the site, have left behind a fascinating legacy of archaeology: pot fragments, cattle bones, spears and tools, but most potently stories. Still, here, as is the case elsewhere, they remain obscure, almost mythical figures themselves. They were forcefully promoted by the fledgling Bunyoro state as their pro-genitors, perhaps, as the critics suggest, to legitimize fragile claims to regional control. For migrants from the Nilotic region to the north that is today South Sudan such a local connection to the Bantu-speaking indigenous population would have been deeply advantageous; or it may be that by the time the Bunyoro state came into being, although the Chwezi dynasty were long gone, a subgroup of their descendants remained at least to influence this region before retaking control. Whatever the truth, the Chwezi left a potent legacy, both in the named spirits who still have a presence in the landscape and as a real royal family to whom the Bunyoro maintain a genealogical link. It may be that on a continent in which historical narrative is traditionally quite fluid and ancestor worship well established there is something in both stories, that these ancestor spirits were indeed real figures. The only thing that makes untenable the consolidation of the two interpretations into one narrative is that the small handful of figures from the oral history cannot stretch across a chronology that is meant to straddle hundreds of years. But perhaps we should be more generous with this history and, like the local people, allow some of the ambiguity and poetry to remain.

Under the canopy of the tree the root buttresses are at their most impressive. A dozen supporting roots divide the trunk into discrete chambers that are used like chapels within a cathedral, separate areas dedicated to particular spirits, each with its specialist area of spiritual focus. Each space is washed with milk and the ground is laid with freshly cut grass. A priestess throws herself down into the hollows between the buttresses and begins to howl as if possessed. She spits milk across the surface of the bark. Another priestess summons a snake from beneath the tree, and like the stories of the Chwezi, one is never sure if the snake is real or a metaphysical analogue. Some of what we are seeing here is said to be a relatively modern confection, possibly based on some remnant of past practice, but like religious practices the world over it has evolved and changed. The core elements of what is happening here are very old, perhaps a thousand years old – as old as the fragments in the Kampala Museum and on the Ntusi mounds, but aspects continue to evolve.

Warmly invited by the matriarch, I kneel among the congregation in a space between two buttresses below a large bulbous root node known locally as one of the breasts of Ndahura's queen, Nakayima. Its nipple is a throbbing beehive that hums with activity, its structure drooping under the weight of honey. We kneel and chant and we are each handed coffee beans to throw into the nape of the buttress. The repetition, the meditation, the obvious dedication and care are aspects I am familiar with from

THE LOST KINGDOMS OF AFRICA

other religious experiences. It is obvious why this place continues to draw people. It is highly affecting.

The site is beautiful too, sitting on a hilltop looking out over hundreds of miles of open countryside, but there is much more to it all than just an awe-inspiring view. Place is what matters, making a relationship with the landscape. The reasons are subtle, but in part it comes out of the demographic and cultural complexity that has resulted from hundreds of years of migratory shifts and regional instability. As different people settled this land, each in turn appropriated these stories for themselves. What began as a Chwezi narrative was embellished by others. This special site is a point of confluence for many people's stories of origin. Many chronologies are anchored here.

Travelling back down the hill on the bus, it is hard to argue against the power of what happens here. Belief and ritual have been a hugely important part of building states throughout history. Whether the Chwezi were real or not does not seem to matter. What does matter is that the Bunyoro believe it was here that their civilization began. This was the claim that infused their kingdom with a power that would allow it to grow and prosper. A common belief system has provided civilizations throughout the world with a shared sense of morality and sense of purpose.

One of the beliefs of the people of Bunyoro is that their Chwezi ancestors were great providers. There is evidence for this – the huge number of cattle bones found at Ntusi clearly indicates that this area was unusually well stocked. Large herds were being kept on Bunyoro's central grasslands four centuries ago at a time when this was culturally quite unusual. There is a reason why Bunyoro could maintain vast herds of cattle, why it rose to prominence. The kingdom had a resource that provided vital minerals for livestock and people alike. Bunyoro had salt.

In a culture where place, the notion of land, is so important, the fact of being able to draw a valuable resource from the earth itself always had a resonance. The fact that salt was vital for life made it all the more potent. This industry was the source of calcium for the cattle, which provided milk for their calves, which enlarged the herds and made Bunyoro wealthy. A plentiful supply of salt meant healthy people and healthy herds. That in turn led to surplus cattle, which in turn allowed for trade.

Getting to the salt fields at Kibiro is an adventure; there is barely a road. Lake Albert, on the western edge of modern Uganda, faces the Democratic Republic of Congo. According to oral history the Chwezi disappeared into the lake, never to be seen again, and it remains a place with a ghostly air. Visitors are so rare that children rush out of their schools to greet cars as they descend the precipitous kilometres down to the lake. It is alarming on the dry gravel paths, but the views draw you on: the orange road against the bush, the tree-crested hills, the vastness of the lake stretching off to the mountains of Congo looming in the far distance.

The Kibiro ash salt industry has not changed its method for drawing the valuable salt from the soil for hundreds, perhaps a thousand years. It is not a beautiful industry. Sulphurous-smelling hot water percolates up to the topsoil of the coastal stretches leaving a crust of salty mud, and all about us the earth is littered with small pieces of ceramic that tell the story of this region's rapidly expanding economy. The salt-refining processes are long and back-breaking. Hours are spent working in the sun, scraping the salt off the surface of the soil, then allowing it to recrystallize before repeating the process. This is done over and over again until almost all that is being scraped away is the powdery salt, the heavier detritus having filtered through the crystals back into the earth. This grey crust of crystals is then carried away. At this stage it tastes like salt but it is still full of grit and dirt. The grey flakes are soaked in water to draw out the impurities, then the rich saline liquid is boiled dry to leave pure salt. Before it sets, the salt is poured into flaky cones, ready to be sold.

By the seventeenth century a major economy had emerged here. Archaeology shows the beginnings of ivory jewellery manufacture and the emergence of a market for prestige goods requiring rich buyers and more sophisticated concepts of value and worth. Natural resources, and a strong sense of identity thanks to the mythology underpinning the kingdom, meant that in the seventeenth century Bunyoro was a highly organized state.

By evening I arrive in the town of Hoima, Bunyoro's capital. Just 20 miles from Kibiro, it once would have been packed with traders looking to sell and exchange their wares for cakes of salt. It feels like it has seen better days; the main crossroad that dissects the old town suggests that it was once a fine-looking place with elegant buildings and shop fronts reminiscent of the old mining towns of South Africa. Behind the old buildings a market still thrives, selling among the fruit and vegetables cones of salt covered in sheaths of twisted leaves; there are also hardware stalls selling buckets and adzes and spears and spearheads, just as I'd seen in the museum in Kampala. It is a place that brings the history, the journey, to life.

I am on my way to meet Yolamu Nsamba, historian and secretary to the current king of Bunyoro. The palace is a modest suburban-looking house, well kept but exuding a sadness. It seems to say something about the current state of both Bunyoro and its monarchy. Speaking to Yolamu in the gardens of the palace, I find him defiant. He tells me with enormous passion and pride how the Bunyoro, of Nilotic origin, came south across what is today Sudan in waves over thousands of years. Many had similar traditions, but each was distinctive enough that discrete waves of migration were marked out by separate clans. Today, there are many dozens of these clans in existence that give a sense of the complexity of this period. The clan chiefs became enormously powerful, they were the custodians of the land, but at Bunyoro's heart was the king, the anchor of the society. And to bring coherence to this quickly developing society they found the traditions of the indigenous Chwezi to bind and rally around. As they did so, the growth of Bunyoro was building its own cohesion. Iron, salt and trade that came from right across central and northern Africa and the Arabian Peninsula began to turn Kitara into a very attractive place for the entrepreneurially minded. Bunyoro became an economic powerhouse, sucking in people from across the region and nurturing technological innovation. It thrived on this cosmopolitan liberalism.

For Yolamu Nsamba, and many Bunyoro, the Chwezi were real people who legitimized through blood Bunyoro's connection to the land. As Yolamu informs me, the very name 'Bunyoro' was not derived from an ethnicity or a place, it connoted senior rank. These Bunyoro people were first Chwezi, but as the region consolidated around a number of newly focused communities so the cultures combined and gradually took on the sole name Bunyoro.

Before I leave, Yolamu is very keen to show me the throne room – the animal skins with spear holes made at the time of the hunt, the state drums, the king's caps, all of which reveal the intimate detail of 'how the kingdom was once organized, the state structures, the systems of taxation, military organization, relations with other powers. They also reveal very vividly how this once powerful kingdom has been laid low by recent politics.' Yolamu once studied history in Britain, but when talking about the court regalia he seems to leave that empirical historical tradition behind. Describing relatively modern headdresses and spears as being thousands of years old, he seems to move seamlessly from the kind of Western history I know into another form of history that is not about dates and chronology but is driven by a need to build a connection to the land, to resolve age-old questions of origin.

Today, listening to Yolamu, it is hard not to feel a little disheartened about the present state of the kingdom. Two hundred years ago, before the arrival of Europeans, Bunyoro was a prosperous kingdom with significant political influence and an evolving culture that gave its people a common sense of identity and belonging. But it wasn't to last. Many of the reasons for that are to be found on the other side of the country, by the banks of Lake Victoria. Here another kingdom was beginning to flourish. To tell that story, I had to return to Kampala.

The old Buganda capital and seat of the Buganda kings is a city of hills. Each hill is topped with a building that seems to represent a facet of the city's history – religious, administrative and monarchical. The old Kampala Mosque, the Anglican and Catholic cathedrals, Lord Frederick Lugard's former colonial base, they all look down on the city from the hills. Without doubt one of the most imposing hilltops is the one on which the old Royal Palace perches. Looking out majestically across the city at the other striking buildings on their respective plinths, it looks every bit a seat of royalty. Facing a mile-long avenue that drops down into the city before rising up towards another hill on which sits the old parliament building – a road that has become known as 'The Royal Mile' – the Royal Palace was built to inspire and impress. And to emphasize the once umbilical connection between Crown and state, each roundabout at the intersecting roads has an entrance and exit across it so that the king, and the king alone, might be free to drive directly from one building to the other.

The Buganda palace is a large white stucco building surrounded by pleasant grounds. The building is imposing but municipal and somewhat soulless. As for the king, he has largely lost his influence. He has given only one interview in the last decade. The state drums, once the symbol of power and continuity for the Buganda people, are said to have lost much of their potency. Today there are no official court drummers, but the descendants of those who once served as royal drummers continue to fight to keep the drumming traditions alive. They play at official functions and have become an unofficial repository of history, a living reminder of the lost magnificence of the Buganda court.

I spend the evening in the city sitting out on the lawns of the palace with drummers whose ancestors were official court drummers, and listen to them play. It is a melancholy sound. The Buganda say 'the drums are never beaten without reason', and today there is a fiery undercurrent of defiance in the playing. In the past each drum was named and had a deep significance; at the height of the empire there were several hundred combinations of beats that were known by most people. These beats defined the people, guided them, informed them when a specific aristocrat was arriving, or announced the death of a king. At the height of the Buganda empire these messages were repeated by drummers in a chain of towns and transmitted all over the countryside. The noise of the battery at close quarters was said to be deafening, a cacophony of mixed beats, but from a distance the qualities and individual messages of each drum could be clearly perceived. Listening to these layers of drumming looking down over the city is a thought-provoking experience.

Within recent history some Buganda drumming traditions have been lost or have fallen into misuse. The temporary dissolution of the monarchy under the Obote regime in the early 1980s only made things worse. From the playing on display here you get the impression that Buganda's dominant position has been secure for centuries, and that rituals like this have been going on uninterrupted for hundreds of years. But Uganda's ancient kingdoms – Buganda, Bunyoro and Toro – were only reinstated in 1993. For decades during Uganda's turbulent modern history, all mention of these kingdoms was banned. They were reinstated to defuse ethnic tensions, and they became regional powers under the authority of the national government. Their return was a moment of great celebration. But there was, for some, a sense of strangely uncomfortable familiarity with the realization that the reinstated borders were based on those drawn up by the British at the end of the nineteenth century, with Buganda dominant. It reflected the status quo, yet no more than two centuries earlier Buganda had been dwarfed by the kingdom of Bunyoro.

Although many of the Buganda drums of communication survived, without official drummers, the drums of state have slowly begun to lose their status. Nevertheless, it is still believed that when beaten, the royal drums increase the vigour of the king. So they are still beaten with an absolute passion. Although like many similar traditions all over Africa, their relevance has been tested by contemporary life.

Among the royal drums the most important battery is the Mujaguzo, a set of hand-carved drums handed down over generations. They were beaten for coronations, or when the royal family embarked on an important expedition, or on feast days. If the son of the king died they were sounded, and when the mourning stopped they were sounded. These moments were wrapped into the drums' history, a part of their cadence. The very history of the royal family was at one with their name.

One of the greatest living Buganda drum historians, Kabenge Gombe, tells me that 'the oldest drum structures are older than the kingship of Buganda'. The rhythms he plays have been played for thirty-six kings of Buganda over hundreds of years. These are passages of drumbeats that migrated with the earliest waves of people into this region, demographic shifts that are still evident in the clan system. Today, there are more than fifty Buganda clans. Mr Gombe, a senior member of the Butiko, or 'mushroom', clan, tells me that his ancient clan drum was instituted at the same time as the clan. 'This was not in origination a Buganda drum, this drum pre-dates Buganda, but it has become a Buganda drum over time. It was brought into being at the time of our forefather, Wagaba, just before his rival murdered him.' Wagaba's body was never found; it is now believed that he did not die, but escaped to the moon. The Butiko still say that if you look at the moon when it is full you will see him carrying a bunch of firewood, and you will see the mushrooms scattered beneath. And so the Butiko instituted a set of drums named Kowuguro that are played every full moon, playing motifs that will entice Wagaba to return.

When the ninth king, or Kabaka Mulondo, came to the throne (according to oral tradition he ruled *circa* 1524–54), he was a baby, still being nursed by his mother. He was far too young to fulfil his duties. So a wise member of the king's court advised its principal members to invent a way of amusing the Kabaka before his subjects. At the time the Butiko clan counted among its members the maternal uncles of Kabaka Mulondo, and had great influence at court. They instituted a set of drums to amuse the young Kabaka. As Mr Gombe says, henceforth 'since the days of Kabaka Mulondo these special drums played for every Kabaka.' They are regarded as a spiritual storage space for the regalia of kingship. The respect that we show to the drums is evident in that we only play them while kneeling. When you play before the Kabaka you must face him, but the player of these two drums will always have his back to the king; something that would have meant death in the olden days. But because of the special historical link . . .' Mr Gombe's words trail off. He seems to be transported by the Mujaguzo weaving their ghostly aural magic.

I reflect on the realm of drum histories that bound these peoples together. They were not just mechanisms for holding histories, they were the basis of jurisprudence, philosophy and so much more. Some of what is contained in these stories occupies the realm of conventional history, but some of it is a kind of mythological rallying point, a means of uniting people around an account of origin and a story of a vulnerable, loved, completely central Kabaka. Key to all of that was drums.

A few of the great Buganda drums did not venerate kings and heroes but gods. Dungu, the god of the chase, had a special drum that was said to have metaphysical powers. It was so powerful that in the colonial era it was confiscated and ended up in the ethno-logical museum in Cambridge. It is a large drum made up of pieces of every kind of animal hunted by the Buganda, and every form of magical charm used in the hunt – miniature weapons and pieces of their traps. Whenever the drum was beaten a medium would be possessed by Dungu.

The history and romance that surround the great Buganda state traditions are palpable. In the distant past the drum histories melt into mythology, but layered within them is robust history. As Mr Gombe remarks, 'they anchor Buganda and hold the narrative of the people. They hold kingship and kinship. Since these drums were instituted they have created a powerful consanguinity. This is a binding force for us. We have a drum for the clan, and each member of the clan has a responsibility to sound the clan drum once they marry and start a home. They offer continuity. When you marry you have to have a drum, a spear and a stick. Your drum is your identity card; wherever you go, you sound it, and we would know you were coming. Your drum is your signature, it is a totem, a motif that will be known as time passes.'

They were dynamic transformative vessels. Drums did not fix identities in aspic, they could redeem. One of the most often told drum stories recounts the origin of the Buganda-Mirembe, a drum made in the reign of Kagula (*circa* 1704–34). According to oral history he was known for his almost sadistic behaviour, even on occasion burying his subjects alive, and his people rebelled against his cruelty. In an endeavour to regain his subjects' favour he instituted the Mirembe, the drum of 'peace', and today there still exists the proverb 'the drum beats for the office, not for the person who holds it'.

This story tells us something about the importance of Buganda's drums; it also gives an insight into a dynamic modern kingdom that learned to balance the power of the monarch against people's freedoms. And it was its freedoms and stability that made it so much more attractive and successful than its peers. The early clan chiefs enjoyed considerable power; the kingship found its place on the hill, but it was constantly aware of other discrete elements of the state. The loyalty of the clans was guaranteed: the king selected his wives from different clans so that his successor could come from any clan in the Buganda kingdom.

Around 1700 the clans of Buganda began their rise to dominance, a rise that was at least in part built on the production of bananas. The high rainfall and fertile land on the northern shores of Lake Victoria had encouraged the clans to settle in the region in the first place, but it was the introduction of the banana that allowed them to stay and grow a state that would eclipse the older Bunyoro kingdom. Bananas require fertile, well-irrigated soil, and the topography of this part of Uganda was ideal. They grew well here, far better than in the higher grasslands of Bunyoro. Bananas were an important foodstuff; along with the fish of the lake, the people of this area enjoyed an extremely nutritious diet. With settled agriculture, a society quickly developed.

At this time of year, mid May, it rains most afternoons in the Buganda region, so the vegetation is a deep emerald green. We have come to meet a woman known by everyone simply as 'Mama'. She is the much-respected matriarch of a very productive small-holding. At first sight the area seems to be almost wild, but when you walk through it is obvious it has been carefully planned and tended. Runner beans and haricot beans grow rampant across the soil beneath trees laden with avocados, mangoes and bananas. Everything is growing with an almost frightening vigour. But the banana is king here, not just for the potassium, iron, vitamins and complex sugars it provides: its leaves are used for thatching houses and for wrapping and packaging, in housing construction itself, its stems for tracing, its fibres for ropes. The fruit can be consumed sweet or as a starchy main course accompaniment, and of course it makes a heady beer and a frankly dangerous spirit. The British expeditionary journalist Henry Morton Stanley remarked that it was 'everything but meat and iron'. As Mama says, 'It has a soft heart, just like the Buganda people.'

Dozens of varieties of banana (or *matoke* as it is known locally) are grown in Uganda, but here on Mama's small-holding they concentrate on half a dozen that have been chosen to make the most of the growing season and offer a range of cooking options. It has been a bumper season. I watch Mama cutting the last few bunches of fruit. Each bunch grows on a different tree; to harvest bananas means cutting the soft fibrous tree near its base to allow a new one to grow in its place. Mama uses a machete to slice through the trunk. She cuts the tree down with little effort. The trunks are made up of layers of fibrous, sticky bark that can be peeled back with one's fingers. The top of the tree separates from the base and folds slowly down towards the ground, allowing Mama to cut off the bananas with ease. She then cuts the leaves from the trunk and lays them in piles, taking particular care to place the central topmost leaf safely in the centre. It is believed that this core of the tree is special, a living metaphor for the flow of historical narrative that lies at the heart of any family.

Mama has asked me to stay for supper to try *matoke*. We sit on the steps of her house, peel the bananas and wrap them in several layers of banana leaves before tying them together in a parcel that is placed in a pot of boiling water. We sit and talk and watch late afternoon lightning forking down to the horizon. As the light begins to disappear the house fills with the comforting smell of our evening meal. As darkness falls we unwrap our piping hot parcel and enjoy the rich, buttery *matoke*. In the countries of East Africa banana consumption is higher than anywhere else in the world. Sitting here with Mama and her family, I am beginning to understand some of that sophisticated, rich context.

Among the banana groves another tree thrives from which the innovative people of this region fashioned one of the earliest homestead industries. The next morning I find my way to Bugerere to see traditional bark-cloth being made by a family who have been engaged in its production for centuries. Nsanga is an isolated hamlet nestling in some beautiful forest about an hour from Kampala. It is the place where bark-cloth has been produced for generations; indeed the bark-cloth from Nsanga has been used by the Kabaka. The town's cloth production is focused on two studios.

The origins of bark-cloth are now obscured by time, but there exists oral history that places its invention deep in the distant past, at the time of Buganda's origins. That is not verifiable, but it was certainly being used in the twelfth century, and had percolated out beyond the aristocracy to be in general usage by the seventeenth century.

As I arrive, the 'old man' Omutaka Kabugozza, the senior craftsman, is leaving to go to a funeral, but he stays long enough to tell me how he has grown up with bark-cloth and has passed on the craft to dozens of younger men. He sees the cloth as core to the Buganda narrative, an ancient but still highly relevant craft. As he says goodbye to me, he leaves me in the hands of a group of middle-aged men who were all trained by him in their youth. Unlike the salt production of Bunyoro, this was a male occupation, passed from father to son.

Emmanuel Ssonko offers to be my guide. I follow him through the heavy undergrowth until we find a mature ficus (a kind of fig tree). I watch as he scrapes off the outer layer of bark and cuts two lines about half a centimetre deep at head and ankle level into the white sappy flesh of the tree. A precise vertical line is then carefully incised down the tree joining the two initial incisions. Using a piece of discarded banana bush sharpened into a wedge,

Emmanuel eases away the outer layer of the tree along the vertical incision.

For me, this is about the people of Buganda's connection to the land and the environment. Just as Bunyoro claimed its roots set it firmly in its territory, Buganda looked for symbols that gave it a sense of place.

Slowly a perfect rectangular slice of foamy, sticky bark is peeled away from the core of the tree. It is wrapped in ever-useful banana leaves and put safely to one side. Then, to protect the naked and vulnerable tree, a bandage of banana leaves is tied around the de-barked trunk. This way a tree can be harvested every six months.

The slither of rectangular bark is then beaten diagonally across the grain with three different weights of mallet: the first to break the fibres, the second to begin to separate and widen them, and the last to refine the texture. At the end of this process a piece of flexible cloth the size of a bed-sheet is left to dry before being finished with a final beating.

I leave the forest with the sound of bark-cloths being beaten echoing through the trees. It is only from a distance that the drum-like rhythm is obvious. Buganda must have been a deeply impressive culture at its peak.

Making a product like this would have allowed families and villages to participate in the emerging wider economy, provided they had some land available to them among the banana groves. By the second half of the eighteenth century, as well as being worn for rituals and ceremonies, bark-cloth would have been used to pay land rates and fines to clan chiefs. People were encouraged to wear it; it had become a badge of identity. The cloth itself was so important that it had trade value. Today, as it has been for centuries, bark-cloth is regarded as sacred.

By the mid eighteenth century, Buganda had grown. The once small groups of cultivators living by the lake had expanded to a significant territory. In a few generations the Buganda kingdom had exploded and it now rivalled its neighbour, Bunyoro. The fiercely competitive kingdom of Buganda realized that it had a chance to become unassailable, although to take on Bunyoro would demand some audacious and fearless thinking. But Buganda was now ready to take advantage.

Throughout the seventeenth century and into the eighteenth Bunyoro had also continued to trade and grow. But it had made the error of a fledgling political power and had not changed its laws to ensure smooth transition between kings. Its administration was still decentralized. With a number of independent principalities still within its borders, this could only spell trouble. In the late eighteenth century King Olimi VIII died, leaving two heirs. Oral history tells us that almost immediately the princes began to argue about whom the drum might choose as king. Rows turned into divisions in the court, which in turn developed into a series of deadly fights for the succession, weakening this once great kingdom. Not consolidating power when it was at its height proved to be Bunyoro's undoing. As the splits across the kingdom widened, princes and senior members of the royal family were given provinces to rule to placate them. Rather than calming the situation, the monarchy had simply given away valuable power, which only served to embolden those on the fringes of the court. It left the kingdom even more vulnerable to rebellion and exploitation by its neighbours.

By the end of the eighteenth century a burgeoningly confident Buganda had expanded to occupy new areas such as Koki and Buddu. These regions that were strategically crucial as they cut off Bunyoro's access to Lake Victoria, and to the vital coastal trade routes. Then in the 1840s came a shattering blow to Bunyoro: the powerful province of Toro declared itself an autonomous kingdom, taking with it one of Bunyoro's most valuable salt fields. Bunyoro was now almost powerless to react. The loss of the king's authority only emboldened provincial chiefs further. It was a devastating blow to the economy of the kingdom. And as Bunyoro threatened to disintegrate, Buganda grew ever stronger.

Buganda had begun transferring power from clan chiefs to the monarch. It had begun to organize its military, collect taxes and tributes, and build roads. In 1844 the first coastal merchants began to arrive in the court of the Kabaka. By the middle of the nineteenth century Buganda had become a serious power with a voracious appetite for expansion. A predatory politics was emerging in the region. The strutting, wealthy Buganda had sufficient power to take what it wanted from its neighbours. Spoils such as ivory – a hugely important export commodity – were collected almost at will. Determined to defend its lakeside border, Buganda also built up a vast royal navy of canoes to patrol and raid across Lake Victoria. The lakeside towns flourished as centres of entrepreneurial activity, drawing in people from across the lakeland region.

The big Buganda boat yard buzzes with activity today. One morning I make the trip down to the lakeside to watch as the boats return with their catches. Bunches of tilapia tied with twine through their gills are thrown on to a low flat block. An auctioneer picks them up and drops them – a firm thudding sound that confirms their freshness. A small man throws a bunch of notes on the table, a younger man grimaces and shouts a higher figure, and another note is thrown. Then a cacophony of bids breaks out, notes and numbers being tossed out one upon another. Each time a new sum is offered the auctioneer gestures at the original bidder to match it. Slowly the pile of notes in the auctioneer's hand thickens; a fat thumb covered in fish slime presses down hard into the wodge of green notes. At last the young man spits on the ground and walks away, and the small man smiles to himself. More boats are bringing in fresh catches, there will be plenty more fish, but the young man is gone. There is an edge to what goes on here.

Behind the harbour in the boat yard, fishing boats are still made in the traditional way. The boats for the most part are constructed from flat planks of soft wood that are slowly twisted and forced to take on the curves of the craft. Seams are patched with strips of aluminium that are riveted into place before the base is sealed with a thick layer of bitumen. The boat builders use simple tools – adzes, planes and saws – but deploy them very skilfully so the finished craft are strong and reliable. And they need to be: Lake

Traditional Bugandan canoe, photographed early twentieth century.

Victoria is not always a millpond. These days most canoes have outboard motors, but many are still propelled with traditional paddles. They are not beautiful craft but they are extremely effective, capable of cutting across the surface of the still lake at an impressive speed and of battling against wind and waves when the weather turns against them. It is possible to imagine how the Buganda navy would have struck fear into their opponents. The full-sized craft could carry between sixty and a hundred men. The navy was deployed to conquer islands and neighbouring lake territories, but the canoes were also used for commerce, bringing traders right into the heart of Buganda. Stanley described the navy on full muster as sixteen to twenty thousand strong. Even allowing for journalistic exaggeration, it was obviously a formidable force.

Arab traders, attracted by news of this growing economy, began arriving from the Swahili coast. They brought something new to the regional equation: they were willing to trade guns, ammunition and other valuable goods for ivory and slaves. The regional power balance had already shifted substantially in Buganda's favour, but this felt decisive. With succession wars weakening their northern neighbour, Buganda seized the opportunity to expand at Bunyoro's expense, and set about conquering much of Bunyoro's lands.

However, further north, things were starting to change too. Bunyoro's clan chiefs still held great power and in times of political instability internal disagreement could reduce the state to chaos. At the end of the 1860s Bunyoro found itself in the midst of its most bloody succession war to date. The king who emerged from this period of instability to take the reins of power has gone down in history as the strongest Bunyoro has ever known – Kabalega. He is a figure who has come to personify a glorious moment in Bunyoro history when the old kingdom got its old confidence back.

There is a shrine dedicated to his memory. The tomb of Kabalega sits in a compound in a thatched building on the outskirts of Hoima. This obviously loved figure was buried in a side-chamber at the foot of a deep shaft below the windowless building. Inside, the floor of the shrine is covered in ruddy-coloured pieces of bark-cloth held in place by nine nails and nine hoes. The number nine, the base number of Bunyoro mathematics, is special. When goods were sold they were traditionally grouped into nines. Here there are nines everywhere; even the stools that sit by the grave have nine legs. Everything connects the visitor to the notion of place: the skinless drums of Kabalega that were designed to resonate in the earth, the stools that were meant to emphasize a physical rootedness, the old agricultural implements – everything complements each other to create a picture of a people who were of this place.

Kabalega was a formidable strategist. He recognized what Buganda had got so profoundly and efficiently right; like his rivals, he introduced new trade routes and began working with Arab traders to bring firearms into the heart of Bunyoro. He set about gaining control of provinces that had been lost earlier in the century, pushing Buganda right back to its original borders. He reinvested in royal institutions and focused on the army, turning Bunyoro into an efficient military machine. Buganda had taken the crown as the great cattle capital, an invading force once having taken twelve thousand cows from Bunyoro. Kabalega reversed that decline, increasing his own herd to more than 150,000.

Policies such as these had a quick impact. The capital at Masindi expanded threefold and Buganda's long-term adversary was once again a serious threat to them and their monopoly in the region. In the 1870s Kabalega began to build links with Zanzibari traders. These traders drove hard bargains for goods such as ivory, but Kabalega wanted guns. A musket worth $1 on the coast was bartered for ivory worth fifty times that in Bunyoro. It was a price worth paying. There had always been trade northward with merchants from the Sudan region, but these Khartoum-based traders had become increasingly involved in local politics, difficult to control and sapping resources and influence. In the 1880s a Mahdist uprising in Egypt weakened Kabalega's northern rivals, enabling him to push the interlopers northward. He consolidated these advances with skilful democracy.

Through the 1880s Bunyoro grew in strength; Buganda, after decades of growth, had entered a period of decline. It had suddenly found itself spread thinly, and its adversaries were able to stretch, counter, defeat and humiliate the great kingdom. It continued to achieve successes in smaller battles and more prolonged campaigns, but its army looked vulnerable for the first time. By the end of the 1880s Bunyoro and Buganda were of a similar stature, almost too big and successful to risk a war. The old enemies squared up for momentous change. Bunyoro was the old power, the kingdom that felt it had a right to rule over its established lands, the salt gardens and the spiritual home to their Chwezi shrines, its new northern trade routes and reinvigorated armies. Buganda was big, a relatively new kingdom, born from empire building, that had grown powerful through bananas, barkcloth, its royal canoe navy and an organized standing army.

With so much at stake and tensions at an all-time high, new players were establishing themselves on the scene. Until the mid nineteenth century this region of central Africa was a blank void on European maps. As Bunyoro and Buganda headed towards a more equal, albeit tense, footing, intrepid white explorers began their first expeditions to the region. Most European trade and exploration had restricted itself to the African coast, which meant the continent's interior remained something of a mystery. Despite being beyond Europeans' reach, it was certainly not beyond their imaginations. It may not have been charted but it had become well known. For many Europeans this was a special place, the possible source of the Nile – the biblical river. This was the body of water that had sheltered the baby Moses from the Egyptian pharaoh; along its banks Mary, Joseph and baby Jesus sought refuge and were saved. The twin pillars of the two Christian testaments had sought sanctuary on its banks, yet its source remained closed to the Christian world.

In an increasingly religious period, the source of the Nile became a tantalizing target for explorers. It was a quest with history and pedigree. Even before the birth of Christ the Greeks had tried to navigate the Nile's lower reaches to find its source.

During the time of Ptolemy II (283–46 BC) a Greek expedition penetrated beyond the cataracts deep into the higher reaches of the Blue Nile. The Portuguese merchant pioneers of the fifteenth and sixteenth centuries traced the Blue Nile to its source in Lake Tana in Ethiopia. However, they knew that even though the Blue Nile gave the river its enormous volume, it did not hold its true source. It was another wave of European empire builders who took up the challenge, the Victorians. For an ambitious generation of British nineteenth-century explorers the source of this biblical river was one of the few remaining romantic quests. And although less written about, there was also the economic imperative of dominating a potential highway from the coast into the heart of Africa. Could this river become the basis for the religious salvation of the African continent while offering a new well of economic benefits for an ambitious generation of Europeans?

In the second half of the nineteenth century a handful of the most driven Victorian explorers joined the pursuit. John Hanning Speke, an ex-British army officer, had already made two unsuccessful attempts to find the source of the Nile; both had ended in near fatal catastrophe and he had been forced to limp home to lick his wounds. But the quest had got under the skin of Speke and his expedition partner Richard Burton, and they refused to give up. In 1858, on their third attempt, while Burton was incapacitated with illness, Speke came upon a vast body of water that he named Lake Victoria. Speke pushed on along the lake's northern edge to locate what he claimed to be the source of the Nile.

It was Burton's last great journey. He was one of the greatest explorers of the Victorian age. He had visited Mecca disguised as a Muslim, travelled along the east coast of Africa and written about his adventures to wide acclaim. But this was different. The journey into the heart of Africa had not just tested them physically and psychologically, it had broken their friendship. They returned to London separately. Speke arrived first, and made his announcement of the discovery of the source of the Nile at the Royal Geographical Society. He was not given the reception he craved. Many who mattered saw it as a premature and unjustified

THE ILLUSTRATED LONDON NEWS.

No. 1211.—VOL. XLIII.　　　　SATURDAY, JULY 4, 1863　　　WITH A SUPPLEMENT, FIVEPENCE

WAR WITH JAPAN.

IF a sarcastic enemy of this country were asked to define what was meant by the advancement of civilisation by England, he would probably reply the opening of new markets for trade at the point of the bayonet. Although, as good patriots, we may reject the sneer, as men of common sense we must accept the fact. Passing by other and less important, though, so far as the theory is concerned, not less significant instances, take that of China. For how many years did we offer civilisation in the shape of bales of goods for sale to a country so benighted as not to understand the symbol; and how long was it that we were kept on the threshold of a land, the exclusiveness of which gave it an air of enchantment to our eyes? But the urgency of our

peculiar principle of civilising the barbarian was not to be denied; and, after a protracted series of mistakes in ravaging the coasts and destroying provincial peasants, who were of less account in the estimation of the ruling powers than so many pigs of the Emperor's own breed, in the course of a third or fourth Chinese war we found ourselves in Pekin; and at last we were understood. It was discovered at the fountain head of Chinese policy that the armed Englishman was only the precursor of the enterprising trader; and, so far as things have yet gone, there is every reason to believe that the Celestial Empire is at length opened to the commerce of Europe, with special advantages attaching to that of England. On the abstract question of general policy involved in the system of

the invasion by the sword to make way for the invasion of commerce it is useless now to dilate; but, in reference to the conduct of the details of that policy, a useful lesson has been learnt from the course of events in our successive operations in China. It has been clearly demonstrated that little wars, even with Asiatics so unwarlike as the Chinese, are mistakes. When we left off something like buccaneering on the seaboard of China, and waged war as between Queen and Emperor, the difficulties were found to be less, and the results actual. As it has been with China, so in seems that it is likely to be with Japan. The latest accounts inform us that, ere this, war has been distinctly declared against Japan by England, France, and Holland, and the question arises how

RECEPTION OF CAPTAINS SPEKE AND GRANT BY THE ROYAL GEOGRAPHICAL SOCIETY.—SEE PAGE 11.

Speke addresses a rapt Royal Geographical Society.

pronouncement. Speke's equipment, his means of verification, had been lost or damaged during the expedition and Burton, with whom he was no longer on good terms, could not, or possibly would not, corroborate his claim.

The controversy and debate served only to heighten the sense of excitement about the source of the great river and the potential of the region, inspiring David Livingstone, a medical missionary, to try to substantiate or disprove once and for all Speke's claim. And when Livingstone disappeared, Henry Morton Stanley followed.

They were all ruthlessly ambitious romantics, each driven in part by the idea of locating the source of the biblical river but each also hungry for fame and everything that might come with it. Burton was an orientalist who simply loved the idea of 'exotic' cultures and alien things to delight and stimulate his voracious intellectual appetite. Speke was a soldier who was doggedly determined to prove himself; with each failure he only became more driven. The devout Livingstone saw himself as beating out a path for religious and intellectual enlightenment, while Stanley, the journalist, simply knew a good story when he saw one. It was storytelling that would really win this race. As Livingstone went westward into the Congo region, Stanley circumnavigated Lake Victoria, confirming Speke's claim by locating falls on the northern bank – the source of the Nile. It was just as Speke had described it.

It was epoch-defining stuff. They all wrote their accounts, but it was Stanley who was lauded and enriched in the post-discovery period. Subsequently, perhaps more so than the soldier, the missionary or the professional traveller, Stanley went on to do real damage to the indigenous population. His book *Through the Dark Continent* helped to paint a picture of a helplessly violent and savage place that could only benefit from European contact. It fed Europe with what it wanted to hear. Perhaps understandably, it was Stanley who was later commissioned by Leopold II, the Belgian king, to devise a campaign to claim the Congo on Belgium's behalf. Stanley fulfilled his brief, opening up the region to some of the most highly organized colonial brutality the African continent ever saw. The drive to save souls, to enlighten the 'Dark Continent', cost many millions of lives. It is one of the darkest chapters of colonialism. The spectres of that period still stalk the land.

Today, the boat trip out to the source of the Nile navigates down between steep-sided banks, thick with creepers, bushes and mature trees. Once this area was an unnavigable set of rapids, but since 1954 when the Owen Falls Dam was built, widening the riverbanks, it has become easier to travel up to Lake Victoria to see what Speke called the source of the Nile. The water here flows glassy flat, but the deep brown colour disguises a 30-metre depth and deadly eddies. The locals fish tilapia and perch from dug-out boats, and the occasional felucca sail can be seen tacking across the flow, but most local people avoid these waters if they possibly can.

Submerged beneath the dammed waters, among the rushes, what the Victorians called the river's source is still evident. Hundreds of gallons an hour of fresh water percolate up through the rocks creating flat plates of clear fresh water on the surface. There is a plain cement marker to draw attention to the spot but little else. It is modest and immense. It takes three months for water to travel the 6,500 kilometres from this spot to the Mediterranean. Many rivers end their lives in Lake Victoria, but only one starts here – the Nile. These waters will flow across Sudan, through the white clay that gives the river its name, and then join the Blue Nile as it passes through multiple descending cataracts into Egypt, defying the heat of the desert before meandering out into the sea.

I retreat 200 metres away to a hill overlooking the river. It is the site of a Victorian monument to Speke; it looks down over a spot that seems to match an engraving in Speke's book. It is a place where Speke stood and surveyed the site of his greatest success, and it's an epic view, looking down into Lake Victoria towards Kenya and Tanzania. But there is also something quite sad about the place. It's not just the faded grandeur of the monument, it's also that it marks the conclusion of Speke's odyssey, a journey inspired at least in part by an ambition to do good but which resulted in the beginning of Uganda's colonial experience. Speke's lasting legacy is a theory he concocted about the reasons behind the success of the kingdoms of this area. He promulgated the idea that these sophisticated peoples could only be descended from the lighter-skinned people of the north, and unfortunately his racist notion stuck and became part of the orthodox history for many years.

After lunch I begin the drive back towards Kampala. In the late afternoon I turn my car off the bumpy road and weave along a tiny lane past children who have just finished school. It is the new moon when, according to Buganda tradition, women are said to menstruate and the blacksmiths are inspired to create special tools. I am heading for a village where a family of very talented black-smiths have been making tools for centuries.

As I arrive the natural light is fading. This is not a town of generators and satellite dishes so as night descends the only light comes from the fire of the forge. The mechanism of the furnace itself is buried in the ground, but above are the glowing coals, hot enough to melt the local ore and turn it into a rough pig iron. The only moving parts of the forge are a powerful pair of bellows that are being forcefully plunged into the ground. The bellows create a rhythm for a new moon dance, and in the flickering light of the forge the women join the men to dance and sing. It is a joyous celebration of ancient tradition that remains passionately celebrated today. A man tries to sell me his metal wares; among the scythes are lozenge-shaped spearheads and barbed arrowheads. This is a modern society, but aspects of its most vivid traditions have remained unchanged for hundreds of years.

It was the journalist Stanley, however, not Speke, who had a truly profound effect on the region. On 15 November 1875 he sent a letter to the *Daily Telegraph* describing this region as the 'Pearl of Africa', and the king of Buganda as a sort of enlightened despot keen to hear the gospel. His letter had the desired effect, and in 1877 the trade routes from the coast brought a new kind of import across Lake Victoria: missionaries.

The missionaries were immediately successful. Many of the Buganda chiefs welcomed Christians; they felt that the kingdom had fallen on difficult times. It had suffered unthinkable defeats to Bunyoro, sickness stalked the land, and Kabaka Mutesa seemed to be blighted by repeated bouts of illness. But the missionaries did not deliver what they expected. As in so many other parts of Africa, the introduction of Christianity in Buganda was by no means smooth.

I get back to Kampala to join the crowds gathering for Martyrs Day, one of the country's biggest annual Christian holidays. The full moon may be the time for traditional celebration, but it has also become the time to commemorate the day in 1886 when twenty-two Catholics paid with their lives for choosing Christianity over Kabaka Mwanga, who had succeeded Mutesa after his death. The beheading and castration of these early Buganda Christians was not just meant to send a message to the people of Buganda, it was also a warning to outsiders that Buganda was still powerful and, when necessary, ruthless. The king reigned supreme.

I join a congregation of at least a hundred thousand others at the shrine of the Catholic martyrs. This tradition may have started as an open-air church service, but today it has grown so big that even a kilometre from the waterside altar the crowds are almost too dense to push through. People gather from all over Uganda and beyond, some of the most devout walking behind cross-bearers from as far afield as Kenya, Tanzania, Sudan and Rwanda. They converge on a handful of streets, joining hundreds of buses, thousands of cars and tens of thousands of Kampala's resident Christians. Even though the communion service is played through a substantial public address system, many never make it close enough to hear the blessing, to pray for forgiveness or to give thanks; they simply want to stand in the adjacent streets and to feel part of a huge religious moment. Like all events on this scale, Martyrs Day is an opportunity to hawk goods, to see friends and enjoy a day off work. It is also, for me, an interaction with twenty-first-century Uganda, a country that is a complex ethnic mix of overwhelmingly young people. It is glorious, a very African mixture of both high and low church, both modern and traditional.

The closer you get to the site the more the density of people intensifies and the tougher it becomes to make progress. But inch by inch, smiling and easing my way between bodies, I edge myself through the last streets down across the park into the natural lake-side auditorium.

The area immediately around the altar glows in ecclesiastical colours. There are important bishops and cardinals here from right across Africa. Immediately surrounding them are hundreds of nuns and novices wearing white, and beyond them, in every direction, the biggest congregation I have ever seen. At least thirty thousand people in my immediate view, but beyond them every street and road is densely packed. These people have brought gifts of goats and chickens, baskets of fruits, boxes of vegetables, all of which are passed down over heads towards the altar. If crowds tell us anything about places, these people, like Uganda itself, exude a certain thoughtfullness. One can feel the pain, the weight and love of history, but also the aspiration to find unifying totems around which to rally.

It is a formal ceremony, a traditional mass, but on a formidable scale. Rather than dishes of communion wafers, here there are large buckets. The sound of hymns ripples out across the city, inviting everyone to join in. It is hard not to be affected. I cannot help thinking about the way Christianity arrived here, but these people have made it their own and it seems to have a power to cohere and inspire that is enormously moving. Sub-Saharan Africa has seen a massive growth in churches in the twenty-first century; it has been widely conjectured that the continent could be the future heartland for Christian thinking. One has to wonder what Henry Morgan Stanley would have thought about that. I have often thought that Stanley and his contemporaries were as much concerned with promoting European culture and economic interests as they were with saving souls. Christianity gave them a moral banner behind which to stand.

I think Kabaka Mwanga understood that. And perhaps in the murdering of those Christians he may have been trying to find a way of drawing a line in the sand. Not just in the face of Christianity, but in defiance of a host of burgeoning challenges and overwhelming encroachments. This was a king under pressure from all sides. As well as being threatened by foreigners from Europe, Mwanga had to contend with King Kabalega; but perhaps worst of all his own chiefs were beginning to see the advantage of collaborating with Europeans and began lobbying the Kabaka to open a dialogue with the British. Lugard went to Buganda in 1890 to secure an acknowledgement of a British protectorate. Mwanga was left with no choice. In 1894, under pressure from his own clan chiefs, the king of Buganda signed a treaty making his kingdom an official British protectorate. It seemed to many like the ultimate capitulation, but for the vast majority of chiefs and aristocrats in Buganda this was a marriage of convenience.

Lugard looked upon Bunyoro as the thornier problem, Kabalega as the more stubborn leader. Kabalega said he would rather wage war than 'allow the white man come into his country'. Lugard took this as it was meant, personally. It was a period when all across Africa Britain was consolidating its territories. In Buganda, the British benefited from the kingdom's well-formed political and social structures that gave them a means to rule. But this wasn't simply a case of the British gaining all the advantage at the expense of the Africans. Buganda had been given an extraordinary opportunity to ensure that they, not Bunyoro, would be the most important of the region's kingdoms. King Mwanga must have known that in signing the treaty of protection on Kampala hill he had sealed the fate not just of Buganda, but of the kingdom of Bunyoro too. He must have calculated that Kabalega, who had spent years rebuilding his kingdom, would refuse to enter into an agreement with the British.

A joint British and Buganda force launched a bloody war on the people of Bunyoro. The imperial invasion force comprised well-armed Bugandan men augmented by Sudanese and led by just eight Europeans. They devastated Kabalega's capital and burned the crops in the countryside for miles around. Kabalega escaped and began to wage a more unconventional war; he could not compete in military technologies, but he could in strategy. He deployed a targeted scorched earth policy, raiding tactically important sites and retreating, and took advantage of the Sudanese soldiers' disaffection to rebuild his offensive potential.

It was a gallant rearguard action, but ultimately the tide was against him. In five years of violence, an estimated two million people were killed and Bunyoro was decimated, both physically and spiritually. For a kingdom that believed in its permanence in this environment, it was a shock. Kabalega's decision to resist the British sealed Bunyoro's fate once and for all. This once great kingdom was relegated to a weakened, humbled position of inferiority, a shadow of its former self.

With Bunyoro now effectively crushed, Buganda fully exploited its relationship with the British and took huge tracts of Bunyoro land. But this marriage of convenience was never destined to be a happy one. By 1899 relations had soured. Mwanga became frustrated at his limited power and began creating problems for the colonial powers and they could see that things would be a great deal simpler with the Kabaka out of the way. The British exiled both Mwanga and Kabalega to the Seychelles. Imagine the scene, these two men, the most bitter of rivals, effectively marooned together on a tropical island in the Indian Ocean. Both thought they had made the right decisions for their kingdoms. Both felt cheated.

The British installed kings they could control, two boys who were later deposed by the colonial regime on a charge of incompetence. The two kingdoms of Bunyoro and Buganda were finally subservient to the British empire, swallowed up into a colony and then a new country – Uganda. The fact that the modern state takes its name from the kingdom of Buganda isn't coincidence, it's a reflection of the influence Buganda had within the British protectorate at the end of the nineteenth century.

All of the region's kingdoms were abolished when Uganda

The Kabaka – one of the 'boy kings'.

gained independence in 1962. For four decades they vanished from the map. But not from the memories of the Ugandan people. Buganda and Bunyoro were reinstated in 1993, along with Toro. The fact that their culture and history so readily returned with them tells us a great deal about what these kingdoms continue to mean to their people.

I do not believe in ghosts, but some landscapes are haunted. The past has been a powerful force for the peoples of Buganda and Bunyoro, sometimes destructive, sometimes profoundly unifying. It is difficult to know if these stories begin as history or as myth, but what is very clear is that as Bunyoro and Buganda jostled for regional supremacy one of the most contested theatres of war was history. Bunyoro needed its links to Kitara and the Chwezi to offer them legitimacy, and Buganda needed an infrastructure of myths of origin that could be shared through drumming. That history was as important to these cultures when they failed as it was in times of glory. Their rivalry inspired them both to great things, but was also fundamental to their downfall, as they began to see their success measured in the other's failure. It was only when it was too late, when the British had used their divisions to forge a protectorate, that they overcame their differences.

The truly remarkable aspect of this story is that a country with such a history of division, that continues to celebrate its ethnic differences, has today found a way to balance discrete regional cultural need with national narrative. In part this is because there is a genuine affection for the country, but it is also because its kingdoms, though ancient, continue to be celebrated, loved, and relevant.

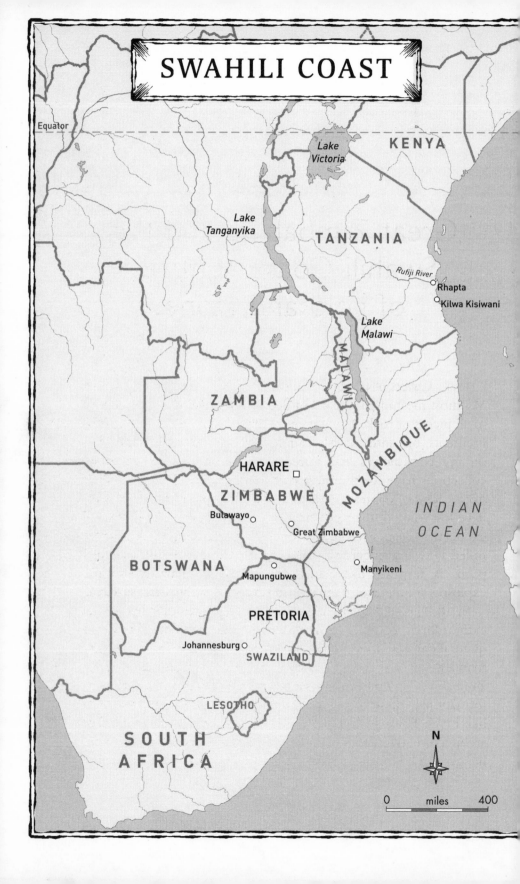

Great Zimbabwe and the Swahili Coast: cultures of gold and stone

I HAVE ALWAYS ENJOYED PICKING UP AND HANDLING STONES. My most meaningful record of decades of travel is a collection of small pieces of rock. Many were collected as mementos of special moments, but some simply caught my eye. After spending years on my bookshelves and stored away in shoeboxes, my stone collections have for the most part become decoupled from their stories. Out of context, extracted from their places of origin, they have lost some of their potency. But like all good stones they still exude that deep need to be touched. Some simply want to be rolled between fingertips, others to sit in the bowl of a cupped palm. A few are like jewels that carry the narrative of the explosive moment of their creation mapped across their surfaces.

In 1871, Carl Mauch, a German geologist, stumbled across an extraordinary complex of abandoned stone buildings. He never quite recovered from what he found: a granite dry-stone city stranded on an outcrop above an empty savannah – Great Zimbabwe. This miracle city sat in a region of dramatic natural rock formations – skyscraper stacks, monumental arches and cathedral-like caves. For a geologist it was already an important area full of architecture whittled by millennia of wind and water erosion, henges and stone defences, barrows and the archaeological detritus of ancient civilizations. He knew that more than two billion years ago when the planet still crackled and fizzed with the heat and radioactivity of its birth, this landscape was disgorged from the Earth's mantle. This was the place where the first bacterial life forms developed in that proto-organic moment of mineral and heat. As the lava cooled into granitic crystalline rocks, frozen sparks and explosions were trapped in the fabric of the landscape – evident not just in the residual radiation, but in sparkling mica, quartz and feldspar. It still feels like it is alive. As the geology stabilized over subsequent millennia, the evolving chemical ecology was perfect for the maturation of rich seams of gold. Great Zimbabwe is, and always was, a special place.

Mauch had no idea who was responsible for what was obviously an astounding feat of architecture, but he felt sure of one thing: the rock architecture of Great Zimbabwe was simply too sophisticated, too special, to have been built by Africans. Like dozens of Europeans who followed in his footsteps, Mauch speculated on who might have built the city: a 'civilized nation must once have lived there . . . I do not think that I am far wrong if I suppose that the ruin on the hill is a copy of Solomon's Temple on Mount Moriah and the building in the plain a copy of the palace where the Queen of Sheba lived during her visit to Solomon.' For Mauch and his generation, Zimbabwe was a multi-layered conundrum; they were intrigued not only by who might have created the site, but also by why it was built and indeed how it was constructed. For a geologist, it was a delicious puzzle. The very rock Mauch had spent his life studying had seemingly, miraculously, transformed into architecture. Great Zimbabwe was a place that seemed almost supernatural, as if a citadel had grown out of the very landscape.

Over subsequent decades European explorers and scientists found that Great Zimbabwe was not an anomaly, it sat as the spectacular head of a chain of dry-stone structures that stretch down and across southern Africa to the Indian Ocean. Although they remain mysterious, there has been a significant amount of study and conjecture about how and why they were built. Through colonialism and then apartheid, these sites suffered decades of skewed and tainted interpretation. Today, as new technologies and approaches become accepted, it is time to reconsider Great Zimbabwe in the light of the latest thinking, and to ask again how and why its creators built one of the world's great wonders.

As I embark on the trip, scholars are for the first time piecing together the fragments of information we have about Great Zimbabwe and its connections to the other kingdoms of pre-colonial southern Africa, building fragile but compelling evidence that suggests these rock sites formed a sophisticated trade network between Swahili traders on the east coast of Africa and the peoples of the interior. This was a network of mutually supported economies held together by the mutually beneficial drive to safe-guard a lucrative gold trade. But one is left wondering, who were the people who drove this trade? And how were these highly unusual long dry-stone walls and exquisite maze-like corridors used?

I decide to begin this journey a thousand miles from Great Zimbabwe, on the eastern edge of the continent where Africa meets the Indian Ocean. I want to trace the trail of gold and goods from the great trading emporia on the Swahili coast to Great Zimbabwe, to gain some sense of the scale and influence of that mysterious culture. I am hoping that I can begin to get a picture of Great Zimbabwe as a political and cultural entity through the kingdoms and civilizations that formed the trading symbiosis with it.

For centuries traders have been drawn to the Swahili coast from as far away as India, China and the Middle East, by the trade in raw materials but over time most particularly in gold. Recent research suggests that this coast was central to an intercontinental trade in gold which originated at Great Zimbabwe. It might be tempting to interpret the beautiful Great Zimbabwe as a symbolic jewel, a vast ceremonial sculpture in stone. But the site must have been part of a complex and significant nexus of economies. To build, organize and drive Great Zimbabwe would have required considerable wealth, power and resource. It must have involved trading partnerships and supply chains that probably stretched from Great Zimbabwe out to the coast and beyond. The Swahili coastline would have been a possible conduit for the importing of trade goods from across the Indian Ocean and for the export of commodities like gold.

Tanzania is the Africa most people are likely to dream about before a first trip – not the Africa of news broadcasts but the Africa of Hollywood and wildlife films. Beyond the cities lie impossibly large areas of gently undulating honey-coloured grasslands, red soil and cloudless skies, and a coastline of immaculate palm-fringed beaches dotted with islands and ancient castles. There is evidence to suggest that traders were coming to this coast from far away as long ago as the first century AD. There are Greek travellers' records which describe and list ports, and major geographical and architectural features that would have been used as guides by sailors and traders of the ancient world. These guides, or 'periplus' as the Greeks called them, mapped out the world at the very edge of knowledge, offering a fascinating insight into their trading priorities and cultural prejudices. Hanno the Navigator sailed from Carthage (present-day Tunisia) right along the north coast of Africa down into West Africa, opening up trade and strategic opportunities to the expanding empire. Hanno sought to build new relationships and test out new supply chains for a variety of sought-after goods, but the dream was gold.

These great voyages were known for their danger, but the rewards were potentially enormous: new and rare goods that could be traded in the markets of Greece, perhaps even gold. At some point between the first and third centuries AD an unknown Greek merchant began an eastern trading odyssey. He set out to forge new links with the Red Sea ports, the west coast of India and the east coast of Africa. For the Greeks, these were places on and beyond the fringes of the knowable world, on the edges of the violent and unpredictable Erythraean Sea, a body of water that would have tested their maritime knowledge to its very limit.

To undertake a successful voyage demanded a very particular range of skills. One of them was undoubtedly self-publicity. The most ambitious and successful accounts became very well known. The language of the original *Periplus of the Erythraean Sea* suggests that the author was not a Greek scholar but a sea-toughened trader who knew how to fashion a salty tale while crafting a vital navigation and business guide. The knowledge accrued on these trips was not only potentially worth a fortune as a guide for future sailors, browsing the maps and reading the descriptions was also as close to exotic travel as most educated Greeks would get. As in the story of Jason and the *Argo*, these sailors were heroic figures, but gold was never far from their imaginations. After travelling sections of these original journeys on local boats, I have developed huge respect for the men who must have carved out these trade routes in ancient times. I can see why the text of the *Periplus of the Erythraean Sea* became significant and well known. Making these early voyages must have been tough and dangerous; these were uncharted waters bounded by unknown cultures.

The people who lived on the East African coast nearly two millennia ago had developed their own maritime technologies that elegantly dealt with the particular dangers of the Indian Ocean. Their fast boats contrasted with the Greek cargo ships. These local craft were designed to be undemanding and easily maintained. Dhows were light, flexible craft with movable triangular sails that could tack very effectively against winds and be easily repaired at sea, and their size allowed them to navigate inland on small waterways. The very fabric of these ships was often porous and could tolerate substantial water penetration. In fact the boards were often sewn together, and this gave dhows an inherent buoyancy and stability. Over generations every element was thought through and refined for sailing and trading in these difficult waters. It is quite understandable how these beautiful craft dominated the Erythraean Sea for thousands of years, carrying gold from the Swahili coast up to the Arabian Peninsula and down into South Asia. The demand they facilitated drove the development of gold refinement in southern Africa. Eventually it drew ancient Europeans to seek a means to build direct links with the Swahili coast.

What the Greeks found here is captured in the *Periplus of the Erythraean Sea*. It describes the East African coast from ancient Aksum down to a place called Rhapta, the most southerly port in Africa that they reached, and at that time the most southerly point known to the Greeks. Rhapta was a well-developed and popular marketplace described as two days' travel south of the Island of Menouthis. According to the *Periplus*, traders from India and Arabia came to Rhapta to buy ivory, fine tortoiseshell and rhinoceros horn; in return the people of Rhapta imported spears, daggers and glass. Could Rhapta be the proto-market that eventually supplied gold from some interior progenitor of Great Zimbabwe?

Unfortunately, as the *Periplus* is vague on the exact location of Rhapta it is difficult to know. But I have always felt that there is enough corroborative material to suggest that Rhapta, the great market, was not a fantasy; something significant was here. According to Ptolemy's *Geography*, one of the most respected ancient surveys of explorers' logs and map material, the first-century Greek merchant Diogenes was blown off course from his usual route to India. After a month of sailing south Diogenes, like the author of the *Periplus*, found Rhapta at the point where the Rhapta river entered the Indian Ocean adjacent to the Island of Menouthis. Where the Island of Menouthis once lay is now unknown, but these descriptions offer us tantalizing clues. The historian G. W. B. Huntingford, who has written at length on the *Periplus*, suggests a number of possible locations for the site of Rhapta but concludes that the Rufiji delta is among the most likely options.

So I am going to begin my journey on the edge of the continent with Professor Felix Chami, someone I have wanted to meet for years. I have read his work and been intrigued by his claims that he has found Rhapta, 100 kilometres south of Dar es Salaam, close to where the Rufiji river diffuses into a delta. The river mouth is adjacent to Mafia Island, just as described by Diogenes. Looking at maps, it seems to have many of the features described by the *Periplus*, and according to Felix he may have found a previously unknown site big enough to have supported a vast amount of ancient trade.

Felix is not as I'd imagined. For no other reason than his huge reputation, I had subconsciously already given him a formidable persona. But the man gesturing me aboard the small boat is friendly and avuncular. He smiles, but I can see he is slightly agitated. 'We have a long journey,' he shouts. The jetty is packed with hawkers and covered with a film of slippery rainwater so I cannot rush.

Almost before I sit down in the boat the outboard motor lets out a scream and we are skimming across the surface of the muddy Rufiji river. Down here, just above the delta, the river is treacle-thick and a deep foreboding bronze. Below us it feeds the biggest mangrove swamp in the world, an ecosystem of intense bio-diversity and richness; above us lies a network of rivers that perhaps once carried Greek cargo ships to Rhapta.

It is too noisy to speak so I spend my time concentrating on the riverbank, looking out for signs of archaeology. It is hypnotic. Monkey calls ring out across the water, monitor lizards bask on the banks, egrets make the occasional swooping dive towards the water, but the impenetrable tangles of mangrove roots and branches form a wall of vegetation that makes it impossible to see more than a few metres inland. Kilometre after kilometre, bend after bend, the outboard screams on.

After an hour we approach an open muddy bank and the boat slows. The only way on is across the mud. Felix goes first, moving on up into the undergrowth. I watch as the professor skilfully finds his way on to firm ground beyond the bank. It's now my turn. We have barely spoken. I want to make a good impression. I try to be bold, but the mud surface breaks like the skin of a cooling custard and with each stride forward I can feel myself sinking deeper into the warm ooze. Felix puts out his hand and pulls me up on to the bank. It looks like I'm wearing waders of crimson mud. Felix smiles, then begins to laugh. We are going to be OK.

Felix Chami's work has been revolutionary and controversial. Carl Mauch's attitude to Great Zimbabwe, his belief that the site could not have been created by black Africans, was a view that was widely repeated; at some point there has been speculation that the Benin Bronzes, ancient Egypt, Sudan and Ethiopia were all created not by Africans but by foreign interlopers. What Felix has argued – he would say proved – is that the Swahili coast that fed the ancient Indian Ocean and Erythraean Sea was driven and controlled by black Africans long before the arrival of Greeks and Arabs. His excavations at the mouth of the Rufiji have produced Greco-Roman pottery, Syrian vessels and Persian glass beads that may date back to 600 BC.

We begin a long hike through the undergrowth, occasionally on paths, but mostly I just follow Felix as he tramps through seemingly untrodden bush. Occasionally we stop for water, or for Felix to tell a blood-curdling story of snakebites or lion attacks, but mostly we just push on. It very quickly ceases to be exciting.

Felix has had his detractors. The ancient texts describe the people of Rhapta as big in size – might they have been Arabs? Many historians have doubted that the indigenous Bantu, a pastoral people, would have had much to do with coastal trade. And if you came from the arable open interior, why would you want to come here? It is humid and the air is thick with mosquitoes and the grass is densely woven with a variety of thorny bushes that seem to be able to penetrate leather. All around I sense but never see substantial wildlife – but we push on.

After more than four hours of walking, the pitch of the landscape begins to alter. If Felix has indeed found Rhapta, this will rank as his greatest discovery yet. It will also prove that this region, which is today a dense, barely inhabited forest, was once a vibrant part of the ancient world. I am intrigued, and between my increasingly laboured breaths I ask Felix why the people of Rhapta would have lived so far from the river. He tells me that the course of the river must have changed over the millennia. I am not sceptical, but I am also not quite convinced. The *Periplus* talks of Rhapta as a great trading centre, a cosmopolitan metropolis where traders from all over the ancient world would meet, buy and barter. It is difficult to imagine such a vibrant place existing here, in this riverside wilderness, with its crocodiles and snakes.

But another hour later, in the dirt beneath our feet, fragments of an ancient world begin to emerge. For the first time Felix begins to speak in an animated, almost emotional way. Buried in the ground in this isolated wilderness, Felix has found shards of pottery – tantalizing evidence of an ancient settlement. He thinks he has found Rhapta because of the age and variety of the pottery. 'This is the beginning of what I call the Rhapta site . . . and if you look down you can see pottery that's two thousand years old.' I sense that he is profoundly tired of being seen as unconventional, of having to fight his corner – he wants the archaeology to make his argument.

Pitted into the surface of the soil are fragments of ceramic, some just tiny flecks but a few are substantial, identifiable pieces of unglazed pot. Felix bends down and scoops up a piece of ceramic that I am dangerously close to stepping on. 'This is a piece of pottery. For sure it is two thousand years old.'

The words stick in my head. Two thousand years, which would indeed make this site contemporary with Rhapta.

'And imagine, actually, if you are able to clean this ground . . . look, you see, another piece there. When we go up I will show you more.'

Felix tells me that this place was the centre of a vast trading network that stretched down along the coast towards Mozambique, across South Africa into Zimbabwe. These pottery shards may have held trade goods from the interior or from one of the ports that bounded the Erythraean Sea. It is his belief that this was a trade driven by Africans, and if they were driving trade networks here on this scale, Rhapta could have been part of a network of interdependent cities that collaborated and cooperated on the manufacture and distribution of a range of goods.

I stop and pick up a pair of thumbnail-size shards. They have come from the rim of the same vessel. 'How old are these?' I ask Felix.

He runs his finger along the rough edge of one of the slithers.

'Two thousand years old,' he repeats. 'Carbon dating for this material is giving us a date of about AD 200 to 300. AD 200 is a common date here for this kind of pottery.'

'Are these imported or are they made locally?'

Felix stops walking for the first time in hours and looks at me. 'They are local.'

This is obviously important to his argument. Not only did the local communities have ceramic technologies, they were probably using these vessels to carry locally produced or refined goods. That would imply quite a complex culture or network of communities.

'Have you found pottery that has come from beyond these shores?'

Felix nods. 'We have found a good amount of ceramics which were brought to Rhapta from different parts of the world.' He shows me a large pinkish piece of very fine clay. 'We have had this kind of pottery examined by experts in Sweden who have confirmed it is from the Nile Valley.' He dips his hand deep into his pocket and pulls out another piece of ceramic. 'Here I can show you good pottery which comes from India, and this pottery has been testified by Indian scholars.'

In his palm lie a handful of shards that give a sense of how this was some sort of trading hub. But combined with the obvious sophistication of the local pottery, it may suggest that this was a complex community that traded across the ocean with an array of peer states. If indeed they were Bantu – African – then it would give credence to the notion that to the south and the west of here lay a cooperative network of communities supplying this coast.

The sun is already beginning to wane so we look for somewhere to camp for the night. At the top of the ridge we put up our tents and sit and talk and watch satellites scuttle across the night sky. Felix tells me more about the site, how he imagines it to be a beautiful city of cosmopolitan merchants who dominated coastal trade. From the flat hilltop, again it is difficult to imagine that this serene and isolated spot was once a thriving hub of commerce. It feels like we are in the middle of nowhere. But the evidence from the pottery – its age, its varied provenance, and the sheer amount of shards – suggests Felix is right. Perhaps this empty place did once play host to merchants from across the Erythraean Sea, from as far afield as ancient Egypt and India. From our vantage point it is possible to make out just how big this city may have been. It is a site that could have supported many tens of thousands of people. Rhapta or not, the pottery is evidence that from the earliest times this part of Africa had established trade routes with the wider world.

We sit up drinking until the early hours, Felix in a silk dressing gown, me cowering under a blanket as rampant mosquitoes buzz about our heads like Exocets. We swap stories of our historical adventures. Whatever I have done with my life is certainly put into context by the career of Professor Felix Chami, someone I will always treasure meeting. Talking to him has opened up a whole raft of possibilities about where to explore next. According to the *Periplus*, Rhapta traded in goods from the African interior like ivory and rhinoceros horn, but there is no substantial sign yet of historical archaeology of the trade in Zimbabwe gold, which is what I'm looking for. Great Zimbabwe is something of an enigma, but its production or control of gold was profound enough to shape the region and its trade relations. Rhapta could not have been its only coastal outlet; perhaps there were other ports that carried gold from the interior.

Before sunrise I am back down the path heading for the river-bank. I have a long journey south. I leave Felix sleeping, perhaps dreaming of ancient Rhapta. As I head back into town on the early bus with the market traders I can hear the buzzing, dynamic legacy of ongoing trade, exchange and contact with a world beyond this coast in the distinctive language the people speak. Swahili may well be a Bantu language, a relative of that ancient tongue spoken by the indigenous people who built Zimbabwe and Rhapta, but it is an African language that has incorporated many words from around the world. Swahili is a linguistic melt-ing pot, an analogue of the region that spawned it. Spoken from northern Kenya to Mozambique, it has touched communities wherever the great coastal trade routes reached, from Uganda to the Democratic Republic of Congo. Following its distinctive sound is to follow the trail forged by the gold trade centuries ago. The word Swahili itself actually comes from the Arabic word for 'coast'. The language contains traces of Indian and Portuguese. Portuguese traders first sailed along this coast in 1498, during their period of aggressive international expansion, and like the *Periplus*, they described a spectacularly wealthy city on an island just off the coast. And that is where I am heading next.

By the fifteenth century, trade between the Indian Ocean ports and the east coast of Africa was flourishing. New trade routes had opened up, carrying gold from the Zimbabwe plateau out beyond the Indian Ocean to China, up the length of the Red Sea and across the Mediterranean into western Europe. The competition for Zimbabwe gold had consistently driven up prices and strengthened fragile trade routes into a robust string of cooperative cross-regional partnerships centred around thriving cosmopolitan ports. Most coastal communities were minting their own gold coinage and could marshal military support when they needed it. After hundreds of years of sustained trade, the east of Africa had been transformed. Today there are the ruins of hundreds of ancient sites along the coast that attest to the money generated by foreign merchants attracted by a variety of trade goods, but mostly by gold.

One of the most impressive of these sites is Kilwa Kisiwani. Early Portuguese travellers described a city of fine coral-stone houses, including the ruler's hundred-room palace, full of gold, silver and precious stones, and streets that overflowed with gold. Kilwa Kisiwani was enormously powerful, a vital chain in the flow of gold; its storehouses, palaces and garrison offered every facility that could be asked for by an inter-continental merchant. The Portuguese also wrote about their Kilwa trading partners as black Moors, Bantu-speaking Africans of a similar ethnicity to the inhabitants of the Rufiji delta who so fascinate Felix Chami. It seems their descendants still controlled the coastal trade a thousand years on. Colonial historians assumed that Kilwa was an Arab outpost because of its Muslim heritage. But there has been an important revision of that theory. It is now accepted that Kilwa was African, that coastal trade was controlled by African Muslims – an interpretation supported by the observations of the famous Arab traveller Ibn Batuta, who came to Kilwa in 1331. Batuta writes about Kilwa as one of the most beautiful cities on the coast and he talks about the local population as being of very dark complexion and describes facial scarification. This was definitely an African city.

It was also a very profitable one that rose up at the same time as Great Zimbabwe to become an outlet for its goods. These merchants knew the international value of the precious metal and bargained hard. As gold flowed through Kilwa, so it grew, and by the fourteenth century the city had become one of the most important, and richest, ports in Africa. If you look closely, some of that wealth is still visible. One of the things that has drawn me here is a copper coin minted in Kilwa in the fourteenth century which was uncovered by archaeologists at Great Zimbabwe, 3,000 kilometres inland. This perhaps is evidence that Great Zimbabwe and Kilwa were two ends of a lucrative trade in goods. Archaeologists have found gold coins here minted by the town's founder, Ali Ibn al Hasan, as far back as the eleventh century. It was the abundant, stable supply of Zimbabwe gold that gilded the great Byzantine and Catholic icons and made Europe's royal jewellery.

The site is still spectacular, sitting right out on a promontory above a reef. The silhouette of a garrison, luxurious palaces and the mosque of Husuni Kubwa beyond remain imposing sights. Approaching on a dhow, it is still possible to see from the scale and scope of the enterprise just how wealthy and confident the coastal merchants had become. Among the ruins are houses that would have accommodated travelling foreign traders who must have descended on Kilwa from across the ocean.

I wade ashore on to a beach covered in tiny fragments of pottery to be greeted by a local guide, Athmani Abdullah. Kilwa attracts tourists today, as it once attracted adventurous travellers and merchants. A small army of young men make a living out of showing around these occasional visitors. Athmani has spent his adult life living and working here, and he knows this place as well as anyone. He leads me over coral-stone ruins into the substantial remains of old Kilwa. I am curious. Why out of hundreds of trading ports on a 3,000-kilometre stretch of coastline did Kilwa become the major conduit for gold?

Athmani points out to sea where the dhows are skipping across the waves, as they almost always have. 'It was easy,' he replies, 'for the traders to anchor from monsoon winds in this sheltered, reef-protected port.' The direction of the prevailing wind on the Swahili coast changes twice a year allowing ships to cross the Indian Ocean and return again within twelve months. Kilwa was ideally situated to serve as East Africa's gateway to the trading networks of the interior.

We wander over the site. More than just being surprisingly intact, it retains domestic architectural details that give it real poignancy. Substantial carving and painting are still evident. The people who lived here lived in great style. It is impossible not to be affected by this intimate detail, particularly in the mosque interiors where some vibrant colours remain, yellow and blue, inset blue and white Chinese porcelain bowls that once studded the ceilings, and fragments of ceramic tiles that decorated floors and walls. The domes may have fallen, but even in their prone state they still do that thing that all great mosque domes do: they still hold and resonate sound in beautiful ways. It may well have been a coast that was lubricated by commerce, but here, for the first time on this trip, I have a sense of an ancient culture and the way people lived. And like the stone sites of Great Zimbabwe, Kilwa Kisiwani was in part held together by the cultural cohesion and beliefs of the people who lived here.

I drop in on an archaeological dig led by Stephanie Wynne-Jones, a British archaeologist who works at Bristol University and is part of a team from that city who have made a long-term commitment to the archaeology of the Swahili coast. Stephanie has studied how Kilwa's fortunes have ebbed and flowed through the ages and I hope she will enhance my understanding of the people who lived in the city.

We meet beneath the vaulted interior of the Great Mosque. It is damp, slightly crumbling, but still imposing. Many of the great buildings of Europe were built around the same time – the Piazza del Campo in Siena, the Cathedral of Notre Dame in Paris – and to my eye the Great Mosque of Kilwa is a match for them. It is a beautiful, partially restored space reminiscent of some of the great ancient mosques of the Middle East. 'It was a congregational mosque where the whole community would have come together,' Stephanie explains. She points up into the huge, dark, arched ceilings. 'One of the things that is quite wonderful about this particular structure is the vaults you can see in the roof. It is a particularly Kilwa phenomenon to have such a plethora of domes and arches.' Coral, the building material, is the defining characteristic of Swahili architecture. There is no good source of stone on this coast, but coral is found in abundance. 'That block you are touching now was once soft living coral under the water,' Stephanie observes. The coral was cut from the reef and carved before it hardened. As at Great Zimbabwe, Kilwa's materials were chosen for more than their physical integrity. These builders wanted to link and re-link themselves to the landscape. They also shared with the builders of Great Zimbabwe the urge to make something more than just a functional building, to construct something that would define a people. As Stephanie says, 'it would have been gleaming white, it would have been beautiful'.

Ambitious archaeology has been going on here for more than fifty years, but only recently has there been a consensus to support the view that like the site on the Rufiji river, this was an outward-looking African culture that traded goods from across the Indian Ocean. The Great Mosque was begun in the eleventh century and was the first mosque built at Kilwa. But as Stephanie points out, one of the things the archaeology has demonstrated is that 'there has been a settlement here since at least the ninth century'. Centuries before Islam became the focus of coastal life, people traded here, perhaps as the Bantu population once did at Rhapta.

These were Africans who were directly integrated into the Indian Ocean system, trading the most valuable of commodities.

Stephanie tells me something surprising: the gold trail did not lead directly to Great Zimbabwe, it first went south.

So Mozambique is where I am headed next. It is a country I know, but which always surprises me. It's the place where the Portuguese merchants who visited Kilwa founded a long-term colony. This region was colonized in 1505, soon after Vasco da Gama's visit in 1498, and remained under Portuguese control until 1975, after which it descended into more than fifteen years of civil war. It is only relatively recently, after recovering from devastating floods and reclaiming its farmlands from unexploded mines, that the country has begun to build a confident sense of itself. It is a place of enormous style; its fashion, architecture, food and music are all very distinctive. I always adore visiting Mozambique. I have travelled its length a number of times, but on this trip I am going off the beaten track, 70 kilometres inland, heading westward towards the ancient gold lands.

I am hoping to find the first outposts of Great Zimbabwe. We know that Great Zimbabwe's heyday was in the thirteenth and fourteenth centuries – just when Kilwa, too, was at its height. But Great Zimbabwe is still two countries, one complex visa application and many days' travel away. Here in Mozambique I am looking for outposts of this gold-trading kingdom that could have maintained a long and complex trade route. There is one in particular, Manyikeni, which is mentioned in the history books and is my intended destination.

Unfortunately I cannot find it on any map. Beyond the coast the countryside very quickly becomes quite sparsely populated, but after several wrong turns I find someone who gives me quite confident directions. I arrive at Manyikeni at dusk. I park my car and before I unpack I explore the site.

Manyikeni lies in a relatively flat region but sits on a subtle hill. The land is scattered with rock, some of it a natural part of the landscape, some the scattered, robbed-out stone from the site. The site is not large, about the size of a football field. Beyond a

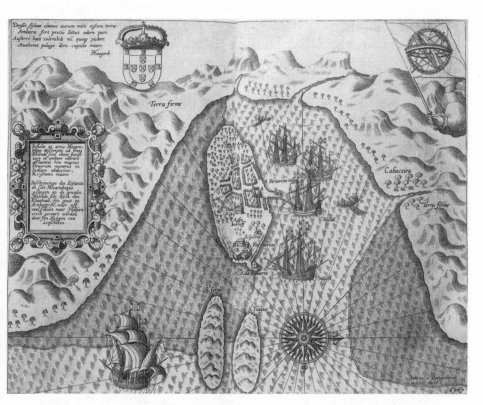

Sixteenth-century map of Mozambique and the Indian Ocean.

low wall, in the final moments of the day's light I can make out what looks like a constellation of small dry-stone buildings. At this time of the day, with the shadows long and fluid, it is as if the place is still inhabited. I imagine ghostly cattle-farmers droving cows towards this stony corral to beat the waning light. The people who live in the adjacent villages say that they still occasionally hear eerie bell-chimes tolling through the night. Before long a damp blanket of pitch-blackness folds in over the site, extinguishing the final vestiges of light and leaving me almost blind. I walk gingerly but quickly back towards my car, half believing the villagers' tales.

I am awoken by the sound of a car. By the light of dawn the campsite is barely more welcoming but I have slept surprisingly well. I dress in my tent and step out to meet local historian Vincent Vilanculos. Vincent is not alone; he has brought with him a number of local people. These are the people who have heard the ghostly sounds of Manyikeni at night and know that the site needs to be respected. Vincent says that they want to bless the site to protect me against snakes, but I have a suspicion that it is spectres rather than serpents they are really concerned about. I share their worries and take the blessed libations willingly. When the brief ceremony is over, Vincent whispers, 'The ancestors have heard us, and they have welcomed us.' With the blessing of his forebears, Vincent and I set off back up the hill towards the ruins of Manyikeni.

An untidy avenue of trees creates a natural path up to Manyikeni. As we walk, I ask Vincent, 'What was Manyikeni's relationship to the coast and to Great Zimbabwe?'

Vincent has a quiet voice but he speaks very deliberately and with great clarity, which lends his words a seemingly effortless gravitas. 'Manyikeni was in between the coast and Great Zimbabwe. People from the coast used to bring goods to trade here, and this was a place of exchange. In fact Manyikeni is a Bantu word which means, the place where people can give to one another.'

For the first time I begin to get a sense of how these powerful sites operated as regional trading hubs that could secure trade routes by their very influence and reputation. The inward–bound trade goods arriving at the increasing number of Portuguese–controlled ports would have travelled down the very route I have driven and found their way here to Manyikeni, this place of exchange. Where Kilwa was a market for sailors from around the Indian Ocean, this was a marketplace for merchants coming in from the coast who wanted to trade with Zimbabwe. Manyikeni was higher up the gold supply chain, and perhaps prices were cheaper here, but perhaps with Great Zimbabwe's organizational muscle they were able to control markets, particularly in gold, driving out competition and standardizing prices.

But such things remain a mystery. The existence of Manyikeni was barely known to scholars until the 1970s. When archae-ologists did come to dig it up they were rewarded with some valuable clues about its past. They found copper wires, blades and beads, and Zimbabwe gold was found in the graves of Manyikeni's elders. But this is a lost history in more ways than one: the museum that housed most of Manyikeni's unique and priceless treasures was destroyed in Mozambique's civil war. There is something about these sites that seems to be steeped in the enigmatic; they almost collude with their own mystery, resist-ing the hard work of historians. But even though that valuable material culture has been tragically lost, aspects of this site's history endure.

We are nearing the site, but Vincent stops to pick up a long stem of grass. 'This grass here is typical of Great Zimbabwe. In Mozambique it can be found in just this place.'

Vincent hands me the single stalk. It is a very distinctive sage-coloured grass with a full feathery head of reddish-brown seeds.

'So this grass, this particular grass, is only found in Manyikeni?'

'And Great Zimbabwe.'

So the people who built Manyikeni and lived there brought their own grass from Great Zimbabwe to feed their cattle and make this landscape truly theirs. There is evidence to suggest that cattle were driven seasonally from Great Zimbabwe and Manyikeni, the mature cattle being culled before they left.

Then I see the wall of the site for the first time in daylight and realize how emphatically the people who lived here wanted to make this place theirs, and for it to remain so. Even faced with the fog of an eroded historical narrative there is something about the materials, as at Kilwa, that speaks to the visitor directly. Seeing Manyikeni at dawn is quite different to encountering the site at twilight. The people who built the site were dry-stone sculptors who obviously loved stone. The walls at Manyikeni appear to have been built using a similar technique to Great Zimbabwe. They have been carefully crafted; stones chosen, sized, aligned and placed with great precision, and held in place by no more than their own weight. I am stopped in my tracks by the completeness of the site. It was occupied between the twelfth and seventeenth centuries and was one of a number of out-stations of Great Zimbabwe that now stand in Mozambique. A few areas appear to have been robbed out, but the walls still describe a number of clearly defined areas: an inner sanctum, areas for cattle and exchange, the defensive wall that would have protected and excluded. The space is not big, but it has been very carefully conceived, just like Kilwa, to safeguard its owners and protect the channels of trade.

On the west side of the site there is a small gap in the wall beyond which there is nothing but open pastures of Zimbabwe grass. These were probably the meadows where the inhabitants of Manyikeni grazed their cattle. This may well have marked the first few steps of the path to the Great Capital, the path from which a thousand years ago traders and drovers would have arrived and left. I am going to say goodbye to Vincent and travel west, towards Great Zimbabwe.

Manyikeni seems to have been a crossing point – in two senses. It seems likely it was a place where gold was traded as a commodity – coming in from Great Zimbabwe, then going out towards the coast, and by boat up to Kilwa – but it also seems to be a place where the attitude to the gold itself shifted: grave findings at Manyikeni demonstrate that gold was not just a commodity, it was buried with the dead – very different from Kilwa.

The evidence that Manyikeni was once a link in the gold trade between the region around Great Zimbabwe and the coast seems compelling; the architecture, the grass, the oral tradition and the discoveries of gold all point that way. But before I head for Great Zimbabwe I want to investigate stories of an even earlier kingdom: Mapungubwe.

Early the next morning I begin the long drive from Mozambique to the modern city of Pretoria in South Africa. I have done this journey a number of times before. It is straightforward, the roads are superb, the border crossing very efficient, the countryside monumental – but the contrast between the two countries is stark and difficult to bridge mentally. The cliché of Latin warmth and vibrancy contrasting with British coolness and distance would be too easy a paradigm with which to see the differences between Mozambique and South Africa, but there is a change in the cultural pitch that is immediately evident as you get your passport stamped.

Though just as African and culturally dynamic, South Africa wears its Africanness with far more restraint. Although Portugal had a reputation for a particularly ruthless form of colonialism, apartheid was devastating to many of the African cultures of South Africa, tidying away the awkward communities from the main highways. The road I drive, along rivers, through canyons and valleys, is probably similar to the path the traders and farmers took a thousand years ago. But while there are still the rocks that might have built houses of stone and fertile grass that could have fed their livestock, there are very few of the communities. This region is today a landscape of beautiful and peerlessly efficient farms, interrupted only by sleepy towns and the occasional awkward township.

Thankfully, the mark made by the communities of Mapungubwe has been carefully preserved. The site is now part of South Africa's Limpopo Province, and fate has been kinder to it than it has been to Manyikeni. The museum where

Mapungubwe's glorious past is now stored is still standing, in the country's capital, Pretoria, the home to an astonishing collection of ancient African gold. I am met there by the museum curator, Sian Tiley-Nel, who is something of an expert on the material culture of Mapungubwe. It is a coveted role, because she has in her collection some of the most iconic ancient southern African objects.

The focus of the collection is a small gold object, a palm-sized grazing rhino crafted from the lightest, purest gold leaf. Unlike a lot of African art this is a representational object, every detail of the powerful-looking animal held in delicate golden suspension. In the gallery light the gold looks so thin that it almost glows. 'The gold would have been hammered out on a gold anvil,' Sian explains, 'and they would have carved a wooden rhino mould and then folded the gold leaf over the wood, and all the little holes you see would have taken golden tacks that secured the gold sheeting to the wooden core. The wood has disintegrated over one thousand years, leaving one hundred per cent pure gold, with a lovely buttery shine to it.'

I am enthralled. I have spent my journey thus far chasing ghosts through materials, left behind by long-dead communities, and for the most part not really getting satisfyingly close to them. But here in this beautifully crafted and preserved object I can, for the very first time, almost see the fine fingertip impressions of the ancient people of this landscape. This was the product of a twelfth-century proto-Zimbabwean kingdom, only a short distance from the gold mines of the Zimbabwean plateau. Its people clearly developed great skill in goldsmithing, producing work that is impressive by anyone's standards. As at Manyikeni, much of this treasure was found in the graves of Mapungubwe's kings. Such burials imply a culture that valued gold for more than its commercial value. The tiny rhino is a perfect essay in gold crafts-manship, the work of a smith absorbed by the possibilities of his skill. As at Kilwa and Manyikeni, getting up close to objects shows how important materials were to the people of this region. This gold is being appreciated not just for its financial value but also

The golden rhino, fashioned from wafer-thin gold. Discovered in the Limpopo river in the 1890s, it may be a thousand years old. (Gus Casely-Hayford)

because of its unique physical and aesthetic qualities, and the art that it alone could make a reality.

It is time to visit Mapungubwe for myself, just a few hundred kilometres from Pretoria. The green fields give way to brown scrubland, and then the landscape becomes increasingly rocky. It is only then that I realize how tired I am after weeks on the road. Camping, driving and trekking has taken its toll on my body. I decide to treat myself and hire a plane for the remaining miles of this journey. It will give me the chance to see the site from the air. In this region of Africa planes are not considered a luxury. The scale of the local farms forces many to learn to fly. Farmer and ex-pilot Jacques Willemse agrees to give me a ride. He has two tiny Cessnas in a hangar by the side of a makeshift runway between two cornfields. I watch as he makes his pre-flight checks, trying to appear relaxed about the experience. For Jacques, flying is his main mode of transport.

We pick up speed and within what feels like metres of the end of the runway we are aloft. Instantly it is possible to see the Limpopo river cutting an extravagant meandering path through the rocky landscape in the distance. This huge river was for centuries a highway that carried people and goods from the interior to the coast. Jacques uses it as a guide, flying its course low enough to see elephants and rhino bathing in the waters, crocodiles and antelope among its rocky pools, and to wave at workmen toiling in the vast farmlands that sit hard up against its banks. Then, at its confluence with the Shashe river, where Botswana, Zimbabwe and South Africa meet, is a 300-metre-long teardrop plug of golden sandstone: Mapungubwe.

The name 'Mapungubwe' is said by many to derive from the Venda and Tshongo tongues and means 'place of jackals' – an allusion to the uncompromising and fearsome rulers who lived on the hill – but some say that it is a Lemba word that means 'the place where rock flowed like water', which could be a reference to a history of smithing on the hill. It is difficult to say what the truth is, but these riddles only enhance its reputation for mystery. Today it remains for many a place charged with a metaphysical power.

On the ground to meet us is a very cool dreadlocked park ranger by the name of Cedric Sethlako, who has agreed to show me around. Today Mapungubwe is part of South Africa's National Parks System, but it still exerts an influence on the people who live around it. Cedric tells me that even in relatively modern times local people 'believed you couldn't even look at the hill itself, they were even scared to look at the hill'. He recounts a tale of a local man who brought the first archaeologists to see the site but refused to look himself, approaching it backwards saying, 'There is the hill right behind me and I am not going there.' After spending the morning looking fairly unrelentingly at the hill from a plane, I am intrigued by these stories. Cedric looks at the ground and adds quietly, 'Some people believed you would go blind, lose your life, die, or something like that.'

Looking at it from a distance, there is something about this Place of Jackals that is a little foreboding. The landscape around the hill is pitted with sandstone rock formations – caves, tors, standing figures, frozen rivers of rock that are particularly distinctive. Over millennia the land has been a canvas for nomads and farmers. There was a tradition of rock art here long before a royal clan inhabited the hilltop. Many ordinary people left permanent records of their daily lives and concerns in the sandstone. The poignant modesty of many of their interventions in the environment is in stark contrast to the uncompromising re-engineering of the landscape undertaken by the people who lived on the top of Mapungubwe Hill a thousand years ago.

Cedric leads as we begin the climb. The people who lived on Mapungubwe Hill were an aristocracy that had grown out of a cattle culture. They wanted to become masters of this tough landscape. Their influence grew over a vast area that stretched for kilometres across the confluence, allowing them to farm, to hunt, to fish, to nurture their cattle and to trade and smith gold. They established a new way to live in this geography, making social hierarchies, exploiting economies of scale, building markets and creating symbiotic relationships with the nomadic cultures that seasonally passed through. It was the prototype for Great

Zimbabwe. Archaeologists believe Mapungubwe's reach spread across southern Africa from the eleventh to the thirteenth centuries, and that after the kingdom collapsed some of its inhabitants returned to their nomadic pre-Mapungubwe way of life; but others may have headed north and founded Great Zimbabwe. It was one of the most complex societies in southern Africa, with a rigid division between the head of state, his ministers and his subjects.

After some minutes of silent climbing we reach the top. Even with the modern convenience of paths and steps it is a precipitous 30-metre climb. Archaeologists now think that thousands of tons of soil were transported up here via the same route a thousand years ago. That speaks volumes for how the society might have been configured. 'The king chose to be buried here with a lot of artefacts,' Cedric says. 'If you look at the inaccessibility of the hill itself, why would people choose to live up here? Look around it, it is just sheer rock. There is no way you can access this hill; there is only one way up to the top.' It's a good question, and from the ground there are no clues to provide an answer.

The top surface is more than 300 metres long and tapers from 50 to 15 metres wide. It is a substantial undulating rocky surface with grassy paddocks and carved enclosures and millstones. The kingdom's rulers kept this space to themselves. Not only did the difficulty of access create an obvious demarcation between the royal family and their subjects, it also conferred defensive advantages. Ordinary members of Mapungubwe society were simply not allowed up on to the top.

Standing on the top, it is easy to understand why they wanted to build up here. It is simply beautiful. Huge flowing rocky vistas pour out towards the distant horizon in every direction.

We wander over the site. There is still a huge amount of physical evidence left by the people who lived on the hill. Archaeologists have found remnants of a grand stone enclosure up here, with buildings for servants and a wooden palisade built around the summit for privacy and defence. It was not simply an occasional retreat for the aristocracy, this was where

Mapungubwe's rulers lived, and died, with their gold. Near the widest end of the site Cedric stops to show me a shallow but wide dip in the rock. 'This is exactly where that little golden rhino came from; it is exactly where it was discovered. This whole area was a burial site. The people were buried in a sitting position facing west and each one of them wore golden bracelets, accompanied by pots filled with thousands and thousands of glass and golden beads.'

Cedric so obviously loves Mapungubwe that before we part company I ask him why it is so special to him. He gives me an answer I will never forget: 'Mapungubwe is the first southern African kingdom. This is where it all started.'

Mapungubwe was once the most powerful kingdom in southern Africa, but by the thirteenth century it seems to have collapsed; the archaeology does not tell us why. There is much more we don't know about the life of the people here – like how power was handed down, or what they believed in. The wooden and stone structures that would have stood on the hill have long since disappeared too, but the gold artefacts in the Pretoria museum testify to this ancient kingdom's existence, its power and its wealth.

It is late afternoon, and with only one fairly scary way down the hill we agree to begin our descent, before the sun begins its own descent. As we walk towards the sandstone landing at the top of the exit stairs, Cedric pulls on my arm. 'I want to show you something.'

We gallop back down to the centre of the site and he sits down facing two rows of cup-sized undulations in the sandstone. 'We have a game here,' he says. 'It was played by the ancient Mapungubwe inhabitants a thousand years ago. It is called Maruba in Suthu, Mafuva in Venda, and in some southern African countries they call it Bao. I understand it's Toro in Zimbabwe.' I recognize it; it's a game played all over Africa. In West Africa, the land of my ancestors, there is a very similar game called Oware. It is a game of strategy that a child can easily learn but which takes a lifetime to master.

I sit with Cedric as the sun slips towards the horizon taking turns to drop pebbles into the cups. I grew up believing that Oware was a West African game, but the fact that variations of it were played here in Mapungubwe hints at connections that extend across the continent. Maybe this was not an isolated kingdom. Maybe Mapungubwe was interconnected with other cultures. By the time we do descend from the Place of Jackals it is starting to get dark, but I now sense a protective warmth about the place, despite its reputation.

Within a few hours we are at the border crossing. There is an inordinate amount of paperwork to complete and an interminable amount of waiting. It is not an uninteresting place. Thousands of migrant workers crammed uncomfortably into vans travel in one direction and vehicles dangerously overladen with electrical and building materials seem to return – everyone in a hurry, everyone frustrated. Perhaps there have always been places like this, conduits like Rhapta, Kilwa, Manyikeni, Mapungubwe and Great Zimbabwe through which money and people flowed. Once it might have been the nomads and farmers like those captured in the rock art, trading from baskets and ceramic vessels, walking these same paths and crossings to find food, shelter or better prices for their goods. Technologies and cultures may change, but humans do not.

The last stamp is pressed into the final sheet of paper and we are free to go. As soon as we cross the Limpopo and enter Zimbabwe, the countryside alters subtly. I say goodbye to Cedric and head on alone. I have not just crossed a river and changed countries, I have stepped up on to the Zimbabwe Plateau. Rather than the sandstone we have left behind, this plateau that stretches north to the Zambezi river, east to the Victoria Falls and west to the Chimanimani Mountains bounds modern Zimbabwe with dramatic rocky features. The plateau is a plug of radioactive granite that was expelled from the Earth during the Archaean over 2.5 billion years ago, when the Earth's heat flow was three times higher than it is today. As this landscape cooled, the minerals and heat combined to provide unique conditions for proto-organic life.

Buganda and Bunyoro

This afternoon Uganda is playing Guinea Bissau. Before the football match a curious clown-like figure appears. The military dictator has become a figure of fun in Uganda – but beneath the laughter there is still profound pain. As many as half a million people may have lost their lives at the hands of President Idi Amin, his officials and supporters. This is a place where the past seems potent and ever present.

Above: The salt fields at Kibiro on the banks of Lake Albert have been producing ash salt for hundreds, perhaps thousands of years. The salt percolates up through the soil and is scraped off the surface into bowls by local Bunyoro women. It is skilled, tough work that is poorly rewarded – but they produce what is a vital and sought-after commodity.

Below left: A Bunyoro ceramicist crafting pots in his workshop, using centuries-old clay-coil technologies.

Below right: The priestess of the sacred Nakayima Fig Tree on Mubende Hill.

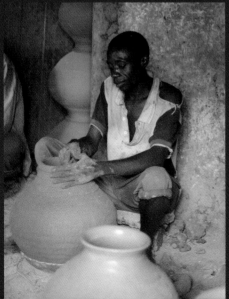

Above: Today, decades after the state drummers of Buganda were disbanded, their descendants still keep the tradition alive. I sat on the lawns of the old palace and listened to the troop playing drumming passages that have remained unchanged since the institution of the Buganda state.

Below left: I spent an afternoon with Mama Namayenji, who grows *matoke*, or plantain. This versatile crop remains a staple of Buganda diets. Its leaves and stems are used in a variety of ways from building to cooking.

Below middle: Bark cloth is still cut and beaten in the traditional way.

Below right: Mr Gombe is the major custodian of Buganda's drumming tradition. Although much of the supporting material culture and political infrastructure might have ceased to exist, these vital drumming customs endure.

Zimbabwe
the Swahili Coast

Right: The early-morning mist rises over the river valley. While the obvious plethora of archaeology suggests an ancient conurbation, is this really the site of Rhapta?

Below: The Husuni Kubwa Mosque at Kilwa Kisiwani is still impressive even in its semi-dilapidated condition. It was crafted from coral harvested from local waters and finished with the finest ceramics and tiles imported from right across the Indian Ocean.

Below right: Beneath the mosque's arches it is still possible to get a sense of Kilwa Kisiwani at its height. These buildings were conceived not just for worship, but to send a powerful message to every trader who passed through.

Above: The dhow to Kilwa Kisiwani, an island once described by an early-Portuguese trader as overflowing with gold. These traditional boats still tack up and down the strait today, carrying goods and people to and from the mainland.

Below: Copper Kilwa coins inscribed in Arabic with the prayer, 'Sulaiman son of al-Hasan, may he be happy'.

The honey-coloured rock of Great Zimbabwe comes alive, almost luminescing, in the early light. From a distance it seems like a natural phenomenon – both its scale and completeness defy initial comprehension.

The first Europeans who saw the site found it an enigma. They speculated over which non-African civilization had created these beautiful walls, and what the site was conceived for.

Great Zimbabwe was built in or around the thirteenth century by Africans, by a people who wanted to make a powerful statement about rootedness. It is an essay crafted in the most permanent of materials: 250 metres of exquisitely built walls, sometimes 10 metres high – a space of awe and reflection.

Within, it is
equally enigmatic:
claustrophobic
passages connect
wide enclosures
and tapering dry-
stone towers. But
all of this beauty
had a purpose.
This was the
centre of a culture
that dominated
the commercial
exchange with the
coast, through trade
routes that linked
its coastal satellite
ports with the Indian
Ocean trade.

Here they used
their wealth to
create something
that mimicked a
defensive building,
but in fluid beautiful
organic lines that
erupt from the
landscape upon
which it sits. It is a
tribute, a celebration
of this place.

Above: Approaching Mapungubwe from the air is one of the most uplifting things you can do – the teardrop-shaped rock is like a vessel rising up out of the plains. At the confluence of two rivers, its strategic advantages are immediately apparent, and scored into its surface is the undeniable evidence of ancient habitation: paths, carrels, and what appear to be the outlines of excavated graves.

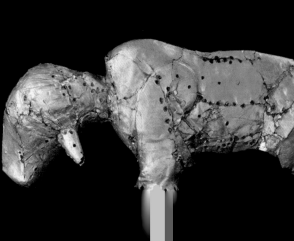

Right: Grave goods excavated from the site show the wealth and sophistication of its inhabitants – an elite who separated themselves from their subjects on the plains beneath. The culture inspired some of Africa's most subtle gold craft. Wafer-thin objects fashioned with the utmost care give an insight into this complex culture and belief system.

Having conquered the Mozambique coast in the early sixteenth century, the Portuguese swept north through this region of southern Africa looking for the source of seemingly endless gold. When they got to Zimbabwe they were amazed. One Portuguese captain described Great Zimbabwe in almost mythic terms: 'among the gold mines of the inland plains is a fortress built of stones of marvellous size, and there appears to be no mortar joining them'. Great Zimbabwe was Africa's El Dorado. It was, and perhaps remains, a place of myth and mystery.

I think this journey has peeled away a little of that mystery for me, revealing something of the geographical and historical context in which Great Zimbabwe was created. I have seen Great Zimbabwe's progenitor, Mapungubwe, and I have grown to understand what change these sites wrought on the landscape; how they nurtured the scale of trade and farming and developed the sophistication of the culture in the region. I've visited the earliest trading centres on the coast – one which pre-dated Great Zimbabwe by more than a thousand years, the other more contemporaneous – and seen how Africans consistently drove and finessed the Indian Ocean gold trade, building a huge two-way trade network for a broad diversity of goods. I've travelled through Manyikeni, one of a number of miniature coastal satellites of Great Zimbabwe and begun to understand the scale, influence and organizational capacity of this culture. But perhaps most profoundly, I have learned how this southern African landscape has informed the culture of the peoples who made their lives here. These were drovers and nomads who decided to settle and did so by making permanent and beautiful interventions in this landscape, marking their respect for this place and its materials. Yet, as I drive the final miles at the end of this long trip, I am still not sure what to expect.

The next morning I am joined at breakfast by Zimbabwean archaeologist Dr Edward Matenga. As well as formerly curating the site, Edward has written extensively about Great Zimbabwe. He has more than an academic interest in the place, he clearly loves it. 'It is the cradle of a lot of people who live in this region,' he tells me. 'The descendants of people who used to live here are now found in South Africa, in Botswana, and in other places.' He leaves me in no doubt about how important the ruins are to the people here. I must have the blessing of one of the site's spiritual guardians, Ambuya VaZarira, before I can get in.

Archaeologists are sure that Great Zimbabwe was a rich trading empire. Digs in and around the site led by Edward and his predecessors have yielded a wealth of trading goods – beads, bracelets, porcelain and glass – from overseas, but also gold that was mined locally. 'There was traffic linking with China, with India, with the Middle East,' Edward says. 'And gold was the material that brought this kingdom incomparable wealth and influence. Great Zimbabwe's rulers became powerful and they started to command people, and build unbelievable structures as an expression of that wealth.' One artefact in particular shows the link between Great Zimbabwe and the wider world: that four-teenth-century copper coin from Kilwa Kisiwani, the great trading city on the coast, a place that derived its wealth from sell-ing on the gold from Great Zimbabwe to the rest of the world. Two ends of the same trading route.

After more than 7,000 miles, weeks of travel and a lifetime of expectation, walking the last couple of kilometres to the gates of the park is somewhat overwhelming. We are quiet. We remain strangely quiet as Ambuya VaZarira meets us at the gate and gives us a beautiful blessing.

For two hundred years the rulers of this place controlled an empire between the Zambezi and Limpopo rivers covering much of modern Zimbabwe and part of Mozambique. This was their capital, their palace and their bastion. From the eleventh century to the thirteenth these people controlled the gold mines of the plateau; here in stone is their expression of that wealth and power. They chose to celebrate their power by constructing something that is more than a series of buildings. They have grafted on to the fawn-flecked grey granite landscape a series of dry-stone sculpted enclosures that demonstrate exquisite care and thought. Walls soar out of the earth and curve and flow around the contours of the

Early Great Zimbabwe excavations.

ground, creating narrow passageways and forbidding enclosures. Great Zimbabwe is a stunning feat of architecture. There is nothing holding its walls together, just extraordinary precision and craftsmanship.

These are some of the largest stone buildings in southern Africa. The walls of the Great Enclosure are more than 250 metres long and 10 metres high and undulate around the complex. They contain domestic spaces and large areas where significant numbers of people might have gathered. Above is the Hill Complex, a group of high-status buildings that have been placed precariously on the boulders, and beneath the Valley Complex, a range of living spaces of varying ages. To describe them in these prosaic terms is to do them a disservice; they are crafted with such skill and care, the product of an almost supernatural imagination. Exhaustion and exhilaration combine to make the first few moments of seeing the site somewhat emotional for me. It feels not just like the culmination of this journey, but like the resolution of the hankering that set me on the path looking for Africa's Lost Kingdoms. It is a place that makes the visitor feel an immediate sense of connection.

When we reach the wall of the Great Enclosure Edward stops. 'This is the highest wall in Great Zimbabwe, at eleven metres tall and six metres wide at the bottom. It is estimated that there are more than a million bricks packed into this wall.' These large dry-stone walls once surrounded stone and clay thatched buildings. At its height, Great Zimbabwe was a medieval city of twenty-five thousand, those inhabitants seemingly divided into social groups. Edward points out that 'beyond the stone walls, and least obvious to visitors, are housing units, dense housing units, that were located outside the enclosures over an area of about seven hundred and twenty hectares'. These would have housed the people who farmed, hunted, mined and protected this environment. Although we know very little about them, in a place where nomadic lifestyles were the norm there must have been good reason for them to stay; there must have been something attractive around which this society cohered. It might have been fear of the alternatives, but I would prefer to believe that this was not just a wealthy state, it also showed some consideration towards the welfare of its citizens.

Just as at Mapungubwe and Manyikeni, the king and his subjects seem to have lived separate lives. It is likely that Great Zimbabwe's immense stone walls ensured that the aristocracy were kept isolated. As we walk along the long dry-stone corridor that surrounds the Great Enclosure Edward explains that 'some people were not supposed to be seen in certain places on the site. The kings, the royal wives, would follow these passages, and the plebeians, the lower sort of rank, would follow discrete routes through the complex.' Yet for hundreds of years this place thrived, expanded and commanded a trading empire over thousands of square kilometres. There must have been a ruthless, uncompromising vision to achieve this, but it must have offered substantial rewards to many of its citizens, or it would simply have imploded. This was an advanced society that understood how to manage its trading relations. What a formidable vision it must once have been to see the gold-rich elite with expensive trade goods from across the region welcoming merchants and vassal chiefs and guiding them through the labyrinthine corridors to meet the royal family.

I have always wanted to see Great Zimbabwe, 'the great house of stones', a site shrouded in mystery for years. But although mystery remains, there is too an overt truth: it is shockingly beautiful. Perhaps I am tired, but as I descend the hill to leave I feel a tear well in my eye. There may well be a great many unknowns that haunt this place, but it is blatantly obvious that it was built to disarm simply by being. Its beauty is partially its purpose, to remind us across time and culture about what we are capable of.

Sadly that very ineffable quality was a vulnerability. For decades the significance of this place – what it meant, and who built it – was fiercely debated. The colonial regime that controlled this part of the world in the late nineteenth century believed and promoted the idea that cultures from beyond this continent, from the Phoenicians to the Queen of Sheba, must have built this kingdom. Thankfully those debates are at an end as carbon-dating technology has ruled out ancient foreign civilizations as being responsible for Great Zimbabwe. There is no evidence in the architecture to suggest that this place was built by anyone other than the indigenous Bantu-speaking locals. What we know of earlier settlements such as Mapungubwe shows an obvious continuity of southern African culture over millennia.

As I walk back to my car after saying goodbye to Edward I notice a coin-sized piece of mushroom-grey granite lying in the sandy soil between stalks of Zimbabwe grass. It is heavy and warm in the palm, but somehow uncomfortable. I drop it back where I found it.

There is so much we still do not know about Great Zimbabwe – the nature of its king or kings, the full meaning of its narrow passageways and formidable architecture. But we do know that this vast city was one of Africa's richest and most sophisticated kingdoms, and the starting point of a gigantic trading network that stretched from these high plateaux across southern Africa to the Swahili coast, and across the globe to Arabia, India and China. When Great Zimbabwe went into decline in the fifteenth century, so too did Kilwa: two kingdoms, connected by gold, and forgotten by historians for centuries. Today the ruins of Great Zimbabwe have given their name to a modern African country. They are a reminder that although ancient kingdoms can be forgotten, they are rarely truly lost. This remarkable kingdom high in the Zimbabwe highlands is an emblem of a continent remembering its past.

I began this journey some distance from Great Zimbabwe on the Swahili coast, thinking that this was a journey about trade, about gold; but it was about so much more than that. It has been an astounding experience to recover an African past from the ruins of lost civilizations. In Africa, the memory of these kingdoms, however fragile and enigmatic, is still celebrated, and rightly so. The past, like the environment, the landscape that made them, is very much alive here. It is a living, breathing part of people's lives, their cultures and identity.

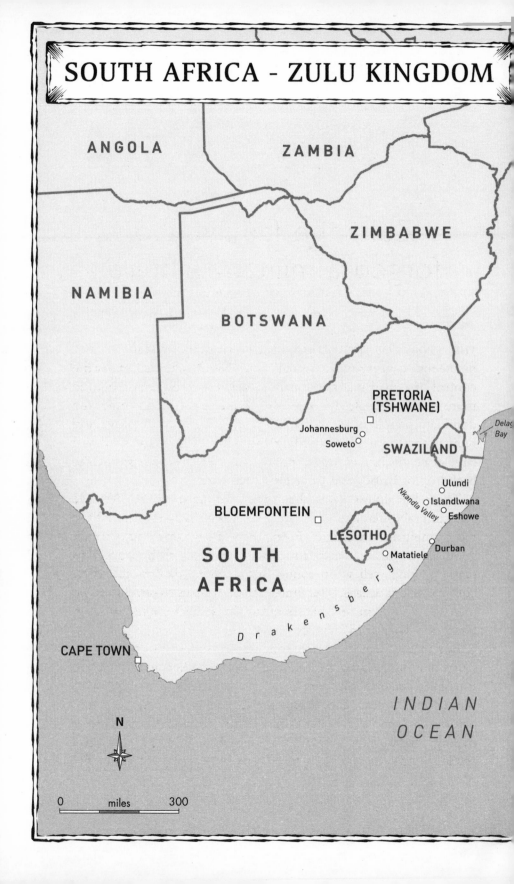

SOUTH AFRICA - ZULU KINGDOM

ANGOLA

ZAMBIA

ZIMBABWE

NAMIBIA

BOTSWANA

PRETORIA
(TSHWANE)

Johannesburg
Soweto

SWAZILAND

Delag
Bay

Ulundi

Nkandla Valley

Islandlwana

Eshowe

BLOEMFONTEIN

LESOTHO

Durban

Matatiele

SOUTH
AFRICA

D r a k e n s b e r g

CAPE TOWN

INDIAN

OCEAN

N

0   miles   300

Zulu: the family who forged a military empire

THE STORY OF THE ZULU BEGINS AT THE DAWN OF THE nineteenth century when a small cattle-based polity fell under the control of a charismatic visionary leader. Over the course of little more than a single lifetime the Zulu grew to become the dominant people of southern Africa and forged a way of life and reputation that is still a binding force for millions today. It is a large-scale history of trade, politics and war forged against the backdrop of British and Boer encroachments.

There has almost always been intercontinental trade. Distance and cultural difference have rarely been worthy adversaries of the most ambitious exchange. From the earliest times sought-after goods have been passed from hand to hand, from market to market, along well-worn routes that straddled deserts, countries, continents and oceans. The fundamental impetus to develop commercial activities means that there has always been some European awareness of African cultures.

But second-hand, remote contact was simply not enough to satisfy the burgeoning commercial impetus. The most ambitious European merchants were driven actually to see Africa. Pioneering Greeks and Romans pushed southwards on often perilous voyages to establish contact with Africans, to build direct trading relationships, to widen the narrow trade conduits and challenge the ancient land-based exchange cartels. During the classical era, African trading and diplomatic pioneers began to make direct contact with Europe, while Carthaginian and sub-Saharan African soldiers serving in Roman armies spread out across Europe, the Middle East and Asia carrying African goods and thinking with them. Over the centuries this two-way curiosity did not diminish. By the fifteenth century Europe's trade with Africa was bolstered by new boat and weapons technologies, opening up a great new era of maritime exchange. While most European merchant pioneers were motivated by the lure of gold and exotic trade goods, others were inspired by the possibilities of new religious alliances or the potential to build new long-term strategic partnerships. But almost all shared an underlying aim: they were driven by cultural curiosity.

In the sixteenth century Rabelais wrote with a mixture of fear and fascination that Africa could always produce 'new and monstrous things'. He, like many of his contemporaries, saw the continent as an undisturbed well of potent possibilities. As a period of intermittent trade gave way to a sustained presence of European bases in many of the most accessible areas of coastal Africa, the quantities and purity of the gold, the quality of the precious stones, the diversity of new foods, plants and animals that the traders returned with, along with vivid, almost unbelievable stories, served only to build a greater sense of attraction and intrigue. But Europe's understanding of Africa remained undermined by substantial unknowns. It was an uncharted continent, a Lost World, an unexplored Eden that seemed almost immeasurably big. It hinted at unquantifiable wealth and magnificent civilizations, but most of it felt hidden from view. At the heart of Africa's mystery was a plethora of under-exploited resources which appeared on the surface to be ripe for the taking.

In the eighteenth century Hegel wrote of the 'African Uplands' as 'a golden-land', a sub-Saharan utopia. He conjectured that 'Africa proper, as far as History goes back, has remained – for all purposes of connection with the rest of the World – shut up; it is the Gold-Land compressed within itself, – the land of childhood, which lying beyond the day of self-conscious history, is enveloped in the dark mantle of Night. Its isolated character originates not merely in its tropical nature, but essentially in its geographical condition.' Hegel saw the continent as having no history, as being in a state that was akin to the infancy of humanity. He was not alone. Many similar conclusions welled up from a long history of misreading the continent; they were compounded by cultural confidence as enlightenment thinking opened up new approaches to traditional disciplines.

The eighteenth-century knowledge vacuum that surrounded Africa drove complex impulses. Some European intellectuals conjectured that they might learn something from the simplicity of Africans' lives, but there were also those who felt a duty to empower Africa with 'modern' knowledge. Almost inevitably it was the latter impetus – the drive to expand influence, to spread and inculcate European thinking, to educate the African, to build trade – that came to dominate the age. Many felt that there was almost a moral duty to intervene, and to be there to reap the mutual commercial benefit of closer relations. After all, from a European perspective, beyond a handful of great kingdoms Africa was only beginning to awaken culturally.

In many ways they were wrong, profoundly wrong. Many of those seemingly virginal landscapes hid thousands of years of complex indigenous intervention. We now know that for longer than on any other continent humans have been making their mark on the sub-Saharan African landscape – some of it subtle, but some of it so significant that it might be read by the untutored visitor as physical geography. Thousands of years of farming and hunting have changed vast areas of Africa's environment, even its ecology; human migration and urbanization have tamed and shaped many of its landscapes, altered and harnessed its watercourses, consumed its forests and developed productive geographies. Some of those interventions have proved durable – Africa boasts some of the oldest surviving cities, universities, religious buildings and markets in the world – but a substantial part of its ancient history has been subsumed back into nature, perhaps now lost to all but the most ambitious and well-resourced archaeologist.

Many of the pioneering European traders visited Africa with a Hegelian filter on their perception, seeking to build trading relationships with communities that shared a similar political and cultural outlook. African cultures, which were not based around models of centralized government and trade, were often overlooked and marginalized; cultures with similar forms of organization and ambition to the Europeans were naturally placed at an advantage, and many grew exponentially in the initial period of trade, until they themselves became obstacles to European expansion. The story of the Zulu is the story of a people who grew out of a period that straddled initial contact with Europeans. They thrived in their trading relations with Britain and prospered through trade with other indigenous populations.

At the turn of the nineteenth century the Zulu were a small ethnic group of around fifteen hundred people, but they grew rapidly to become a powerful kingdom of almost quarter of a million whose territory stretched across a vast swathe of southern Africa. At its peak the scale of the Zulu empire and the effectiveness with which it was governed earned them a fearsome reputation. In the space of just twelve years they created a sophisticated society with a unique, inclusive identity that has shaped aspects of South African history ever since. Long after the Zulu empire lost its independence, its reputation as a fearsome adversary continued to thrive, inspiring dozens of travellers' accounts, novels and even films. The reality in certain respects is even more impressive. The Zulu organizational and military expertise was more than a match for all of their African adversaries. Their defeat came only when changes in European weapons technology rendered their military tactics moribund. After this the permanent presence of a British colonial administration triggered a cascade of significant economic changes that transformed the sociology of Africa in profound and devastating ways. In spite of this, what the Zulu had achieved in little more than a lifespan changed southern Africa profoundly.

★

KwaZulu-Natal is the ancient homeland of the Zulu people. Bounded by the Drakensburg Mountains in the west, Swaziland and Mozambique in the north, and the Indian Ocean to the south, it is a landscape of rolling hills, deep river gorges and fertile grasslands. I decided to begin this trip by experiencing one of the most spectacular events in the South African calendar, an ancient ceremony that's as old as the Zulu kingdom itself: the First Fruits Festival. It's one of the many times during a year that the Zulu gather with their king, Goodwill Zwelithini KaBhekuzulu. This event is being held in Eshowe in the substantial grounds of one of the king's palaces. Goodwill Zwelithini KaBhekuzulu has a number of similar compounds across the region in which state events can be held, where his people can gather and where he can house his substantial herds of cattle. Although he no longer has the power of his forefathers, under the Traditional Leadership Clause of the South African constitution he continues to be both a spiritual and paternal focus for many Zulu, and seems to remain both respected and loved.

There are almost eight million Zulu in South Africa today. Many are Zulu in no more than ethnicity, but a significant number still feel a strong draw to the Zulu monarchy and its traditions. The First Fruits Festival celebrates the first harvested crops; there you can enjoy the first beverages that have been brewed from marula, a lychee-like plummy fruit almost uniquely found in the region. Once upon a time the festival was an opportunity for rival groups of young Zulu soldiers to be tested by killing a bull with their bare hands, to show strength and bravery. Rival regiments would compete to put down the bull in the most efficient manner, their sergeants barracking and mocking the weak and cowardly and the king rewarding the brave. But pressures from animal rights groups and the drive to modernize forced the tradition (along with many other customs that time had rendered unpalatable) to end. As I join the throngs of people gathering in the fields around the king's house I wonder if such compromises have led not just to the dilution but the loss of a critical and substantial part of their belief system.

But I am heartened when I see the old and obviously senior men in their traditional Zulu costumes carrying their spears, fighting sticks and shields with deep pride. They wear their belts hung with twisted lengths of fur and skin breastplates and stand in a line waiting for the king to begin the fruit blessing. As they wait they joke and jostle one another in a way that belies their mature years. They still seem to exude that solidarity that only soldiers share.

An old man steps forward from the line and starts hitting the earth with his shield and dancing low to the ground. This is no joke – it clearly means something. Then the whole line breaks out in song, a sad, soulful tune of a battle lost. One at a time, the senior Zulu officials dance; size, age or level of intoxication are no impediment to taking a turn.

Eventually the king in full regalia – two long feathers fluttering from a headband, a leopardskin breastplate and full belt of twisted cords of antelope skins – comes out of the palace to greet his senior men and invited guests. He is joined by a number of traditional leaders from across Africa and representatives from government. All have gathered to celebrate the coming together of the Zulu. The Fruits Festival is more than a celebration of the harvest, it is a celebration of Zulu culture, a very public affirmation of the power of the monarchy, an acknowledgement that the king is the embodiment of the nation, the guardian of its identity, and the keeper of its soul. He's a living link to the legendary monarchs who created the Zulu kingdom.

Every year in late summer, the first fruits are brought to the king. Traditionally, the king's subjects could not partake of the harvest before first offering it to the king. Any soldier who ate the first fruits before his leader was said to grow weak. As leader of the nation, the king must be the first person to accept the harvest from God on behalf of the Zulu kingdom. During the ceremony, the king eats a special mixture of herbs and vegetables prepared by one of the kingdom's spiritual leaders. He thanks the ancestors for the gift of the harvest and requests their blessing for the coming year. The main part of the ceremony finishes with a display of dancing and drumming as everyone is invited to enjoy the harvest and give thanks. But the party goes on until well after sunset, the damp evening air full of the sweet smell of marula beer and the sound of singing. There is plainly a continuing powerful pull to the Zulu traditional way of life.

Before I leave, I manage to speak briefly to His Majesty Goodwill Zwelithini KaBhekuzulu. I query him about the contemporary role of a king of a warrior nation. He is not cross, but he does not seem pleased with the question. He looks me in the eye and tells me that 'the Zulu were founded on solid principles that remain as relevant and effective today as they were in the days of the Zulu empire'. As I weave my car through the crowds and leave Eshowe behind, I am left with the king's words running through my head. What were those original principles that thousands were prepared to die for, and which remain so obviously important to the Zulu today? As the landscape opens up into the vast theatre of green that is so particular to South Africa, I am left to ponder.

The Zulu have dominated this south-east corner of South Africa since the nineteenth century, but their forefathers did not originate here. The Zulu's ancestors were farmers who migrated south from the area around the Great Lakes of central Africa some time in the fourth or fifth centuries AD. It was a period of flux during which the truly ancient ways of life were put under stress by massive demographic change across the continent. Nomadic communities who had low-impact transitory relationships with the landscape were suddenly forced to compete for resources with an influx of farming communities. It was a process that continued for more than a millennium. In the mid seventeenth century the Nguni people, the cultural and racial group that the Zulu belong to, settled in present-day South Africa, the region that would become their permanent home.

Although the detailed origins of the Zulu are not recorded, oral history tells us that the original Zulu polity was established in the late seventeenth century when Malendela, the founding patriarch, moved to the region. It was his son, Zulu, who gave his name to the clan. The word Zulu means 'heaven', and they became known as the amaZulu – 'the people of heaven'. The amaZulu gave birth to a strongly patriarchal society led by a series of powerful chiefs and kings. As King Goodwill Zwelithini KaBhekuzulu, the current monarch, implied, running deep into the bedrock of Zulu society is a coherence conferred by key traditions and institutions, especially the monarchy and the army. It is understandable that the Zulu quickly became a highly militarized society and the authority of the king became its lynch-pin. The male leader, the patriarch, became the defining feature of Zulu society, from the institution of the monarchy to the most fundamental constituent, the family.

In those early days, the fragile Zulu were one of dozens of peoples that co-existed with the indigenous nomadic peoples which included the San. What early Zululand was like is not really known, but the first Europeans to reach the area described grassy plains filled with herds of game that stretched as far as the eye could see.

Although most of the game has now disappeared, the scale of landscape is as it ever was. The countryside is monumental – blue-green epic hill-scapes that undulate out towards the horizon. I am heading for the Nkandla Valley right in the heart of KwaZulu-Natal. The landscape is peppered with traditional Zulu homes. This is a region where despite nearly two centuries of colonial interference and everything that followed, the circular homestead remains a popular facet of Zulu life.

By the end of the eighteenth century, this area of KwaZulu-Natal was a patchwork of hundreds of discrete clans living under larger chieftaincies. The huge numbers of cattle grazing the countryside had changed the landscape, and the Zulu were thriving. New Zulu homesteads were spreading out from their limited heartland. The basis of initial Zulu success was archi-tectural innovation. It is easy to mistake a homestead for a small village, but each homestead housed a single extended family, and by 1800 there were hundreds of them. I'm going to visit a traditional homestead and meet the family who live there. I want to see for myself the basis for Zulu expansion.

I drive down into the Nkandla Valley in search of a traditional homestead. I drive on way beyond the point where the road fails. When the track becomes undergrowth, I go on by foot. I battle my way down into a thorny valley and over a river and then up on to a truly isolated hillside. After an hour of walking I find myself in a beautiful homestead perched on the leeside of the hill. Under a tree I find an old matriarch sheltering from the hot midday sun. She leaps up to greet me. She speaks no English but communicates through a wistful smile, making it clear that she would be happy to welcome me into the homestead and show me around.

The design and construction of the traditional homestead have remained unchanged over centuries and seem to reflect the wider pastoral culture. The cattle carrel sits in the centre of the buildings, surrounded by the circular houses. The circle is important as a symbol of security and continuity. Each small, circular one-room building is covered by a thatched roof. There are no chimneys; these buildings were designed to vent smoke through the doorway, carrying insects with it. The various buildings are utilized like individual rooms in a Western house rather than as single dwellings. The construction traditions are probably older than the Zulu people. The walls are crafted from clay and wattle so they are warm in winter and cool in summer and the floors are made of polished, compressed cow dung, which is soft underfoot. The effect is very homely.

Standing in the doorway of one of these homesteads, hearing but not understanding my guide speaking in Zulu, I am struck by how humble the lives of many South Africans remain. South Africa is a regional economic powerhouse. Its cities offer the choices most other international cities offer their inhabitants. But these are people whose rural lives are simply not part of that world. These communities rely on technologies that have remained unchanged for centuries; their day-to-day existence focuses around pastoral ways of life that were developed when the first Nguni and Zulu communities settled here, or perhaps even before that time. I find it deeply thrilling that a traditional way of life like this continues to remain viable to people who have some level of choice, but it is also impossible not to be shocked by just how tough their lives are, and must always have been. It is easy to become intoxicated by the quiet rural isolation and the simple beauty. Aesthetically it is a lifestyle that seems idyllic, in the way the Pre-Raphaelites saw beauty in rural lifestyles. The warm comforting smells, the closeness of families working with their cattle and sharing resources, all of this is deeply inviting, but other than the social mechanics there is little else. These are, and were, people who have very little other than their families, their homes and their cattle. Their material wealth, the objects they possess, are few.

It is a reminder for Westerners that people with seemingly very little material wealth to tie them to a place nonetheless choose to remain. It must be that for the majority there are some real benefits to this way of life. Going into the old matriarch's house, seeing a domestic environment that was loved, smelling walls rich with the aroma of decades of cooking, and walking on dung floors shiny from barefoot use, it is obvious that being close to family, sharing jeopardy and intimacy every day, builds profound cohesion. Zulu culture is one that on the surface built its narrative out of the threat from the outsider, but here in these domestic environments where the Zulu women are the anchors there is a counter-balancing story, of love and cultural cohesion. It might not be the story that prevails, but it must always have been there. The great Zulu kings all relied upon strong women, the threads that bound these societies together.

The warmth of the maternal homestead was balanced by the highly patriarchal and traditionally polygamous broader Zulu society. Women may have held these traditional homestead communities together, but they were politically focused around key men, and their dependent relatives. The patriarch's house was located at the back of the enclosure furthest away from the entrance and was always the largest dwelling in the homestead. Depending on his wealth and status, a man could have many wives. These wives differed in status. The wife with the highest status was called the 'Great Wife'. She was the mother of his appointed heir. Her house was located immediately to the right of the patriarch's; the other wives' homes stretched away to the left in lessening order of status.

Traditional homesteads became the building blocks of a highly centralized and hierarchical society; they were microcosms of the whole culture. It is impossible to visit one of these homesteads and not come away without some understanding of the importance of cows to the Zulu. Even today cattle remain at the heart of Zulu culture. Not only did the Zulu use them for trade, they were a source of meat and milk, and the hides were used for shields. They became a symbol of the nation. Traditionally, Zulu women might even be exchanged for cattle in a barter process called *ilobola*. Cattle were the currency of the Zulu economy, integral to regional politics; they could be both a source of conflict and one of the ways in which warring factions made peace. Immense pride was taken in animal husbandry. Men looked after the cattle while the women were responsible for the cultivation of crops. The one feature of a homestead which more than any other element reveals the focus and priorities of Zulu society is the cattle pen. Cattle were located in the heart of the homestead, with the family's houses built around them. This was partly for security – any thieves would have to pass through the family quarters – but it was also indicative of the central place of cattle in Zulu society. Only men were allowed in the cattle carrel. The pen itself had a spiritual status. And sacrificing cattle became one of the most potent ways of communing with departed ancestors.

It was and remains a system that works. The design and social structure of homesteads like these have remained largely unchanged for hundreds of years. The beautiful long-horned cattle that are still bred today are the descendants of those that were driven here with the initial migrations. For over a century after the clan was founded the Zulu people lived in relative peace here, close to the land, developing this way of life. But it was a way of life that was coming to an end. By the last quarter of the eighteenth century the socio-economic landscape was beginning to change profoundly, and the catalyst was trade.

In the late eighteenth and early nineteenth centuries, among a variety of goods, beads were bartered widely across the region. For hundreds of years African traders had been supplying the Nguni people with beads that had been manufactured in North and West Africa, south-east Asia and the Middle East, but with the arrival of the Portuguese, glass beads in a dazzling range of colours and patterns began to be imported. The range of goods being exchanged exploded. The new demand for trade grew into a turbulent economic force that transformed this region. Rival southern African ethnic groups started competing ever more aggressively for access to the trade routes to the Portuguese-controlled Delagoa Bay to the north of the Zulu coast. Trade with the Portuguese became a vital way for chiefs to consolidate their power and influence. The distortion to the local trading ecology that was created by the introduction of European trade goods would only deepen and intensify. There simply was not room for everyone.

The Portuguese introduced maize, which was easier to cultivate than indigenous African crops and helped to fuel a rapid population growth. So much so that by 1800 Zulu clans were running out of land to graze cattle. A catastrophic drought around that year brought famine to the region and spurred an increasingly desperate pursuit of resources. In the space of a few years the region began to tip into inter-ethnic conflict. The peaceful existence the small Zulu clan had enjoyed up until then was shattered.

Out of the turmoil emerged a single charismatic individual who would change Zulu culture profoundly. By turning conflict and upheaval to his advantage, he would transform the Zulu from one of a number of small competing ethnic groups into a superpower. His name was Shaka, the first king of the Zulu.

Shaka is a fascinating figure, a king, a soldier and the father of the Zulu nation. In the space of twelve years in the early nineteenth century he single-handedly masterminded the transformation of a small clan into an all-conquering regional power. What is frustrating for historians is that there are hardly

William Bagg's illustration of 'Shaka, King of the Zoolus', 1836.

1849 illustration of a Zulu homestead or Kraal.

any contemporaneous written accounts of his life. To piece together his biography we must rely on second-hand descriptions and oral testimonies that are often conflicting. But there is one thing that most writers will agree on: Shaka's life story was played out on a huge scale. He was born in 1787 outside Eshowe, where the current king maintains a palace. In this tumultuous environment of dynamic migration and the new competition for trade, many rulers feared potential rivals, even their heirs. Shaka, the illegitimate son of an aristocrat, was shunned. His mother had tried to hide her pregnancy, claiming her swollen belly was caused by an intestinal beetle – a *shaka*.

Shaka spent his enforced exile being raised by the Mthethwa, a small but highly militarized rival group. He learned and adopted new military thinking and rose up through the ranks to a position of prominence in the Mthethwan army. His exceptional military skill helped the Mthethwa consolidate, and then expand, as inter-ethnic conflict erupted. As he grew into manhood he returned to the Zulu clan, seized the chieftaincy and set about transforming the nation.

One incident from Shaka's early life is said to have defined him. Like most Zulu boys he was expected to spend some time looking after the family goats, taking them to find new pasture. Young boys were given this task to engender a sense of responsibility and to make them think about their future paternal roles. Shaka was said to have lost his flock – a terrible mistake, but an incident that would shape his life. The lesson Shaka learned from this experience was that the herdsman must pay attention to every animal in his care and must never let his guard down. He seems to have spent the rest of his life compensating for this loss with an overriding drive to shepherd his people, to unite them in discipline and security.

In the turbulent inter-ethnic conflict of the early nineteenth century, Shaka realized that it wasn't enough just to protect his own people. For the Zulu to survive, they had to consolidate and create regional stability – to conquer or be conquered. To achieve this, Shaka initiated a project that would define his reign: the radical transformation of one of the most important institutions of Zulu society.

When Shaka assumed the chieftaincy of the small Zulu clan from his father in 1816, he built on the recent innovations of local chiefs. He introduced military conscription, organizing his troops into regiments called *amabutho* that revolutionized Zulu society. Under the *amabutho* system young men left their families around the age of fourteen to join military regiments where they received rigorous training that imbued them with the values of loyalty and discipline. By separating young men from the main body of the clan, the *amabutho* system shifted the allegiance of young men from their family or clan chief to their military regiment and to the king, so the *amabutho* system was used by Shaka not only as a system for the external defence of the nation but also as a strategy for internal social control.

One of Shaka's key reforms was the reshaping of Zulu marriage traditions. During his reign, men engaged in military service were not allowed to marry; they could only do so once they had distinguished themselves in battle and had reached the age of maturity, which under Shaka was around the age of thirty-five. On reaching maturity warriors were awarded a head ring called an *isicoco*. Unmarried men could be subject to whatever national service the king might demand. Once they had completed their military service they were allowed to disperse and build their own homesteads. Only then could they keep their own cattle, which they received from the king as a reward.

With the creation of the *amabutho* system with himself as commander-in-chief, Shaka transformed Zulu society into a centralized military machine. He next turned his attention to fighting techniques. Until the end of the nineteenth century battles between different clans were largely ceremonial affairs. Warfare was conducted with spears at long range and with few casualties. The defeated clan usually lived to fight another day. Shaka's army was instructed to fight to the death. The key to victory was hand-to-hand combat. No soldier was allowed to let go of his spear. No soldier could turn his back on the battle. A wound in the back was the ultimate sign of cowardice, punishable by death. Shaka also introduced a new battle formation inspired by the cattle that were the symbolic heart of Zulu society. It was called *izimpondo zankoma* – the horns of the buffalo. Under Shaka, the army in battle had four distinct elements: the chest, the loins, the left horn and the right. The chest, containing the fiercest warriors, attacked first, luring the enemy into combat. Once the enemy was drawn in, the chest dissolved into two horns, spreading out to envelop their prey. Finally the loins moved in for the kill. It was a formation that proved stunningly effective.

Shaka's final military innovation was the transformation of Zulu weaponry. To get a sense of that I visit a traditional barracks to handle some of the cold steel for myself. Simon is a small man, gruff and wiry, who seems to have been born to his role. Yet he is not a traditional sergeant major type; he does not shout and bully, he leads by energetic example, constantly rallying the young men in their songs, leading the chants and exercises and telling stories of great Zulu battles. It is when he is thrusting and parrying with a spear or telling off a young soldier that his eyes start to sparkle and it becomes obvious that a softer man lurks beneath the tough exterior. The group he works with, about fifty young men and twenty women, have become like the palace guards you see in old European cities: they look, dress and behave as they always did, but their core function has become lost as time has moved on; today, dressing up and retelling stories is the thing they seem to do best. Though each of the Zulu men I meet is as Zulu as those that followed Shaka and many hold traditional posts in Zulu society, they do not spend their time with cattle or in battle, they perform for tourists.

I can tell Simon is subtly looking me up and down when he meets me – and he sucks his teeth as he does it. Perhaps I'm a little paranoid, but I do wonder if he's thinking I look a bit soft. In one hand he holds a short stabbing spear and an almond-shaped cowhide shield. They look like objects a tourist might buy. As if he were reading my mind, the first words he speaks are 'These are real weapons of war', thrusting the business end of the spear

Zulu warriors, 1875.

towards me. Then he smiles and offers me a spear and shield.

Before Shaka, most inter-ethnic conflict was conducted with long-handled spears, which were thrown from a distance. Shaka introduced this shorter wide-bladed stabbing spear, perfect for close-quarter fighting. He called it the *ikwla*, a name which is meant to sound like the sucking noise the spear makes when it is withdrawn from the flesh of its victim.

In the hand, the craft and love involved in creating these objects becomes obvious. The weapon is perfectly weighted for holding two-thirds of the way up its length. The lozenge-shaped blade is like a jewel, and where it is bedded into the handle it is woven with beads. It is the result of hundreds of years of use and refinement and it simply feels right. The shield is light and only cardboard thin but it has been tautened and toughened to almost a Kevlar hardness. They are made from cattle hide stretched along a tall frame, interwoven with strips of leather. Shaka introduced large shields that were nearly the height of a man. The size of the shield was dictated by the height of the soldier. In the days of Shaka shields remained the property of the king to enforce loyalty. The colour of the shield indicated the age and regiment of the soldier. They are easy to hold, but clearly not as easy to use well.

Simon thrusts his blade towards me. I try to parry with my shield, but he twists his blade and rams it into the surface of the shield. The vibration of the impact judders through the shield sending jolts of pain into my wrist. I know the shield is meant to be used offensively as well as defensively. Shaka taught his warriors to hook its left side around the left side of their opponent's shield, exposing their opponent's left side, which could then be attacked with a thrust from the short stabbing spear. Simon smiles. 'Lesson one,' he says. 'Force the blade away from you with your shield. Don't meet it head on, push it away from you, and while they are disarmed, use your spear thrust!' As he says the word 'thrust' he presses the cold steel of his blade against my chest. We are very close. I look into his eyes. Inside a deep brown iris is an inner circle of pale, cold grey that surrounds a polka-dot pupil. In that moment he is not joking.

But then suddenly Simon drops the blade, begins to laugh, and walks away.

For a few moments I'm not quite sure what has just happened. Then the world beyond the hair-raising incident begins to filter back into my consciousness. First the sound of the young soldiers laughing, then the vision of ranks of young men looking on. It is not the laughter of bullies, they are looking and laughing with me – I have passed an initiation. I begin to understand the Zulu sense of camaraderie.

It is hard to overestimate the impact of Shaka's military reforms on Zulu society. The biggest transformation was the creation of these regiments that placed the military at the heart of Zulu society. This led to the instilling of a mindset of total discipline, courage and fearlessness. The greatest fear was not the enemy but the potential punishment for cowardice. The army became an integral part of Zulu cultural identity, the framework around which the whole society was structured. Indeed, spending just a short time with Simon and his men has given me an insight into the powerful sense of brotherhood the army must have brought to the Zulu.

Over the course of a hot afternoon Simon ushers me into the Zulu way of thought, talking about the old battles, showing me how to stick fight and wear battle dress. I am even given protection by a sangoma, a traditional priest, who throws a handful of shells on to a mat to help him divine my future. It is quite dark when I leave. The last thing Simon says to me is to remember that the 'Zulu have no time for losers – being a Zulu is about defeating your enemies'. As I drive away it strikes me that I will have to work hard not to apply my ethical cultural standards to the Zulu. What Shaka built was a very effective army, and by the end of this process of reinvention he had turned himself into an icon and the Zulu into a ruthless military machine.

The military reforms Shaka initiated gave Zulu culture the power and confidence to take on other ethnic groups in the battle for trade and territory. He lost no time in imposing his will on southern Africa. Within a couple of years of becoming king he had decisively defeated his chief rival and enemy, the aggressive Nwandwe, to become the dominant power in the region. Now he had the monopoly on trade with Delagoa Bay.

For the Zulu this was the beginning of a golden period in which they expanded territory and their trading relations. The consequences for their neighbours and the indigenous San were not quite as rosy. Over a period of four years Shaka led a highly efficient campaign of conquest, annihilating a series of indigenous competitors across a vast swathe of territory. Thousands of people were driven from their land in a series of massive forced migrations that entered folk memory and became known as the Mfecane – the Crushing. The defeated had two options: death or incorporation into the larger Zulu nation. Most opted for the latter. Conquered chiefs could keep some power if they co-operated with Shaka, by assigning him their soldiers or by allowing their daughters to be married off to other clans to secure political alliances. In the space of twelve years the Zulu nation expanded from around 1,500 people to around 250,000.

Hardly any physical traces of the Mfecane remain, but in one of the more remote areas of South Africa anthropologist Benjamin Smith has discovered an exception. The reserve at old York farm in Matatiele is very isolated, set right up against the mountains that mark the border between South Africa and Lesotho. It is a ghostly place of abandoned farmhouses and wide open, bleak and empty vistas. It has always been an in-between place, a badlands. Many of the old farms were bought by the apartheid government as part of a policy to try to control the transit of ANC agents between the south and Lesotho, but it has always been a place that attracted dangerous types and cattle raiders. The myriad paths that disappear into the mountains offer multiple routes for the pursued to disappear. Today thieves still slip over the mountains by night and steal horses and cattle in a highly lucrative, almost unprosecutable crime. Stealing livestock here is an ancient tradition.

In the time of Shaka these mountains were the refuge of the San. The San were an indigenous nomadic people who over generations of suffering the encroachments of Nguni groups and the British were forced into these inhospitable pockets. Their name is derived from the local word for 'thief'. They maintained what they thought were their aboriginal rights to nomadic passage through the land and to the livestock that grazed upon it. This put them in direct conflict with the British and the Zulu. Across the whole of southern Africa they were hunted, persecuted and forced to retreat. Where they were not known as 'thieves' they were known as bushmen – not just an ethnic categorization but a tainted term that came to imply that they were subhuman.

Here at Matatiele they struggled against the turmoil of the Mfecane, because as people were pushed off their land they began to relocate into areas traditionally used by the San. The San were pushed further and further into the hills where they left a record of their retreat and the perpetrators of their persecution in a glorious body of rock art. Benjamin Smith, a professor at Witwatersrand University, agreed to guide me to the secret site of one of these paintings. Most are painted under overhangs and so have modest protection from the weather, but as natural salts leach out of the rocks the surface crazes, cracks and falls away. These fragile, beautiful works of art are slowly disappearing, taking with them a unique record of and perspective on this tumultuous period.

I follow Ben out across the hill. As we set out an ominous flash of lightning strikes on the horizon and a cold wind picks up. 'We must hurry, it is going to rain and the going may get tough,' says Ben.

As head of the Rock Art Research Institute, Ben has studied rock sites across Africa in some of the remotest areas of the continent. If he says the going may get tough, it is a cause for concern.

As I look back down the hill into the valley a low rumble of thunder peals out. Dark vertical bands of rain are marching across the valley floor towards us. Then the rain starts; there's no drizzle to forewarn us. Within moments of it starting the air is a stinging sheet of fizzing water, the ground is sodden and waterfalls begin to appear all about us down crevices in the rock. Every surface, grass, rock and mud, is suddenly fluid – but we walk on, in near silence, up over the hill, bracing our bodies against the wind and horizontal rain, concentrating on every foot placement. To fall would be so easy, and potentially fatal.

We work our way beyond the hill bridge down on to a river-bank to find shelter, as the San once did, beneath a small overhang. The vertical rock beneath the overhang is like the wall of an ancient fresco, flakes of burgundy and blood-red paint hanging delicately to the cracked surface. There are areas where a number of nearly adjacent remnants of paint clearly describe the leg, torso or head of an animal, but for the most part all that remains is bare rock: this important site is being eaten by the weather and the mountain. As that process of erosion goes on, the damage intensifies and quickens. The vestiges of this great work were found by the last farmer to work this land, in the 1960s. He stumbled on this remote place while trying to find some lost live-stock. Today, with the farms long abandoned, very few people walk these paths and see this place. As the painting is so unstable, Ben knows that each visit might be the final time he sees this work.

For a few minutes he scans the surface. He gives nothing away. I stand back and let him do his work. I notice that in the earth around my feet are dozens of knapped stones and arrowheads. This is a rich site, but like thousands of others in this region it is unlikely to receive particular archaeological attention. The nomadic San, the indigenous people of this landscape, were simply too mobile, too prolific, over too great a period to make it viable to excavate all the sites; many of them have no doubt already been lost.

Then Ben gestures me forward and we stand in silence gazing at a beautifully crafted figure, painted around 1820, at the height of the Mfecane. One of the San's principal subjects was game, which reflected their way of life. They particularly focused upon eland, a spiral-horned antelope believed to possess a spiritual power. In the nineteenth century other figures started to appear. The figure Ben is showing me is a palm-sized silhouette painted

*Striding Nguni figure copied from a rock surface on the border
between South Africa and Lesoma. (Gus Casely-Hayford)*

in charcoal black. He is obviously Nguni; he has the feathers of a chief and in his left hand he holds a spear. The weapon's length is impossible to discern because its shaft disappears behind the body of the figure, so, frustratingly, it is difficult to know if they had adopted the latest Shaka-inspired military technology, the short stabbing spear. In his right hand he holds a shield, almost the size of his body. It is not the classic Zulu almond-shaped shield, it is like a fat-waisted figure eight. Ben suggests that the demographic pressures produced by the Mfecane pushed the Zulu and other Nguni ethnic groups into this region; this rock art records the arrival of these new peoples, and it is also laced with protective power – a form of spiritual weapon. But sadly for the San, these beautiful paintings were simply not enough and they were forced further and further back from viable and habitable areas. For a period they resisted, but the combined force of the Zulu and the even more concerted efforts of the British were too great for them to resist. Faced with an active campaign of genocide, and assimilation by other ethnic groups, they disappeared from this landscape. A whole people and a whole culture eradicated like pests.

When Hegel wrote that Africa was without civilization and the early Europeans saw this country as uninhabited, it was the measured, sustainable interventions of indigenous communities like the San that they overlooked. What they have left behind in their rock art reveals a culturally complex and sophisticated people from whom we could have learned a great deal. The oldest surviving San paintings are believed to be around eight hundred years old. The San people retained their traditional way of life right up to the time of the Mfecane. Although the period of 'the Crushing' still lives on in folk memory, there's virtually no physical evidence of it. The only evidence is the absence of physical evidence, and these beautiful and haunting images.

The fate of the San people was a powerful illustration of the consequences of resisting and an incentive for others to join the Zulu. The San were hunter-gatherers who had a fragile way of life, with no tradition of demarcating territory of their own. The

Zulu

The nomadic San left a rich record of their presence on the landscape of southern Africa. This painting of an interloping Nguni man carrying a shield and spear offers a powerful indication of San concerns at the changes they felt were coming

Above: Simon (*right*) runs a highly efficient *amabutho*, or military company, training young Zulu men in traditional military skills.

Top: Isandlhwana, the site of the Zulu's celebrated victory against the British, where twenty thousand warriors armed with spears and shields surprised a small but well armed column of British soldiers and annihilated them.

Above left: Today the site, studded with white cairns, is both a monument to the greatest Zulu victory of the Anglo-Zulu war and to the one thousand three hundred British troops who lost their lives on the slopes of the hill.

Above right: Cetshwayo was the King of the Zulus from 1872 to 1879, briefly turning the tide of Boer and British encroachments, before finally succumbing to defeat at the battle of Ulundi.

Benin

Top and above: From a distance the Tellem granaries appear to defy gravity, clinging to the sheer rock face of the Bandiagara escarpment. The most ancient may be two thousand years old. For hundreds of years these cliffs supported a substantial community of people who traded, farmed and hunted before mysteriously disappearing. The floor of the cave is covered in a plethora of pottery and bones. At its peak this landscape must have been a hub for complex inter-regional trade.

Right: Kene and I drive across fords and unpaved flooded roads, weaving between traffic and cattle on our way to Bandiagara.

Above: As we begin our descent from the escarpment into the town beneath, the Dogon begin their dance.

Below: The great mosque and market at Djenné is one of the most impressive sights in Africa. The market attracts people from hundreds of miles around – merchants from across the Sahara and traders from gold-rich southern forests converge here to exchange their goods and stories as they have for centuries.

The Benin Bronzes capture the inner working of the Benin court. These are not just to be judged aesthetically or symbolically – they record specific episodes and personalities. The figure on horseback is thought to be Oba Esigie, who used Portuguese weaponry to wage war on his rivals and build Benin into an unrivalled power. Though known as bronzes, they are actually crafted in brass, using a lost wax process. They were confiscated as part of the reparations after the British invasion.

The veranda beneath which these men stand is beautifully made. It is recognizably part of the same structure seen in the background of the photograph on page 209. Here the veranda shades senior members of the Oba's court; in the photograph it shades the invading British forces.

Bronze head of an Oba.

Below: The thirtieth-anniversary cloth of the present Oba of Benin, who came to the throne in 1979.

HAPPY 30TH CORONATION ANNIVERSARY

OMO N'OBAN'EDO UKU-AKPOLOKPOLO EREDIAUWA

HRM

OBA OF BENIN

people who farmed the land here did not want to go back to the precarious existence of hunter-gatherers. Shaka was offering people security and stability. If they joined him, he would assure their future and the future of their children.

In a handful of years the ruthless expansion of the Zulu under Shaka transformed the landscape. While there were those that benefited, many rival and neighbouring clans suffered huge hardship during the years of the Mfecane. It was a period that cemented Shaka's reputation in the imagination of his loyal followers and his enemies. But it was a short-lived period of near unquestioned dominance for the Zulu. In May 1824 six young British men landed in a swampy lagoon on the Indian Ocean coast in search of adventure. Their arrival triggered a chain of events that would change the economic dynamic of the Zulu kingdom.

Led by an ex-naval officer, Captain Francis George Farewell, these men had been instructed by the British authorities at Cape Town to survey the coast of Natal and identify trading opportunities. They were determined and imaginative young men and immediately saw the potential of the mangrove swamp. Today it is the city of Durban, the capital of KwaZulu-Natal.

Under the stewardship of Farewell, the British began trading textiles, metals and beads with the Zulu, which they exchanged for ivory, animal hides and maize. The British settlers offered Shaka a more convenient alternative to the Portuguese at Delagoa Bay, so he granted them the use of a small area of land to expand their trading station. Natal, and the volume of goods that flowed through it, grew rapidly. The Zulu were in many respects perfect trading partners: they offered a semblance of regional stability and a consistent flow of sought-after goods. But, with so much at stake, the difference between trading allies and strategic rivals became increasingly fluid. The British were grateful for the stability the Zulu offered, but they craved greater trading freedom and autonomy. Slowly the cordial British–Zulu relationship unravelled. The accounts of the British traders reflected their resentment of Shaka and shaped his reputation for decades to come.

These are some of the only surviving contemporary written accounts of the Zulu in these early days. In 1836, after Shaka's death, one trader, Nathaniel Isaacs, published an account of his dealings with Shaka that fixed an image of the Zulu kingdom in the British mind for nearly a century. 'Chaka seems to have inherited no redeeming quality; in war he was an insatiable despot and exterminating savage, in peace an unrelenting and ferocious despot,' he wrote. 'The world has heard of monsters – Rome had her Nero, the Huns their Attila, and Syracuse her Dionysus; the East has likewise produced her tyrants; but for ferocity, Chaka has exceeded them all.' Another trader, Henry Francis Fynn, one of the first settlers at Port Natal, had extensive early contact with Shaka. Thirty years later he wrote a blood-curdling account of Shaka's grief-stricken execution of thousands of his own people following the death of his beloved mother. 'Those who could not force more tears from their eyes, those who were found near the river panting for water, were beaten to death by others who were mad with excitement. Toward the afternoon I calculated no fewer than seven thousand people who had fallen in this frightful, indiscriminate massacre. The adjacent stream, to which many had fled exhausted, to wet their parched tongues, became impassable from the corpses which lay on either side of it; while the kraal in which the scene took place was flowing with blood.'

It is important to contextualize these accounts by remembering that they were written by Shaka's competitors, and those who felt victimized by Zulu control. For a long time Isaacs' account was the standard work on Shaka and the basis for many fictionalized and mythologized colonial depictions of the Zulu. However, like many British settlers' writings, we must consider their motivations. They had a commercial agenda, and Shaka stood in the way of their ambitions. There were other perspectives on Shaka in this momentous period. Beyond the victims of the Mfecane and the partial accounts written by British traders, I am keen to find out what the Zulu and their collaborative neighbours really thought of Shaka. These were the people who knew him best.

The Killie Campbell Library in Durban contains a collection of documents which historians have come to regard as the most faithful and impartial records of Shaka's reign. The Killie Campbell collection is kept in a neo-Cape Dutch style house in old Durban. Outside, pergolas of jacaranda; inside, oak-lined walls and floors filled with the fruits of a lifetime of collecting. It is obvious that it was begun as a personal endeavour because beyond being African, beauty is the main thing that connects the objects. Drums, beads, ornaments – some wonderful finds in a series of grand domestic spaces that became a public museum when they were left to the University of Natal by Killie Campbell, the daughter of a Natal sugar farmer and politician.

At the end of the nineteenth century a British colonial official named James Stuart took a keen interest in Zulu culture. Conscious that much of the extraordinary Zulu history of the 1800s could vanish for ever because Zulu history was never written down, Stuart learned the Zulu language. Between 1897 and 1924 he travelled around Zululand recording oral testimonies from nearly two hundred Zulu elders, many of them alive in Shaka's time, or with parents or grandparents who had lived under Shaka's rule. Some of these accounts are conflicting because they are from people who were on both winning and losing sides, but they paint a more accurate and nuanced picture of Shaka's reign than those of the British settlers.

Shaka was a driven man, at times almost vulnerable. In a testimony by Jantshi Ka Nonogila we get an insight into a Shaka who could be reduced to tears by the insults of others, of someone who is provoked and pushed into brutal action by his equally aggressive rivals, and when he does react is devastatingly effective and unforgiving – 'as the enemy fled, Tshaka directed his warriors to follow and continue stabbing them until they had driven them home'. Stuart's interviews give us a flavour of the chaotic context in which Shaka forged his empire, a sense of a fluid and rapidly changing political landscape of demographic instability and shifting political allegiances. He is undoubtedly aggressive, perhaps pathologically predisposed towards violence, but he seems to reflect the time in which he lived. He monitors constant plots on his life and throne through the deployment of an intelligence network, but remains vulnerable to assassination attempts. To offer people the stability they must have craved in this atmosphere of uncertainty he may well have decided to fight the ambient instability by ruling with a rod of iron. As Jantshi says, 'My father said Tshaka was a great King and very clever, because he defeated all chiefs in every direction. He was very resourceful in his plans for overcoming his rivals.' The account of Ndlovu Kathimuni, recorded by Stuart in 1902, provides another fascinating insight. It praises Shaka as a great leader and defends him from accusations of brutality, arguing that 'people were concocting stories about him'. Ndlovu paints Shaka as a charismatic, gifted and brave leader; before Shaka the Zulu were 'nothing' but during his reign they 'developed and became a people'.

What these intimate descriptions collected by Stuart reveal is a complex picture of an uncompromisingly ambitious regime led by a charismatic leader. Later in his life Stuart compared Shaka favourably with his contemporary Napoleon. He felt that 'beginning with a small and little-known tribe he by degrees lifted it together with many surrounding tribes within a five hundred mile radius into becoming a great nation'. Shaka was a layered man, obviously capable of strategic and seemingly random cruelty, but not without a hinterland of intimacy. Having been into homesteads, it is easy for me to imagine him not just as a warrior but as a family man surrounded by those he loved and cared for, a man who was prepared to go to extreme lengths to protect the culture that he built. Indeed, he saw the drive to fight for Zulu identity as fundamental to their way of life.

Shaka died in 1828 as he had lived, murdered by his half-brother Dingane, who succeeded to the throne. His considerable achievements could not be erased. Despite Stuart's efforts I don't think we'll ever discover the real truth about Shaka, but by sifting through the ambiguities of his legacy, by identifying the contradictions, the light and the dark, I sense we are getting closer to it. Shaka undoubtedly caused great pain, but he forged the identity of his nation. This was perhaps best symbolized in his institution of a symbolic ring of the sweat, blood, hair and saliva of his soldiers that he kept in his compound, called the *inkhata*. He created a palpable sense of belonging, a cultural gravitational force to bind his people. It was a legacy his successors would find difficult to live up to.

Shaka's death marked a break with the past. One of the first decisions of his successor was to move the Zulu royal court away from the British settlers, about whom Dingane was becoming increasingly suspicious, and back to the traditional Zulu heartland, the Emakhosini Valley. Driving up to Umgundhlovu today it is easy to see why: Dingane's royal compound is set on a beautiful hillside with a 360-degree view to distant horizons. In recent years it has been partially reconstructed, but when it was built in 1829 it would have been awe-inspiring.

The Umgundhlovu enclosure is an interesting reconstruction. It is the central area of the original site rebuilt on the excavated foundations of the original buildings. It feels both faux and authentic. The large multi-acre site occupies the same footprint as the original Zulu enclosure and reconstructed houses sit on the very baked foundations that were burned when the Zulu abandoned the site for strategic reasons. Today there are twenty or so circular dome-shaped houses sitting on the side of the hill. They have been reconstructed in the same materials, layers of straw tied taut by lengths of rope that descend along the outside edge of the building from a central nipple on the crown of the roof. The ropes visually slice the building into segments that descend to the ground. They are simple houses, but disarmingly beautiful. The compound is tiny compared to what it once was: 1,500 small buildings used to stand on the site housing between five and seven thousand people, clustered eight-deep around the central cattle pen that would have doubled as a parade ground. Today the site's focus and feel are different. The gentle camber of the landscape carries the visitor's eye down to a single, particularly large building that sits on the edge of the reconstruction –

Dingane's house. The reconstructed conurbation is breathtaking and still probably quite unlike the large and complex metropolis it must have been in Dingane's time.

It is easy to be left with a very limited spectrum of ideas about the Zulu in this period. An enormous amount has been written about their military-oriented culture and their love of cattle. But here in these buildings are clues to a cultural hinterland. They are structures of real efficiency and utility that have been made lovingly and beautifully – a fitting and affecting memorial. Step inside one of the houses, bending your back low to get through the waist-height semi-circular door and waiting for your eyes to adjust to the lack of light, and they cease to be pastiche; they come alive as domestic spaces and they begin to reveal something of the Zulu way of being. You are overcome by the warm smell of earth and drying straw, the burnt umber light, the intimacy; these were loved spaces, centred around a low circular fireplace in the centre of the floor. Built with a deeply considered aesthetic, circles within circles; indeed the whole circular site sits on the crown of a hill that seems to resemble a dome of one of the houses. Sitting inside one of the houses gazing at the round hearth, it is easy to reflect on the coil of the *inkhata* that bound and wound its way spiritually through and around these communities, inviting them to look inward to family and history for mental sustenance. It was said that the Zulu chose the circle because it meant that no spirit or enemy could lurk in a corner, but the single inner surface of these houses also had a more nurturing effect: it gave everyone a powerful sense of the focused vision of the Zulu, drawing its strength from its heart, its centre.

When Dingane seized the throne, the Zulu kingdom was at its zenith. In the twelve years of his reign Shaka had expanded Zulu territory from 10 square miles to nearly 12,000. The population of the new Zulu nation was around a quarter of a million, with a standing army of forty thousand soldiers. But the kingdom was facing a new threat, which reached its climax up here at Umgundhlovu.

In 1834, a group of Boer settlers, descendants of Dutch,

German and French farmers, frustrated with British rule at the Cape, set off into the African interior in search of new lands on a journey that became known as The Great Trek. By 1837 they had arrived in the southern reaches of Zululand, and their presence threatened King Dingane. He realized that the Boers' weapons, enormous herds of cattle and hunger for land had the potential to destabilize the Zulu kingdom. After a succession of skirmishes he decided to negotiate with them, and in 1838 agreed to cede them some territory in southern Natal in exchange for cattle. To confirm the agreement Dingane invited their leader, Piet Retief, and seventy of his fellow Boers to join him in the royal kraal in Umgundhlovu.

The Boers' arrival on 3 February 1838 to confirm the deal was provocative. They rode into the royal enclosure on horseback, firing their guns into the air in a display intended to overawe their hosts. It was a demonstration that shocked the Zulu and which Dingane interpreted as aggressive and insulting. Nevertheless, the Zulu continued with the planned ceremonies. Zulu soldiers performed ceremonial displays, and the women of the royal compound danced for the visitors. By the third day the mood had changed. Before their departure the Boers were invited to Dingane's house for a final leave-taking. As part of the traditional protocol they were asked to leave their weapons outside. Then, while two Zulu regiments were performing a ceremonial dance, Dingane stood up and called out, 'Seize the wizards!' The Boers were removed from the compound by Zulu soldiers and one by one were clubbed to death. Their leader Piet Retief was the last to be executed. The Boers were buried outside the royal compound.

In the late afternoon, just as the sun is setting, I climb the hill to the Boer graves. A memorial sits on the site where the Boers were killed, turning a place of execution into a shrine. It became for many Boers more than a war memorial, it was a site that went down in their reading of history as a place of grave infamy. On the day I visit there is only a single decaying flower on the grave – perhaps a mark of the slow erosion of the power of this place and a sign of the ongoing power of reconciliation.

Dingane's execution of the Boers was provoked by their arrogance and insulting behaviour. The Zulu felt they had tried to reach an accommodation with these visitors who coveted their territory, but their efforts were thrown back in their faces. Nevertheless, the manner of the Boers' deaths was extreme. The event went down in Boer history as an outrageous atrocity, reinforcing Boer views of the Zulu as violent and treacherous. It was an act the Boers were determined to avenge.

Nine months after the massacre of Piet Retief and his compatriots, the Boer trekkers appointed a new leader, Andries Pretorius. He organized a commando of 470 Boers to take the fight to the Zulu. By 14 December 1838 the Boer party had advanced deep into Zulu territory when they encountered a Zulu advance guard. They set up camp on the banks of the Ncome river. What happened then became a legendary event in Boer mythology.

The Boers had created a defensive strategy to cope with attacks from the indigenous populations they encountered on their trek. By binding their wagons together in a circle, filling the gaps with scrub and wooden gates and firing out with muskets and small cannons, the Boers could protect their families and their livestock inside a sort of temporary fortification. They called it a laager.

The Zulu attacked at dawn. They deployed their 'horns of the buffalo' battle formation, but two things were against them: the geography of the site and the weapons of the Boers. The Boers had chosen their position carefully and the steep sides of the river enclosed the site on two sides. On the opposing sides the circle of wagons was broken at three points by small cannon loaded with gravel and small pieces of metal. Between the wagons were fences packed with scrub from behind which the Boers could fire their rifles. Volleys of rifle fire were coordinated to crackle out between the cannon.

It was a temporary fortification, but for the approaching Zulu, armed with spears, it was close to impregnable. It was unlike any defensive strategy the Zulu had ever seen deployed, but they made a decision to stick to their traditional strategy of attempting to encircle the laager with their two horns. But the left horn broke away, advancing before the centre and the right horn were ready; they were almost immediately repulsed. With each burst of rifle-fire the Zulu were scattered and eventually pushed back into the river that ran along the edge of the encampment. They'd thought the sheer banks of the river would offer them cover; they also left them vulnerable.

The Boers advanced on the trapped Zulu and fired down into the riverbed. The Zulu did not have room to respond with their spears. The right horn of the army broke up and the parties of Zulu warriors were either shot or forced to retreat. According to the Boers, the final Zulu body count was around three thousand. Their bodies filled the riverbed and turned the water red. In Zulu history, what happened here became known as the Battle of Blood River. After nearly two decades of military triumph during which they'd swept away nearly every opponent in their path, the Zulu were suddenly faced with defeat. The exposure of the fallibility of the Zulu battle strategy must have rocked its people – this was a culture that was founded on the belief that they were invulnerable, that working together they could achieve anything. Perhaps the future would be different.

The loss sent shockwaves through the Zulu army for the Boers had identified their Achilles heel: firearms. The Boers had fielded a force of just 470 men compared to the thousands of Zulu warriors, but they had rifles and they used them mercilessly. The Zulu were mistrustful of guns. For them, a true warrior had to confront his enemy up close, in hand-to-hand combat. Guns were the weapons of cowards, a form of craven sorcery; a real soldier would look into the eyes of his enemy. To use cannon loaded with stones for maximum coverage against the spear-armed Zulu was despicable. Even today the Zulu sing a slow lament to remember the battle, about which there is still bitterness.

In the 1980s, at the height of apartheid, Afrikaners constructed on the site where the battle took place a lifesize monument to commemorate Blood River, an austere but nevertheless affecting bronze sculpture comprising a 100-metre-wide circle of dozens of wagons. Each wagon is joined to the other on the circle's outer edge by wooden fences, just as it was at the battle. Today it seems as much an assertion of power and self-belief as the mythology of the original Boers. Even from a distance, sitting on the floor of the vast valley it can be seen not just as a noble war memorial but as a powerful statement that along with the massive loss of life something changed here.

Blood River was certainly catastrophic for the Zulu. It shattered their psyche. Shaka had promised his people that if they gave their allegiance to him he would give them security. That was the covenant of the Zulu kingdom. Blood River was the first great challenge to that. If the founding principle of Shaka's Zulu kingdom no longer held true, what did the future hold? And not only had they been humiliated in battle, they had to withdraw from their territory too. The lands that Shaka had conquered were taken from them. Perhaps the worst consequence was civil war. Dingane's brother, Mpande, took half the Zulu army and made peace with the Boers. With Boer support he attacked Dingane, who was forced to flee, and Mpande assumed the Zulu throne. Two decades of conflict followed.

The Zulu were only just recovering from this period of instability when a chance discovery 120 miles south of the town of Kimberley triggered an economic earthquake that would destabilize the Zulu kingdom even further. In 1866 at Hopetown, 800 miles away from Zululand, a Boer farmer named Schalk Van Niekerk acquired a white stone from a local shepherd who had found it near the Orange river. The stone was a diamond, and it turned out to weigh a massive 21.25 carats. It was named the Eureka and was described by the British colonial secretary as 'the rock on which the future success of South Africa will be built'.

The discovery of the Eureka, and a series of even larger stones, set off a massive diamond rush. By 1873 an estimated ten thousand prospectors had descended on the region, transforming a small farm owned by the De Beer family into the biggest diamond mine in the world. The town around the mine became known as New Rush. In 1877 it was annexed to the British Cape

Colony and renamed in honour of the British colonial secretary, Lord Kimberley. By the middle of the 1870s the town of Kimberley was the African equivalent of the Wild West.

When surface mining was exhausted the land was excavated at sites like the Big Hole to depths of more than 800 metres. Incredibly the first 240 metres of that was dug entirely with pick and shovel, making it one of the largest man-made excavations in the world. To accomplish such a feat the mine owners had cultivated an insatiable appetite for labour. The European prospectors who descended on Kimberley turned to local Africans, many of them members of clans and indigenous societies. The Africans' traditional way of life was a source of irritation for the mine owners and impeded their profits. Migrant workers could be called back to their homes for military service at a moment's notice, leaving their mining posts and their employers in the lurch. They often used the money they earned to buy guns which they brought back to their people, causing deep unease among the colonial authorities.

The impact on the migrant workers themselves was even greater. Young men who had only ever experienced a barter economy suddenly found themselves working for cash, and were subject to a range of new temptations. Traditional African cultures that had endured for hundreds of years were being eroded. At the McGregor Museum in Kimberley, curator Colin Fortune has a collection of photographs of African migrants who came to work at Kimberley in the late nineteenth century. The images tell an arrestingly sad story that began in the 1870s when the diamond industry was in its infancy. Zulu migrant workers could come and go, retaining a certain bargaining power with employers. There are photos of young men arriving for work excited by the opportunity. Then the mine owners instituted the Pass Laws, a system of rules designed to restrict the mobility of the workers. Workers had to live in prison-like compounds which confined them, forcing them to work. Thousands of native Africans died in the mines, facilitating the profits of immensely wealthy European businessmen.

Duggan-Cronin, one of the guards at the mines, was fascinated by the stories of the migrant workers. He took photographs of the Zulu miners and followed many of them back to their homesteads. The contrast between the images of these migrant workers in their traditional homelands and traditional clothing and those of them working as miners at Kimberley is a poignant reminder of a traditional way of life under threat.

Beyond the human impact of the mining industry was the financial effect. Kimberley became the scene of enormous economic opportunity and competition. British businessmen and adventurers, including Cecil Rhodes and Barney Barnato, fought for possession of the mines here, with millions of pounds at stake. The discovery of diamonds kick-started a South African industrial revolution that rippled right across the region and impacted indirectly on the Zulu. A few years later, gold was discovered near Johannesburg. Railways needed to be built, agriculture needed to be improved, and labour needed to be organized – all to feed the insatiable mining industry.

Indigenous African kingdoms like the Zulu, with their cash-free economies and traditional way of life, represented a clear ideological impediment to the sort of economic progress the colonial authorities were keen to advance. At the end of the 1870s, the lands that were producing such abundant mineral resources, those with so much potential for wealth creation, were located in a patchwork of independent Boer, British and native African-controlled territories. With other European powers all scrambling for a piece of the action, it was a situation the British authorities in the Cape were keen to regularize. So they hatched a plan. By federalizing the territories into a single British-controlled South Africa, the British would consolidate their position and secure the resources of the land. By the mid 1870s South Africa was no longer a strategic outpost for the British on the route to the Far East, it was a potential source of untold riches. Faced with ever-increasing pressures from other European colonial powers with African ambitions, the British empire could no longer delay the industrialization of South Africa. The independent Zulu kingdom, with a standing army of forty thousand soldiers, stood in the way.

The Zulu were now faced with a more aggressive and powerful enemy than they had ever squared up to before. In 1878, a number of minor Zulu infringements on the border of the colony of Natal were cited by the British as examples of the Zulu kingdom's aggressive intentions. The British authorities mischievously hinted that a Zulu invasion of Natal was imminent. On 11 December that year, beneath a fig tree on the banks of the Tugela river, the British issued the Zulu with an ultimatum. They had a number of key demands: the disbandment of the Zulu army, the break-up of the traditional Zulu regimental system, and the presence within Zulu territory of a British diplomat to enforce colonial policy. It amounted to a demand for the dismantling of the Zulu nation. The army had been the backbone of Zulu society since the time of Shaka. The *amabutho* regimental system had been the key to Zulu success and nation building. The disbandment of the army was a demand the new Zulu king could never have countenanced.

Cetshwayo had inherited the throne from his father in 1873. During his reign he rebuilt relationships with the British and unified the Zulu nation after several decades of trauma and infighting. After the defeat by the Boers at Blood River and the civil strife that followed, the Zulu nation was once again a powerful military force. King Cetshwayo was not about to give up his nation without a fight.

Cetshwayo was fully aware of the scale of the imminent British attack and devised his military strategy accordingly. He had established his royal compound at Ondini, deep in the heart of Zulu territory, and it became the nerve-centre of the Zulu military campaign. In 1879, when the British declared war on the Zulu, many of Cetshwayo's elite troops were housed in this compound. In recent years it has been reconstructed, but only a fragment of the original complex, which would have been enormous. Over a thousand thatched houses were contained inside a huge enclosure, accommodating the most important *amabutho* regiments. It was both a royal court and an awesome military barracks, and it was quickly put to the test.

On 11 January 1879, three columns of British soldiers led by Lieutenant General Lord Chelmsford moved into Zululand. This invasion force consisted of five thousand British troops supported by eight thousand African levies. Cetshwayo identified the central column, personally led by Lord Chelmsford, as the most serious threat and decided to target it with twenty thousand of his troops, including some of his finest *amabutho* regiments. Before they set out, the Zulu army were ritually prepared for battle in a series of traditional ceremonies. For many of the soldiers this would be their first experience of combat and they were eager to demonstrate their courage. On 22 January they got their chance.

Two days earlier the central British column led by Chelmsford had set up camp deep in Zulu territory. They chose a wide expanse of land beneath the mountain of Isandlhwana. It is late afternoon when I arrive in this vast long open valley surrounded by an uneven wall of ominous hills. At its head sits a strange-looking hill. The British who camped beneath the hill on the eve of the battle thought it looked like a sphinx; the Zulu felt it looked like one of their traditional houses. Its name, Isandlhwana, derives from the Zulu phrase 'looks like home', which proved to be strangely portentous. As the site of the last great Zulu victory in the Anglo-Zulu war it has become a place of homage, but it also still feels quite eerie. Today it is covered in white cairns that mark the places where skeletons were retrieved years later. The area where the battle took place is huge, and every feature necessary to replay the battle remains intact. As I walk over the site I imagine thousands of Zulu covering hundreds of metres of this ground at high speed in the final stage of their attack. The sun soon begins to set and the wind picks up, filling the air with fine flecks of sand. As the light fades the white cairns seem to fluoresce. I stay until the sun dips down over the horizon and the last dregs of lights are wrung from the sky. The only light to guide my walk back is the ghostly radiance of the cairns.

The battle started with a catastrophic military error by the

British. Lord Chelmsford believed that the Zulu would be unwilling to fight, so he decided to take the fight to them. He split his forces here at Isandhlwana and led half of them away to the east to search for the Zulu. It wasn't long before a few Zulu were spotted, scattered on the hills. By pursuing them with his forces he believed they would lead him to the bulk of the Zulu army. But the Zulu had played him for a fool. They were actually waiting a couple of miles from Isandlhwana, readying themselves to strike.

When four British scouts on a routine patrol came over the hill they came upon the twenty thousand Zulu warriors sitting in complete silence. The Zulu commanders had managed to lead this enormous force undetected to within a couple of miles of the British army's base camp. As soon as they spotted the British, the Zulu broke ranks and pursued the scouts back to the camp at Isandhlwana, where the battle took place. As the British infantry lined up to shoot, the Zulu fell into their classic 'horns of the buffalo' battle formation. The chest region, containing the army's toughest warriors, descended on the British infantry while the two horns spread out and enveloped them from both sides. The result was carnage. The British were completely overwhelmed and their camp was destroyed. Eight hundred and fifty British troops were killed, plus over four hundred native levies.

The Zulu success at Isandlhwana was partly due to the failures of the British, but primarily due to the masterful tactics of the Zulu. Moving en masse, all twenty thousand of them, to within a couple of miles of the British camp before being detected was an extraordinary feat, and a decisive one, for their attack took the British completely by surprise.

The battle of Isandlhwana was the Zulu army's finest hour. Their nation had been invaded and threatened with destruction and they had responded with laser-like focus and discipline. By embracing the legacy of Shaka they had shaken the British empire. It was a victory that would be short-lived. Before the two horns of the Zulu army had met and fully enveloped the British a band of survivors retreated and made their way to a small British field

Late-nineteenth-century view of Rorke's Drift.

hospital set up in the home of a Swedish trader, 8 miles away on the banks of the Buffalo river. It was known as Rorke's Drift.

Even today this remains an emotionally difficult history to navigate. Rorke's Drift is an event that permanently eroded the Zulu's sense of themselves, of their capabilities, and to make it worse it occurred only hours after one of their most decisive victories. Even today it is a charged place. I find it, like many before me, impossible to visit, and remain detached and focused.

The field hospital at Rorke's Drift was in what was the British-controlled colony of Natal. Cetshwayo had expressly forbidden his troops to venture into British territory. But, fired up by their routing of the enemy at Isandlhwana, around four thousand Zulu soldiers who had made up the loins of the Isandlhwana battle formation disobeyed their king's orders and moved off to attack the hospital, fully expecting a repeat of their earlier victory. The British realized there was no point in trying to flee. They barricaded themselves in and turned the buildings into a fortification. With thousands of rounds of ammunition stored inside and a large selection of state-of-the-art rifles, the British were able to see off the Zulu attack. The Zulu withdrew, but not before 875 of their troops were killed.

Rorke's Drift went down in history as a legendary British success. Eleven of the soldiers who defended the site were awarded Victoria Crosses, the highest number ever for a single battle. But it was a catastrophe for the Zulu. Before I visited I had read the received history, looked at the battle maps, pored over the contemporary accounts and come to understand it as a battle. Based on that history I had interpreted Rorke's Drift as a place where the superior weapons technology of the British finally told, setting off a cascade of seismic political events. That remains true, but it is only part of the story. Actually to see Rorke's Drift adds a layer of important nuance to that interpretation; the minute scale of the site, the almost intimate setting of the tiny, almost quaint field hospital isolated within a vast hilly landscape, changes the quality of the humiliation into something deeply astonishing and far more culturally profound. The critical stages of this defining engagement took place in a space no bigger than two or three tennis courts. Thousands of Zulu soldiers in such an area must have seemed a completely overwhelming force, an absolute statement of a single possible result: a devastating Zulu victory.

The significance of the astonishing outcome was undoubtedly manipulated by the British for broader political needs, but the complete victory of one form of weapons technology over another marked the beginning of the end of a military culture. It was a challenge to the very idea of military solidarity that underpinned the Zulu way of life and so began the unravelling of the core Zulu metaphysic. The Zulu defeat was far more profound in its effects than the British victory. The loss broke their sense of invincibility, of the rightness of their cause, which raised questions about methods, perhaps even their leadership. The sense of vulnerability that it generated acculturated itself deep into the Zulu psyche.

King Cetshwayo was furious with his troops. He had been elated by the victory at Isandlhwana, but Rorke's Drift was a shocking defeat. The disobedience of a small contingent of the Zulu army came at a heavy price. At Rorke's Drift the Zulu came up against the reality of modern weaponry. All the courageous hand-to-hand combat, all the brilliant battle formations in the world couldn't match it. After Rorke's Drift the writing was on the wall for the Zulu. It would be impossible to hold back the tide.

In June 1879, five months after Isandlhwana, the British army returned to Zululand, twenty-five thousand strong, determined to finish the job. After a series of battles the final blow came in the town of Ulundi, the capital of KwaZulu-Natal. The compound where Cetshwayo gathered and rallied his troops before battle sits on a hill overlooking Ulundi, the site of the final defeat. It is a beautiful place with long hilly vistas that look down into flat fertile valleys. There is a strain of Zulu history that is immensely sad, and like Dingane's compound which was burned before his retreat, the reconstruction here somehow feels like a memorial. It too was burned to the ground, not by the withdrawing Zulu but even more humiliatingly by the British. The flames consumed the great *inkhata* that Shaka had instituted. It was as if the spiritual and philosophical link that connected Shaka and Cetshwayo, the sense of pride in the values of Zulu culture, the drive to expand and protect the nation as a priority, was unravelled here in this peaceful valley, and that pall of sadness still hangs over the site. It was Cetshwayo's home; perhaps as an indicator of his personal priorities, it was also the place where the elite of the army lived. At Ulundi the fluid, sweeping 'horns of the buffalo' that had served the Zulu well in the past were simply no match for the impregnable British block formation, backed by fearsome artillery. Fifteen hundred Zulu were killed but just thirteen British soldiers died.

What followed was a tragedy. Using their classic divide-and-rule strategy, the British broke the Zulu kingdom into thirteen separate chieftaincies, each led by an enemy of King Cetshwayo. The kingdom was plunged into a bitter civil war in which more Zulu died than in the whole of the Anglo-Zulu war. Cetshwayo was captured and imprisoned. He eventually made his way to London to plead his case for the restoration of the Zulu monarchy with Queen Victoria. She granted him a small parcel of land, but he died in 1884. The nation Shaka had built from nothing had been systematically destroyed.

Today all that marks the battlefield at Ulundi is a quaint memorial to the British dead. It was designed in 1946 and makes an attempt to be conciliatory: the plaque sits opposite a dedication to the 'Old Great Zulu Nation'. It is a place out of its time. It feels like a memorial to colonialism. The suburban British architecture and the niceness of the garden that surrounds the site bely the reality of what happened here. Like the old Zulu compounds, the site has ironically become a memorial not just for the dead but also for the loss of a way of life. The British empire itself eventually crumbled and was reborn out of its constituent parts. Here, the South African colony was replaced by apartheid.

South Africa's complex contended histories are fundamental to the country's modern identity. Twenty-first-century South Africa

Romantic late-nineteenth-century British image of Zulu warrior.

has found a way to celebrate its population's differences without constantly regurgitating the painful baggage that was fundamental to crafting the country. The Zulu culture came into being as new technologies and trading opportunities became available. In less than a century their dramatic rise and fall was driven by a handful of individuals. And under uncompromising and brilliant leadership the Zulu grew from one of a number of polities into an unrivalled force ruling over a vast territory. The British and the Boers presented the Zulu with unanswerable military challenges, but their problems were undoubtedly exacerbated by internal politics. Today we can wander the sites of the great Zulu, Boer, colonial and apartheid struggles and still sense the pain, but feel somewhat reassured that the pain is not generally being misused to fuel mainstream contemporary politics. It is admirable and fascinating. But it has left the Zulu a warrior nation in name alone. The spears and shields remain badges of cultural identity, but the edges of the blades have grown dull and the shields brittle with age. The symbols of the warrior nation are today simply that – symbolic. It is laudable, but it points to a passing of a particular kind of cultural potency. These people have lost so much, and that loss has been woven into their cultural narrative, lending a kind of richness to their equally powerful history of victory. The drama of life played out against these two polar possibilities is, and always has been, profound, requiring belief to make it truly viable. Perhaps that is something to celebrate and to mourn a little. Like the ghosts of the lost San, the indigenous people of this land, these beliefs will never truly die.

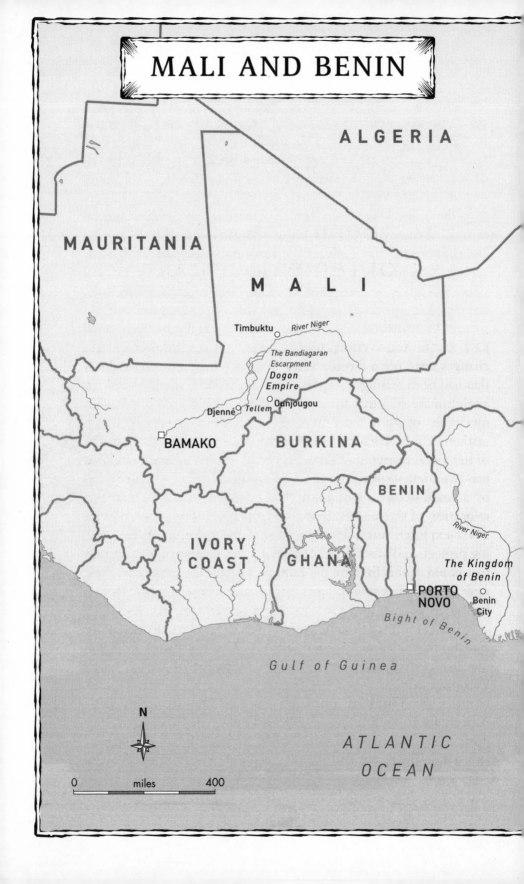

MALI AND BENIN

ALGERIA

MAURITANIA

M A L I

Timbuktu ○ *River Niger*

*The Bandiagaran
Escarpment*
*Dogon
Empire*
○ Ounjougou
Djenné ○ ○ Tellem

□ BAMAKO

B U R K I N A

BENIN

IVORY
COAST

GHANA

River Niger

*The Kingdom
of Benin*

□ PORTO
NOVO ○ Benin
City

Bight of Benin

Gulf of Guinea

N

*ATLANTIC
OCEAN*

0 miles 400

Benin: the art
of remembering

JUST OVER A CENTURY AGO, EUROPEAN ART CHANGED. THE
changes were not a further resolution of the aesthetic conundrum
that had been teasing European artists for centuries. This wasn't an
evolutionary step that took us closer to understanding the subtle
mechanics of paint and canvas. This was the discovery of a new
aesthetic aim, a paradigm shift from trying to resolve the physics
of the visual to trying to come to terms with its metaphysics. The
pre–twentieth-century waltz of oil on canvas was over, replaced
by a visual debate about being, living, feeling and questioning; a
relocation of the self, the individual, the artist. The single viewer,
as self-explorer, was suddenly pushed to the forefront of the painting project, and a new kind of painting became possible, paintings
that could evangelize and exorcize and then fill your psyche with
new ghosts. They weren't pictures of other people, pretty people,
bourgeois people, they were paintings of our pain, our joy.

It is a fascinating time when a number of factors fall into place
and the trajectory of a discipline alters. There is little debate that
one of the major catalysts for the development of abstraction in
European painting was contact with African art. The Fauvist artist
Maurice de Vlaminck adamantly asserted that he 'discovered'
African art in the summer of 1905 when, in exchange for buying
drinks for customers in a café, he carried off two sculptures
and a mask, objects that transformed his work. Henri Matisse

maintained he was the first, dating his finds to the same period; so did Félix Fénéon, Georges Braque and André Lhote. Elsewhere in Paris, after a visit to the ethnographic collection at the Trocadero, Pablo Picasso wrote about the disturbing and uncomfortable feeling that seeing African sculpture prompted in him. He used and reused words such as 'shock', 'revelation', 'charge', terms usually characteristic of a religious experience, of a moment of conversion. He could at last see a potential path through the maze of the then uncompleted *Les Demoiselles d'Avignon*. It was a moment that changed art history.

It was not just confined to art. The turn of the twentieth century was a period of increasing Western fascination with Africa, a fascination that permeated many areas of European and American cultural activity; it seeped across class and discipline to capture the popular imagination. It was triggered in part by a series of events that took place in 1897, when the British embarked on a military campaign in Benin, an influential city-state east of Lagos in what is now southern Nigeria. It was a decisive moment in the history of British colonialism. The invasion led to the annihilation of the Benin monarchy and its court, the trial of the Oba – the head of state – the removal and execution of senior court dignitaries, the razing to the ground of the royal compound and the torching of a number of principal towns. It was a ruthless and devastating campaign that showed the colonial machine at its most effective and unforgiving. The world sat up and noticed. It is quite understandable why this became the inspiration for Joseph Conrad when he began to write *Heart of Darkness* the following year. But from the smouldering embers of the sacked Benin emerged an unlikely story of astonishing beauty that was in stark contrast with the accounts of horror: the European discovery of the bronzes, carved plaques showing aspects of life in a centuries-old, highly sophisticated kingdom.

The Benin Bronzes amazed and confused Europeans. It was art that was deeply enigmatic, that exuded intrigue, that was as complex as anything produced in Rome or Greece – but this art was African, a sensational thought at the end of the nineteenth century.

The British invasion force and the Benin loot.

Some of the subjects depicted in the bronzes were animals. Traditionally the people of Benin were animists, believers in the idea that souls and spirits existed not only in humans but in animals, plants and the earth itself. But there were also people captured in the plaques, including Europeans, whose clothing seemed to date the bronzes to as early as the fifteenth century. To produce each one, the artist would have needed to know how to make and fire a clay mould, and how to mix and melt the metals to pour into it. It is an incredibly difficult skill to master, even more impressive if indeed the bronzes were fifteenth century.

Over subsequent decades the amazement developed into scepticism and then hardened into the idea that 'they could not have been made by African artists'. The skill involved in making these artefacts simply did not match the European view of West Africans. The invading British forces claimed that they found evidence of human sacrifices in Benin City. How could such primitive barbarians create such exquisite and complex art? Where did they get the materials from? How did they acquire the ability to create something as perfect as this? These were objects made during the European Middle Ages but they were as good as, if not superior to, anything produced in Europe. The intrigue and excitement they provoked did not just inspire Conrad and Picasso, it became part of a new wind that blew through culture, changing many aspects of the popular world, from music to fashion. Something of that enigmatic aura still hangs over the Benin Bronzes.

Keen to find out the truth about these bronze casts and to investigate how these beautiful things were actually made, I begin my trip not in Benin, nor even in Africa, but at the British Museum, home to many of the most beautiful of the nine hundred plaques seized in 1897. There is a part of me that is still not comfortable with the bronzes being here, even after decades of marvelling at them in this setting. But whatever my misgivings, they are certainly loved and looked after by the British Museum. And the knowledge accreted after decades of being in close proximity to the bronzes is vitally important for someone trying to find out something about their history.

I seek out Claude Ardouin, the curator of the British Museum's West Africa artefacts, to show me around. There are now more plaques in the British Museum than anywhere else in the world. These objects may be mute, but perhaps just being close to them, breathing the same air, is as good a way to start the quest as any. And so I join Claude sitting on a bench in the Africa gallery gazing up at the bronzes, wondering what the journey might throw up.

Up close to the bronzes I am struck by something very prosaic: these iconic things were made, constructed. I am so used to seeing them in books and films, where they feel so complete, it requires a real leap to imagine that someone built them, that they describe the lives of real people, and that I might soon be meeting some of their descendants and perhaps discovering how and why they were made.

Claude explains how each brass (not bronze) plaque was created with an extremely high level of skill and artistic ability – this was the technological apex of a highly sophisticated tradition of brass-casting. In order to realize their highly particular artistic aspirations, the brass (not bronze) casters of Benin developed a new technique of casting. The initial crude cores were crafted in clay around which a finished surface was applied in wax. The surface had all the detail, subtlety and texture of the finished work. Around the wax sculpture a layer of clay was moulded, before the wax was melted to leave an internal void. Copper and zinc – molten brass – was then poured into the void to create the plaques that we know, each one paired but unique.

They depict everyday and mythological scenes, images of great political, military and ceremonial importance. It is obvious that they are historical documents, but they have become symbolic of the enduring continuity of historical narrative. There is conjecture about some of them. For example, the powerful-looking figure on horseback is said to be Oba Esigie returning triumphant from battle with the Ogana, with his retinue. Oba Esigie bolstered the kingdom of Benin with the help of the Portuguese, who provided mercenaries for battles. The Portuguese also brought the metal that enabled the casters to immortalize the exploits of their Oba. Before the Portuguese arrived the copper is thought to have come from trading merchants much further north. The bronzes were court diaries and records of the kingdom. But the manner of their removal from Benin has robbed them of the subtle meaning they obviously once conveyed. Academics from across the Western world have speculated about that meaning, have worked to decipher and deconstruct them. Claude points out that we do know that 'these pieces are closely connected to the idea of kingship and the divinity of the king. There is certainly evidence that the people who made them had a special status within the court or in the society. They were a way of recording history, but beyond that, we can only really conjecture.' Some scholars have built romantic formal interpretations of the plaques; others have ascribed much more utilitarian readings to the bronzes. Academic thinking has undoubtedly pushed us closer to understanding these enigmatic objects, but there are still aspects that remain a mystery.

It is amazing and frustrating that we know so little about the Benin Bronzes. These plaques are regarded today as hugely significant pieces of West African art, of an extremely high standard that would be difficult to replicate even today. I want to find the answer to the question that puzzled the colonials: where did these skills and materials come from, and what was the significance of such beautiful objects within the broader context of West African cultures?

Claude leaves me and I sit and look at the plaques until an attendant tells me that the museum is closing soon. They are beautiful, beguilingly detailed, but they are haunted by a sense of not knowing that I find quite sad. I spend my last few moments sketching the plaques and taking a few quick visual notes (the snake, the leopard, the crocodile) to carry with me. I leave thinking defiantly, why couldn't West African people have developed the know-how that led to the creation of the bronzes? And if these cultures were significant enough and wealthy enough to produce such artefacts, what on earth happened to them?

I have always thought that there is an art to research, and so, more on a hunch than real evidence, before I go to Benin, the home of the bronzes, I decide to explore the place where the skills and craftsmanship seen in the casts may have originated, which means travelling to what is now Mali. Until relatively recently it was thought that Mali, on the edge of the largest desert in the world, could add nothing to our understanding of ancient Africa. It showed no signs of having been populated until relatively modern times. But I was aware that the history of Mali had had to be revised and rewritten thanks to some recent discoveries. Perhaps within that new body of thinking on Mali there may be clues that can take me closer to an understanding of ancient Benin and the trading communities that lived adjacent to them on the banks of the Niger.

Ounjougou is in an area of southern Mali dominated by tributaries of the Niger. The source of this great river complex is way up in the Guinea highlands. By the time the third longest river in Africa gets to the flat landscapes of Mali it is broad and slow-flowing, meandering in a huge stately crescent before disgorging huge amounts of fertile silt into the massive coastal delta at Benin. The coastal delta in Nigeria covers 35,000 square kilometres and is the largest in Africa. The rich agricultural lands fringing the Niger, and particularly its inland delta, have served as the 'bread-basket' for a succession of civilizations beginning at least as early as AD 300. Its ecological cycles of flood and retreat encourage a complex web of human economies: fisher-folk who live on or beside the river, rice agriculturists who plant on its banks, millet farmers who plant far from its floods on sandy ground, and pastoralists who enter the delta at the time of low waters after the harvest to graze their cattle. This river has always been a trading highway between communities on the edge of the Malian Sahara and on the coast, like the people at Benin. In the absence of any significant knowledge of ancient Benin, perhaps there are clues to be found here amid the burgeoning archaeology of Mali. And Ounjougou is a fascinating place to start. Here a nexus of rivers has defined this landscape for millennia. But recently after a storm a riverbank collapsed, exposing a seam of archaeological finds that have rewritten the history of this region. It is an archaeologist's dream: a cross-section of a mud-bank revealing strata of a vast and important span of history − some thousands of years. In 2002 an international team began to find evidence of prehistoric human activity buried in the layers.

Part of that team during the initial excavations was Adamo Dembele, and he has agreed to meet me and show me around. He is late. Ounjougou is beautiful, but it feels very far from human life. Mali is a buzzing country of highly cultured, very visually oriented people, but this place is nothing like that. It feels remote. The soil is terracotta orange and it screams against the lush green reeds and grass. Other than the sound of the river and the birds, there is complete silence. By the time Adamo arrives, I am very hot and almost bursting with built-up expectation.

He is a lot younger than I'd expected and brimming with excitement and energy. You can tell that this site has lost none of its sense of romance for him. Almost without saying hello he leads me, tripping and falling, down the bank towards a stretch of highly striated and contrasting horizontal strands of earth. 'This is one of the sites where the team has been working,' he tells me. 'We've been working our way down through the sediment and we have discovered layers of sediment from different ages, including shards of pottery and different pottery types.' It is possible to see the tell-tale layers of charcoal and the variations in tone in the mud that point to sustained periods of ancient habitation. This quiet spot in an isolated valley amid a web of rivers is the site of some of the most exciting West African archaeology of recent years.

Archaeologists have found pottery fragments here which seem to be a quite staggering 11,400 years old. On the edge of the bank there are dozens of small, sharp shards of ceramic. I stop and pick one up. It is no bigger than my thumbnail but it has the imprint of woven cloth pressed into its unglazed surface. It was obviously a modest vessel, but it was also obviously carefully crafted. This is ceramic activity two thousand years older than anything else found in Africa to date, the same age as the earliest known pottery in the world, in Japan. I always love holding these things, getting close to ancient objects of utility. They may appear humble, but people were using this pottery here eight thousand years before it appeared in Britain. The discovery has forced historians to rethink the pace of development that this part of Africa experienced. It is an inspiring place to begin a journey. West Africa was way ahead of its time. These were a people who harnessed furnace-based technologies millennia ago. Perhaps their descendants and trading partners were the people who made the bronzes. It is not beyond the realm of possibility.

Unfortunately, while Adamo's research into some of the earliest surviving ceramic technology continues, there is not much else that can presently be gleaned about the people who lived here nearly twelve thousand years ago. However, not far from Ounjougou is a place that gives us a clue as to how this new technology developed.

For the next leg of my journey I have been recommended a guide, the wonderful Kene Dolo. He is a round and effusive man who has been showing people around this area for generations and seems to know absolutely everyone. The only thing I'm unsure about is his chosen mode of transport: an ancient Chinese motorbike with bald tyres and no working suspension. Kene tries to comfort me by telling me that he rarely has accidents, but as we round the first corner at speed and the back wheel skids laterally across the soft sand road, I begin to doubt him. Soon we are travelling at such speed that death seems inevitable and I start to let go of my blind terror, open my eyes and look about me – if these are going to be my final moments I am keen to see them.

We are in a curious region where the Niger bends and diffuses into a myriad of smaller rivers feeding a vast savannah, a region that is defined by a 100-mile-long sandstone escarpment that stretches 500 metres above a green valley. Kene shouts over his shoulder, 'In the ditch we have crocodiles.' The back wheel of the bike quivers under stress yet again, but I have ceased to care. I am in an Eden-like spot of fertile plains, dramatic cliffs and canyons with plunging waterfalls. This is the Bandiagara Escarpment, and it holds the key to understanding a crucial development in early West African culture.

Kene is Dogon, like most of the people who live up here. The Dogon have lived here for more than a thousand years and have made this region well known for their richly preserved traditions. But a thousand years before the Dogon this area was inhabited by the Tellem, and they left a fascinating and enigmatic legacy: dwellings built into the escarpment itself. 'All this place was a forest at that time and there were more rains than now,' says Kene as he pulls his bike to a juddering stop. 'All this was green. The people would go hunting and get many animals: elephant, pig, monkey . . .'

But Kene has not finished terrifying me quite yet. We are parked on the very top of the escarpment; hundreds of metres beneath us the unbroken green valley floor stretches out towards the horizon to the south. The view is monumental – but we do not spend any time enjoying it. Kene begins to climb down the near sheer face of the escarpment. 'A belief endures that the Tellem had the power of flight,' he shouts out as he disappears over the edge. I am beginning to understand why. The cliff-face is a loose collection of near perpendicular rocks and thin, smooth and slippery ledges – how could anyone have lived up here? But I know from my history books that nestled under the cliffs are one of the wonders of West Africa, so over I go.

The escarpment is studded with a honeycomb complex of caves, some natural, some extended by Tellem before the time of Christ. The Tellem were farming communities who grew crops and hunted down on the valley floor and then retreated to caves up here on the escarpment walls. And what they left in these caves offers a stunning insight into their world. There are areas of the escarpment where slabs of overhanging sandstone create natural passages and openings; some have an enormous, cavernous, cathe-dral-like volume. This is where the Tellem made their homes.

Despite the precipitous nature of the terrain, we make our way about 100 metres down without incident into a large cave that contains more than a dozen earth-built granaries. I have seen these structures in books. The cave is big, tall enough to contain an average suburban house at its highest point, tapering to a number of thin paths at either end; in the many recesses and set against the back wall are the fawn-coloured, room-sized, circular grain stores. The Tellem adobe granaries were built using rich ochre-coloured mud from termite mounds. It is a highly resilient material that has been protected by the natural shelter of the cliffs, so the granaries are as well preserved as the Ounjougou pottery. Their function demonstrates a continued incremental development from the first uses of ceramics. As Kene explains, 'In some of the buildings they stored fruit for lean times and trade. In other granaries the Tellem hid secret things, like traditional medicine, like the fetishes, so the spirits would take care of them.' The ability to make pottery for storage and trade, as we saw in Ounjougou, was developed by the Tellem into the construction of large adobe structures to store food away from the heat of the sun. Up here, away from predators and competition, the Tellem could hold their grain to use in lean times; they had created a way of storing energy. It shows that the Tellem could dedicate time to doing more than just farming and hunting, and these structures are not just elegantly built, they have been decorated too.

Getting up close to the granaries is very special. The outer surface of these stores is covered in chevrons pushed into the wet surface by ancient fingers – the pattern is reminiscent of those that decorate the Benin Bronzes. It is just wonderful to be able to place your fingers in the marks made by someone possibly two thousand years ago. The people who lived here could afford to think about style as well as practical function. The caves are the site of a modest renaissance, a moment when things changed. With the development of these granary stores, the Tellem no longer had to be just hunters and gatherers. They bought themselves the time to create art. Archaeologists have discovered carved headrests, pottery, necklaces, rings, bracelets, and even metalwork in these caves. Some objects have made it into museums; many were looted from the caves.

The existence of prehistoric pottery and the appearance of decoration and jewellery in West Africa two thousand years ago is very significant. It is hard evidence of indigenous development of an artistic culture many generations before the bronzes were made – something the colonial British thought impossible. But is there a connection in Mali to the technology required to make the bronzes? Do the cultures of this area share similarities in the use of symbols in their art? And what do those symbols mean?

The Tellem disappeared from this area and it isn't known how they died out. There may have been an overlap with the Dogon; perhaps they competed for the same resources. But over time these Tellem caves became Dogon caves. The Dogon used the granaries and created burial chambers up here, a necropolis built into the rock face. The floor of the cave is covered with bleached bones; scattered, smashed, splintered human bones. It is difficult not to step on them. I tread with care, but every solid object underfoot sends an uncomfortable shudder into the pit of my stomach. I am not sure how to raise it, but how can I not?

'Kene, I've noticed that there are bones on the ground – so are these human bones?'

Kene's reply is perfunctory: 'It is Dogon bones.'

I push a little. 'The idea that we are walking on a surface of human bones here is slightly eerie. Are bodies still brought here? Is it something that is still done now?'

He is barely more forthcoming. 'Yes, yes, until now the Dogon people use the Tellem houses to put dead people. We use until now the tombs.'

I get the sense that this is a sensitive area, so I drop it. I am not sure if I have offended him, but for the first time Kene becomes reflective and quiet. I take the hint and follow him as we begin the long, tough descent to the valley floor. I hope I have not upset Kene, but his silence has reminded me why I am here.

The more I study it, the more I think that history is a minefield; the potential to offend unwittingly is enormous. The network of cultural connections between objects and peoples can be subtle, tender, fragile, yet crucial to identity. That is why I love history. I may feel I know every line, every texture of the Benin Bronzes, but without the kind of knowledge that made them important to those who created and used them, perhaps in fact I barely know them.

The tombs sit high above the rivers' floodplain, above the Dogon town of Ireli. It is one of around thirty Dogon settlements clinging to the lower reaches of the Bandiagara Escarpment. The long, silent walk down gives me time to think. If West African art did begin in these cliffs, it will be interesting to see how it developed with the Dogon people. I also want to see whether their ancient culture gives any hint of a connection to the bronzes of the kingdom of Benin.

We round a path and catch our first sight of Ireli. It is late afternoon and the light is beginning to fade but I can make out a small town of perhaps two hundred people who live in rows of small, steep-sided, thatched-roofed houses with granary stores on the valley floor. They are preparing for a ritual called Dama, part of a funeral ceremony. The first drumming passages are starting to beat out across the town and the sound bouncing off the walls of the escarpment echoes out across the valley. This is a scene and these are traditions that may have lasted unchanged for several thousand years.

The light seems to fail in jolts. A stumble on some rocks might make you cast your gaze downward for a moment, only to notice as you look up that the afternoon has become evening, or the evening has become twilight. Somehow we make it down to Ireli without injury, by which time the town is alight with fires and the ceremony has begun.

There is almost no audience because everyone in the town is involved in the performance. Young men dressed in indigo pantaloons and raffia burgundy smocks are gathered in groups around an opening between the houses. The drumbeats quicken, a bass drum begins thundering out a steady rhythm that resonates through the earth, a number of smaller drums and xylophones join in, altering pace and tone in perfect synchronicity, and lastly a handful of small, almost discordant bells create a jarring accent across each constellation of beats. Then the young men start to dance, almost blind behind their carved and cowrie-shell-encrusted masks. They dance in groups; lizard masks go first. To alternate beats of the bass drum the dancers pull their arms and knees into right angles at the joint, mimicking the silhouette of a basking gecko. Giraffe, antelope, snake and dragon follow, re-animated through dance and masks. Five-metre-high flexible giraffe masks bend and twist with the dancers, arching back over our heads and down to the ground to flick up wisps of dust; stilted dancers mimic antelope. It's the ecology of the valley floor captured as funerary masquerade.

I ask Kene as we are surrounded by a new group of dancers, 'These are snakes?'

'Yes,' he replies, 'and all of this group dance the lizard mask. They are dancing to keep the bad spirits away from the village. The mask touches the ground, it cleans the village and bad things go away.'

This is art with an obvious religious dimension. It is also a clear celebration of cultural identity. The Dogon may date as far back as 10,000 BC – no one is certain – but these cultural traditions, these mechanisms for forging social cohesion and marking important events, have certainly remained unchanged for centuries. Standing in the midst of the dancers as they wheel, leap and somersault in the most acrobatic ways is breathtaking. I have seen dancing all over Africa but this is without doubt the most spectacular. Dogon oral tradition says that they fled their original home of Manding, miles to the south-east, before settling here. Masquerades like this one may well be mechanisms for keeping aspects of that ancient tradition alive. Their history and the compulsion to protect it are also reflected in their craftsmanship.

With the light gone I will have to camp here in Ireli and wait to find out more in the morning. I am exhausted, but find it impossible to get off to sleep. I can still feel the wind created by the sweeps of those giant masks as they roared past me, still smell the sweet aroma of raffia, and hear the thud of that bass drum. My mind spins . . . Did I offend Kene?

Just as I feel I'm about to drift away, a distant cock crows and a low fat beam of sunlight pours over the horizon. This morning Kene is taking me to see the granary belonging to the village chief, or Hogon. Over a breakfast taken as we make our way through the Ireli backstreets past women bathing babies in bathtubs, Kene tells me that he is going to show me some traditional carved decorative door panels that feature some of the animist symbolism I saw in last night's dance. He smiles, he is excited; perhaps I am forgiven.

The streets narrow, and then Kene disappears into a doorway. I follow, into an old courtyard. It is then that I understand what Kene has brought me to see. It is a small wooden granary door, no bigger than the flat side of a briefcase, set into a wall. These are fairly common and are not ancient, but they are part of a tradition that is extremely old. The surface is covered in low relief carvings of figures and animals in rows. It seems to be telling a story, but what? Kene points to a figure seated at one edge of the frame. 'This is the Hogon, the chief. He is the oldest person in the village. And over here all this group are wearing masks representing the *kananga* mask.' I realize that by *kananga* mask Kene means the lizard mask I saw the night before. Suddenly it occurs to me that this is not simply a depiction of something mythic, these are also scenes of everyday Dogon people living much as they do now.

Kene points to a woman. 'There is the woman, she has transformed herself into a bird in the night time flying to the cliffs to listen to the village in the night time.'

'So she transforms at night into a bird, like a demon?' I ask.

But Kene is on to the next piece of the story. 'So this is one of the original Dogon families migrating from Manding.'

Each piece of the panel tells another aspect of the Dogon story, and links that history to the supernatural. The power of animals, the story of Dogon migration, of their genealogy as grand parable, the design of the panel, and its purpose as a permanent reminder of history and a way of passing stories on to future generations, all of this bears in its iconography and form a striking resemblance to the Benin Bronzes.

Dogon granary door.

At last my thoughts are beginning to gain traction, but I want to find out whether the symbols the people use here have a similar meaning to the symbols used in the kingdom of Benin. So I make an appointment to see some elders in a neighbouring Dogon village, a mile along the bottom of the Bandiagara Escarpment. I love walking, but tripping over boulders at the foot of the escarpment is not fun. We stop every now and then to take on water and to shelter from the hot sun. The Dogon have constructed *togu'na*, open-sided shelters made from thick tree stumps that support thatched roofs, for exactly this purpose. But despite regular stops it is a very slow, tough mile. Eventually we arrive at a squat, low *togu'na* that sits on a very prominent boulder to the side of a small square. On the walls of the square are carvings showing depictions of a chief and some animals. For the second time today I am reminded of the kinds of images contained in some of the Benin Bronzes.

The big man, the Hogon, is keen to show off the decorative murals carved into the sandstone. There is a particularly striking and familiar image of an obviously powerful man astride a horse. There are lots of symbols on the walls that show at least a superficial similarity with those that were used in Benin. I do not know how, but there is obviously a connection.

I want to find out what other connections there may be. I sit with a group of old men in the shade of the *togu'na*; I do not share their language, but perhaps there is another way. Buried at the bottom of my rucksack are the sketches I made at the British Museum. I dig them out and point to the leopard. The Hogan smiles and gestures at a small man sitting in the shadows.

'The leopard represents his ancestors,' Kene says. 'If anyone harmed or killed a leopard it would cause a huge problem for his family.'

I am reminded of how in Benin the leopard protected the king, so I ask, 'And the leopard – does it protect you as well?'

Kene then tells me how the leopard could predict imminent death in families and would sit on the roof of a family home the night before they lost someone, knowing that the end was close.

'What about the king on the horse?' I ask. 'In many of the Benin plaques, when the Oba goes to war he's riding on a horse.'

'It's the same,' Kene responds. 'The horse is not for everybody. It is for the chief – the famous people travel with the horse.'

Every Benin symbol I point to seems to have a resonance for these men, drawing out complex stories and mythologies. Perhaps by coincidence or perhaps because there is a common root, these symbols created hundreds of miles away and hundreds of years earlier hold meaning for the Dogon. At the very least there are parallel patterns of connection to the natural world, but perhaps there is something more; maybe we have here some insight into how the bronzes formed a cultural anchor for the people of Benin. What has become clear is that in Dogon villages, as well as their pottery, there is a sophisticated tradition of metalwork.

After a brief lunch we go to visit the blacksmith. There is only one blacksmith family in most Dogon towns – smithing is a skill that is guarded and kept within families. Iron has been forged from the ore found in the area for many centuries. The special place reserved for craftsmen in Dogon society is reminiscent of the guild of metal casters in the kingdom of Benin. But the Dogon smiths are carvers too. These are the men whose forefathers would have carved the masks and the door to the grain store. And like the Benin smiths, maintaining the traditional stories and culture of the Dogon people was integral to their role. They captured and preserved the communal narrative in metal and wood and were often seen as having harnessed a kind of magic.

Sitting with the smiths watching their almost alchemic skills, turning scraps of rusted metal into a golden glowing liquid using little more than charcoal and bellows, is a wonderful end to a long couple of days. It is understandable why metalworkers were regarded as magicians. They do seem to have a transcendent power. They are able to turn ore from the earth into molten metal, and then create tools and weapons, and forge stories and spirits. Archaeologists believe ironworking skills in West Africa date to around 1500 BC, older than any metallurgical activity elsewhere on the continent, and some of the oldest in the world. But however spectacular, these isolated, special pockets of metalworking over a vast area do not really explain how the technology spread, or how it gave birth to the Benin Bronzes. I want to find out whether the answer lies in understanding more about ancient West African society.

After an evening of liquid goodbyes followed by a very good night's sleep, I am back on the road. Seventy miles south-west of Bandiagara and Dogon country, on the banks of the Niger, lie the remains of the earliest-known and most important lost city in sub-Saharan Africa, Jenné-jeno. I am going to miss Kene – he was a scary but wonderful man. But I am on my way to Jenné-jeno with another guide, Amadou Cisse, and a local archaeologist, Mamadou Samake, who has been part of a number of recent digs at Jenné-jeno. For centuries this area had lain ignored, its real history and significance completely unknown. All there was were old stories, rumours and children's tales. The local people believed that the city was cursed by an evil spirit called Jinn Samereuse who caused the waters of the Bani river to overflow and flood the town. Djenné-po, the hero of the tale, sacrificed his daughter, Tempama, in an attempt to save the people. She was told to plait her hair and wear her best jewellery and clothing and allow herself to be buried alive inside the walls of a house for the good of the town. Even today the children of Djenné say, 'Djenné est construit sur une jeune fille qui s'appelle Tempama Djenné-po' ('Djenné was built over a young girl whose name is Tempama Djenné-po').

Jenné-jeno is not like other archaeological sites – there is no need to scan and search the landscape for architectural clues, no need to scour the ground for the remnants of material culture. There is archaeology here in such abundance that it is almost overwhelming. A thick carpet of pottery fragments covers acres of the landscape. As we walk across this ceramic carpet I am driven to ask, 'Mr Samake, can you tell from these shards of pot what periods are represented here? There seems to be pottery of so many different types, so many different kinds of decoration.'

Amadou looks down and motions with his foot towards the rim of a vase: '850 to the eleventh century.' Mr Samake gestures with his hand towards the base of a large dish: 'This one is eleventh century onwards.'

I stop and kneel down for a moment. The range of pot fragments is immense, some plain, some decorated, some with that woven texture imprint I saw in Ounjougou, others slip painted and glazed. I pick up the base of a heavily decorated pot. This is Jenné-jeno at its height. People demanded a complex and sophisticated range of pottery to serve a complex and diverse culture. They were probably trading with people right across the region and obviously the scale of the pottery collected here is an analogue for the economic pull and dynamism of this place. In 1977, a team of scientists working here found that what was previously considered an unassuming 5-metre-deep mound of earth was in fact archaeological material. The mound contained evidence of sixteen centuries of human occupation that began around 2,250 years ago.

Jenné-jeno was obviously a significant city, and it is evident everywhere, even in the remains of its city wall, which is 3 metres deep and runs almost 3 kilometres around the city. Its sheer size suggests that Jenné-jeno was once a major urban centre, and archaeologists believe that there could have been as many as a dozen settlements of similar size in this area. What has been left behind here tells us a great deal about the sophistication of these people. It is a discovery that has shattered previous assumptions about West African society.

We walk downhill to an area that is shaded by trees; beneath them are the terracotta tops of buried pots. They are the rims of interred funerary urns. This cemetery dates to around the fifth century and shows a level of municipal organization few people thought possible until very recently. The people who made Jenné-Jeno were animists. I ask Amadou, 'Did burying people in these pots have significance?'

'Yes of course,' he replies. 'Animist practice is based on respect for the landscape and nature and so the dead are buried in the position of a foetus. We come from the earth and when we die we have to become earth.'

But this was more than a ceramic-based culture, these people also smelted metals from ores excavated from the Dogon mines, and there is still some archaeological evidence of how they made use of it. The excavations which revealed that the earliest inhabitants were using and working with iron found evidence of a smithy constructed around AD 800 to forge iron and to mould copper and bronze into ornaments. The fact that metalwork seems to have been concentrated in the same area for a further six hundred years suggests that craftsmen had become organized in localized castes – just as they are in the Dogon villages. The skills of furnace-based arts were as fundamental to the making of this city as trade. How could they not have influenced the traditions of their coastal neighbours in Benin?

Artefacts found here suggest that Jenné-jeno was trading with neighbouring regions from a very early period until around the 1400s. The wealth of the great ancient Ghana and Mali empires derived from controlling the trans-Saharan trade routes. The desert was an almost impenetrable barrier to trade; even the Romans and Carthaginians managed only a trickle, despite West Africa's vast mineral wealth. But when the North and West Africans began using camels to transport goods around AD 750, new trading routes exploded – and that is what made Jenné-jeno a great city. Materials and skills were exchanged from far and wide. This new mobility brought other things to this area, including Islam.

It is this religious influence that may have contributed to the decline of Jenné-jeno, and the rise of the city that sits just a river crossing away – Djenné. Between the twelfth and fourteenth centuries trade, wealth and ultimately people moved from Jenné-jeno across the Bani river to the new city. Djenné sits near the inland Niger river delta, a lattice of 6,000 square kilometres of water. Its position between the grasslands to the south and the desert to the north made it a melting pot of different cultures from the thirteenth century to the present day. It became a trading

Mecca, attracting people from across the Sahara and up from the coastal regions. What is bought and sold here has not changed much in several centuries: salt, pepper, textiles, metalwork and jewellery.

A ferry carries us the short distance across the river. After the serene beauty of Jenné-jeno, its brash younger relation is a bit of a shock to the system. Even before we get off our boat people rush towards us, trying to sell us cloth, CDs and jewellery. There are people rushing everywhere in fact, carrying goods, weaving in and out of the adobe houses. There are hawking cries and the air is thick with the smell of charcoal fires and roasting peanuts. I follow Amadou through the tiny paths between the terracotta-coloured buildings until the track broadens into a road and then opens out into a huge market square. People have gathered from all across the region, the variety of faces, clothes and goods is confusing, and everyone is shouting, trying to get someone's attention in the crowd. This is one of the great markets of West Africa and it thrives today as it did in the fourteenth century.

Something catches my eye, and I stop by a stall. 'These are beautiful beads, and they're old. I know beads have been found here that are more than two thousand years old. They may have come from India or China.'

Amadou, who lives with these things every day, is less than impressed. He does not stop. He is in a hurry. He wants to show me something.

The main Djenné market stands in the shadow of one of the most impressive buildings in West Africa. We round a corner, and there it is, the Great Djenné Mosque. It is no coincidence that the market and the mosque are found here. The trade generated in this marketplace supported the development not just of the mosque but a huge commercial and cultural infrastructure which drew people from miles around. And because of this cosmo-politanism the architecture of Djenné is striking, featuring elements from across the region. There are clear North African influences – the result of the arrival of Islam from across the Sahara – but local traditions are evident too.

There has been a mosque here since the city was founded in 1200. It fell into disrepair in the nineteenth century but was rebuilt in its present impressive form in 1906. The mosque is constructed from sun-baked bricks and mud mortar and coated in an earth plaster that gives it a smooth, organic finish. It is huge, completely dominating the Djenné skyline. And the entire population of the city contributes to its maintenance. It is an uplifting building with a form of construction somehow reminiscent of the Tellem granaries on the Bandiagara Escarpment. And like the granaries, the architecture isn't just functional, it is glorious. The collaborative dynamism that ensures the mosque's maintenance and the trade that plays out in its shadow might well give an insight into how Benin operated at its height and how the plaques may have been a communal rallying point.

After lunch we spend some time wandering through the streets of Djenné. Many of the private houses are as old, or older, than the grand mosque. They use the same visual vocabulary as the mosque – the adobe techniques, the organic forms – but on a domestic scale. Amadou says that each of the features on the houses has a particular significance; the number of vertical columns on the facade denotes the number of wives taken by the original owner, and above there is a single pillar for each of his children. There is a story in each building, one that can be retold and adapted. Like the central mosque, these houses have to be repaired every year so they are constantly being adapted to tell the story of the present owner. As Amadou points out, 'When there is a new birth or someone dies, we change the house.' Djenné has a guild of builders who conserve and preserve these buildings. Like the smiths and the potters, these men come from a single family and their skills are protected aggressively. Craftsmanship is regarded as a special skill here, just as it was in the Dogon villages, at Jenné-jeno, and in the kingdom of Benin.

But there is an even more intriguing aspect to the masonry here, for despite the clear impact of Islam on the culture and the architecture, the ancient and indigenous traditions have not been forgotten. Amadou introduces me to a mason friend, Tamusa, who shows me how the historical aspects of those animist house-building traditions are maintained. We sit on the muddy foundations of a house he is building and Tamusa gathers the vital protective ingredients: rice, charcoal and a white powder. He combines them with water and earth and makes five bricks from the mixture, one for each corner of the building and one for the centre, thereby creating a protective ring around the house. Tamusa explains that these practices are carried out as a kind of insurance to protect these adobe buildings against the heavy rains and baking sun that this part of Mali is known for. These belief systems bind these masons to their craft. As the ironworkers of West Africa were regarded as magicians, so too the masons are given a special status because of their ability to call on the spirits. And like those other craftsmen, the masons of Djenné administer the communal histories and protect the old ways of doing things. This is what all of the creators of West African art were doing, including the makers of the bronzes.

The ownership of history in West Africa was passionately contested during the period when Djenné was established. It was a time of instability and flux in which a variety of ethnic groups were migrating down across the desert and up from the coast, attracted by the trading potential of this new town. In a relatively short period of time competing medieval empires with no fixed geopolitical boundaries or singular cultural identities rose to dominance to be superseded by rivals. They may not have had fixed capitals but their followers were unified around strong leadership, family and the trade routes they sought to control. Across six hundred years West Africa saw several kingdoms and empires come and go. When one empire fell, another rose to prominence in its place. Family and ethnic allegiances were constantly being renegotiated with the changing regimes, but those who could held fast to their stories, building a variety of mechanisms to give them permanence.

In the thirteenth century, the influence of Islam and the deepening trans-Saharan networks spurred the growth of one empire in particular. Even though Djenné was enormously successful as a city, it was ultimately superseded by a new trading and intellectual powerhouse. So after saying goodbye to Amadou, Mr Samake and Tamusa, I begin the next leg of my journey – to the great city of Timbuktu.

It is a wonderful drive to Timbuktu; the landscape gets greener and the roads busier. This has been a trading highway for millennia. From the 1300s Mali was the most powerful kingdom in West Africa, and these roads were the gold-paved arteries that carried goods and ideas from all over the region to Timbuktu. Its emperor, Mansa Musa, was at one time thought to be the richest man in the world, famed for his vast gold reserves and for sending envoys to European courts. Timbuktu's wealth and power developed because the city became the hub of the most lucrative trans-Saharan trade routes. The city began life as a seasonal settlement where traders would gather, but as trade routes consolidated it developed into a major trading hub. Arab merchants brought goods such as salt, textiles and new metals into West Africa from across the desert. It is thought that in the fourteenth century the camel trains brought refined copper from North Africa, which then made its way south towards Benin. But if this was the source of the bronze casters' metal, I wonder if there are any other hints as to the meaning of the symbols I saw in the plaques.

These Arab merchants brought Islam as well as goods, so after a good night's sleep I meet a local imam who works in one of the old libraries in the shadow of the old mosque. I want to show him some pictures of the Benin Bronzes. After intuiting connections between a number of ancient Malian civilizations and the plaques, I want to ask some questions of someone who may be able to confirm my thinking with facts. He invites me into his study and for some time sits behind his desk poring over the images in complete silence. I look around the room. Within these ancient adobe houses many people have fashioned very contemporary-looking environments. The imam's study is not unlike any modern office – white and light and spotlessly clean.

Then he starts to speak. 'Islam forbids us from making objects with the human form, so for us it is geometric designs, calligraphy and pottery. Islam introduced writing and therefore we've had nothing to do with images and sculpture.'

I am disappointed, but I understand what he is saying, and it makes perfect sense. Timbuktu has a completely different feel to Djenné, and Dogon. It feels much more Islamic. Timbuktu was famous for its libraries and university. At its peak in the sixteenth century the university was as big as anything in Europe, attracting twenty-five thousand students – and that was in a city that numbered only a hundred thousand. It cemented Timbuktu as a centre of learning, but a very particular kind of learning, focused and driven by Islam. There are twenty-four private libraries in the city containing books that are hundreds of years old, and the vast majority record history from events during the ancient Mali empire to the movements of the stars. I sense that the ancient indigenous storytelling craft that has brought me here was long ago overtaken by the confident and intellectual might of a Qur'an-focused writing tradition. The modern storytelling tradition of sixteenth-century Timbuktu centred on writing, not ironwork or guilds of masons or families of blacksmiths; it was a carefully controlled history mediated by teachers.

But religion was not the only thing that came across the desert and influenced this part of Africa. This was a hub for Arab traders who brought new metals from beyond the Sahara, metals that could be melted and mixed with others to provide alloys well suited to casting. They brought the metals and the technologies that ultimately produced brass. Brass was a wonderful alloy for casting. It allowed for greater temperature control during the smelting process and so revolutionized what smiths were capable of. It made possible the lost-wax process so loved by the makers of the Benin Bronzes. The new trading networks of West Africa provided new materials and techniques. The region already possessed the traditions of storytelling through objects, art and architecture; it had already developed the skills and the appetite for beautiful things. Now it had the wherewithal and the know-how to make some of the finest artwork in the world, and display the wealth and power of its kingdoms.

I think the time has come. I pack my things and begin the long journey south from Mali to Benin in Nigeria. It has been fascinating learning how some early West African visual traditions were developed and shared; how many similar symbols and animals used in the brass plaques are still used by the Dogon; how smithing may have been a vital component for bringing coherence to communities and holding history; and how the brass for the plaques followed the path that I am now taking, down the river from Timbuktu into the coastal delta at Benin City.

Although today Benin City is a modern metropolis, it was once the seat of a kingdom that traced its roots to the thirteenth century. Its king, the Oba, took centre stage. And its artwork reflected the Oba's power, and the history of the kingdom. Benin may have changed a lot, but for the keen-eyed there is still evidence that this was once a powerful kingdom. Earth walls thought to have encircled the city and to have been constructed at the empire's height are still observable in many parts of the city. There may have been a staggering 5,000 kilometres of walls built here between 1450 and 1550. They wove around the city, breaking up the centre into forty wards. The network of walls stretched from the city and enclosed the surrounding villages, too, to a radius of over 100 kilometres. In all they enclosed over five hundred compounds and at their highest were 9 metres tall. There was obviously wealth worth protecting here. The kingdom flourished between the fifteenth and seventeenth centuries driven by a trading partnership with the Portuguese that helped Benin grow rich as a lucrative cog in the slave trade with Europe for two centuries. The city and kingdom declined after 1700 with the waning of the European slave trade, but revived in the nineteenth century with the development of palm products.

The history of this city has captivated many before me. At its height Benin exerted political, military and economic control over an area stretching almost 40,000 square miles. To understand how such an empire could have been so humbled, I want to begin the final chapter of my quest at the National Museum of Benin. But I find little to compare there with the spectacular displays of the British Museum. Other than staff, I am the only person in the museum, and looking at the visitors' book, I am the only visitor for a number of days. The museum is very tired, and for the home of the bronze plaques the displays contain only a handful of works which are quite poor. It is depressing. But perhaps it is a fitting epitaph.

In 1896 the British were planning to bring the kingdom of Benin under their protection. It was perhaps understandably, after a number of local incidents instigated by the Oba, an attempt at colonization. Early the following year the Oba's soldiers ambushed a column of British soldiers and killed all but two of them. The British responded with 1,200 well-armed troops who ransacked the city. At the Royal Palace they found the bronzes. Almost two thousand objects were taken, sold and distributed to Western museums. The Oba was deposed and died in exile. Today, Benin's National Museum is stalked by the same ghosts as the British Museum, both tainted by the same terrible event. By forcibly removing the bronzes, the British removed the history and the power of the kingdom as it had existed for over five hundred years, and left behind an administrative husk and a cultural vacuum. In 1914, in an attempt to help manage the complex regional politics of the country, the British colonial administration reinstated the monarchy of Benin. But some of the subtlety of the historical narratives and contextualization that would have given the bronzes meaning were simply lost.

I have been granted a royal audience, an opportunity to attend the Oba's court, where hereditary and appointed chiefs gather each day. The current Oba's palace sits on the same huge compound in the centre of the city which was burned to the ground by the British. Rather than being a complex of beautifully ornate buildings and shrines, the contemporary palace is quite municipal and plain. It has none of the grandeur one may imagine from the historical accounts, or the visual sophistication you can see depicted in the bronzes. Instead it feels like a government ministry.

The courtroom is modest too: three banks of carved chairs facing in towards a strip of red carpet that leads up to a carved throne where

The Oba of Benin manacled and on the boat to exile.

the Oba will sit. Either side of his throne are young attendants, and on the walls are paintings of previous Obas. It is intimate, but still quite stately. The court is full of senior figures dressed in their finest cloth. There is a low hum of conversation. Then we all stand as His Royal Majesty the Oba of Benin enters and the chiefs greet him loudly with 'Oba a'topeh!' ('God save the king!').

This is more than a symbolic institution. The Oba and his chiefs rule on issues brought to them by ordinary people. Their judgment still carries authority and has jurisdiction in parallel with the Nigerian state. And the Oba looks the part, with a symbolic protective leopard at his feet and standard bearers at his side; it's like one of the bronzes come to life. This is the kind of occasion he believes the plaques were designed to mark.

The Oba knows why I have come. He gestures towards me. I stand up, but do not know the protocol. I say, 'Oba a'topeh!' The court seems to approve and echoes, 'Oba a'topeh!'

Before I can ask a question, the Oba begins. 'Those bronzes were not made for museum pieces initially in the absence of writing or photography, they depict certain events,' he says.

It is thrilling to hear the Oba talking about this obviously contentious issue so frankly, but I want to address the question of who made the bronzes. 'How important are the bronze casters, the smiths, the people who actually make these objects?'

'They are a guild,' the Oba responds, 'a royal guild, specifically to make these things in the olden days.'

The court has two important cases to deal with so I am politely gestured towards the back and then outside. I perhaps should feel frustrated at not getting any real answers, but being honest, I did not expect the Oba to be so forthright and I know that there simply may not be answers to some of my questions about the early history of the bronzes. But the bronze casters' guild still exists. Their main business may be tourist souvenirs, but they are still an exclusive group of craftsmen with high social status. Membership of the royal guild remains hereditary. So before I leave I want to spend some time with them and watch them working brass in the way their ancestors did.

Among all the tourist shops I find Ikponmwusa Inneh. His family have been bronze casters for as long as anyone can remember. He invites me behind his shop to a small makeshift smithy. For someone who works with metal every day, the set-up is quite modest. Most of the work is done on a ground-level furnace where the charcoal is pushed with bellows to fantastic temperatures. While the charcoal is being prepared the clay core is covered with a finished wax and then encased in soft clay.

Mr Inneh loads a jumble of scrap metal, including car aerials and discarded metal from previous castings, into a crucible and then pushes it deep into the white-hot centre of the charcoal. In the heart of the furnace, the metal can reach 1,000°C. These bronze casters have an impressive range of skills: they need to understand pottery and metallurgy and to have artistic ability. The same skills would have been required five hundred years ago to cast the Benin Bronzes – something the Victorians could hardly believe. In the sixteenth century, the craftsmen melted down copper bracelets brought by Portuguese traders; nowadays a variety of modern scrap is used. Mr Inneh keeps the temperature high, pumping his foot bellows while scraping the impurities off the surface of the melting metal with some tongs. Once the wax has melted and run out of the mould, in flows the golden molten brass, just as it was done for the Benin Bronzes.

In these days of brasses being sold for the most part to tourists, do they still feel connected to the Oba and his palace?

Mr Inneh replies emphatically, 'It remains this year, next, and for ever.'

That may well be true, but much like the Oba's court, the bronze casting is not quite what it once was. The contemporary bronzes do not reach the standards of their sixteenth-century equivalents; like so much of the history connected to the plaques, the subtlety of the skills was lost with the sacking of Benin. But culture is still profoundly important to people in Benin and that has to be admired. And after visiting the Dogon I have a sense of how these plaques may once have been the focus of a shared narrative, how the smiths who made them would have been important figures, repositories of a history. In Timbuktu I saw how stories and history could build and bind these communities, and in Djenné I learned how creative fraternities could be a society's backbone. But perhaps most importantly I saw for myself in Ounjougou how important beautiful things have always been to West African people, how there has almost always been a deep and rich aesthetic tradition.

Perhaps I am a little closer to the bronzes, and to understanding why the people of Benin have never given up the fight for their return. Benin was a formidable culture that exerted massive influence over a vast swathe of West Africa for more than three hundred years, and it built a metropolis that compared with anything with which they traded. For three centuries it was unassailable. And during that glorious period Benin developed some of the most significant cultural traditions Africa has ever seen. But as Europeans moved into legitimate trade in the eighteenth century Benin's economic might was challenged, and it eventually fell, like Zululand, Bunyoro and Buganda, to the voracious economic and political appetite of the British empire machine.

As I drive out of Benin on my way to the airport I notice a statue in the centre of a roundabout. I ask my driver to stop. It is a monument to the catastrophic defeat for the kingdom of Benin at the hands of the British. But terrible defeat is not the impression you get from this modern monument. It is not a memorial to the loss. It shows a Benin warrior standing victorious over his dead and dying British enemies. It is hard not to admire it. Perhaps in a sense they are right – the people of Benin did win here. This is a monument to the triumph of narrative. In Benin, it seems that history is not written by the victors, it is written by the artists.

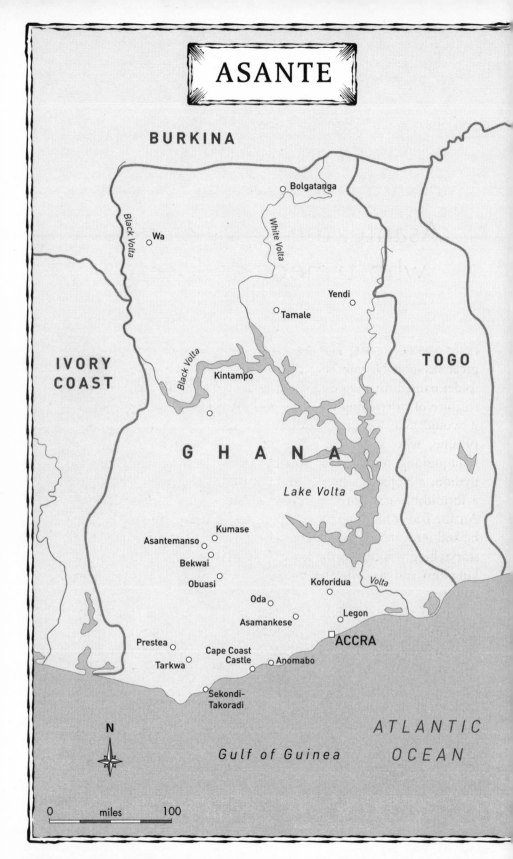

ASANTE

BURKINA

Bolgatanga

Black Volta

Wa

White Volta

Yendi

Tamale

IVORY
COAST

Black Volta

Kintampo

TOGO

GHANA

Lake Volta

Kumase

Asantemanso

Bekwai

Obuasi

Koforidua

Volta

Oda

Asamankese

Legon

ACCRA

Prestea

Cape Coast
Castle

Tarkwa

Anomabo

Sekondi-
Takoradi

N

ATLANTIC
OCEAN

Gulf of Guinea

0   miles   100

Asante: the story-smiths
who tamed the forest

ONCE UPON A TIME, BEFORE THERE WERE STORIES, WHEN THE great sky-god Nyame held the whole world's narrative, a brave spider named Ananse pondered how he might be able to wrest the treasure of storytelling from the gods. Ananse asked Nyame what it would take for him to loosen his grip on the world's tales. Nyame, who knew the value of words, set a high price for relinquishing his control: Ananse would have to bring him a python, a leopard, a hornet and a dwarf. This would have been a formidable task for the bravest creature; as a lowly spider all Ananse had at his disposal were guile and trickery. But one by one he laid intricate traps to catch each of them. And so the power of storytelling was lost to the gods. It spread out beyond the animal kingdom and became the precious lubricating force of human cultures.

I have always thought that Ghana was a nation created by romantics and storytellers. Its name was taken from the great ancient West African kingdom; its flag was derived from the Pan-African colours. Building narrative rootedness is at the heart of so much of its history and culture. Its myths of origin and parables of trickster spiders and sly foxes percolated into the New World and permeated traditional children's storytelling. Ghana's history, a narrative of story-crafters, is suitably fascinating: the first sub-Saharan British colony to gain independence, the place that produced the first African novel, the African colony that sponsored biplanes that flew over enemy lines in the First World War, that had challenged colonialism from the outset and fought it to the highest British courts. Ghana is the home of the Golden Stool, the symbolic focus of the Asante state, and of luscious kente cloths. It is a place driven by a need to declare its own story, to define its cultural footprint – and its history is a battle of stories.

I first visited Ghana when I was seventeen; it was my first time in Africa, my first time out of Europe. For someone seeking his own narrative it could not have been a more fitting place. I travelled the length of the coast, from the buzz of the capital in the east through the fishing towns and slave castles to the new industrial ports of the west. It was an electrifying trip that changed me, and opened me up to Africa. Perhaps my most vivid memory remains visiting the town of Anomabo at the time of the annual flag festival when the traditional military companies parade their young initiates and dance with their flags. That afternoon every street, alleyway and door lintel was hung with brightly coloured appliqué flags, the air full of the sound of cotton and rayon straining and slapping in the sea breeze. It was wonderfully uplifting – truly old flags of translucent red silk and cotton fluttering alongside new flags of dazzling synthetics.

Then from among the flag lines a single flag-dancer appeared. He began to twist and pirouette, twirling a flag in the air. Even for an initiate it was obvious that the flag festival was a celebration of communal continuity. Every flag told a family's history, promoted its own particular story. The flag-dancer was an animation of that combined history, of time flowing through space. With every third step the flag-dancer arched his body forward, allowing the flagpole to role across his sloping back into his other hand. With the help of an assistant he unfurled and brandished the flag, pulling the surface tight, letting the wind tense and flex the surface image. I knew the symbol on the flag well – the Obaatan, the multi-breasted mother who suckles her community. The Obaatan figure is a synthesis of opposites that is said to combine all the attributes of traditional male and female leaders. The actual word Obaatan means a deep, still water-vessel, a reservoir of knowledge and continuity for the community. It is said that for those who seek her she offers an unlimited well of wisdom. She is said to be the mother of time and from within her depths new histories and possibilities can be forged.

In the centre of the group a man dressed in a white jacket and cap pulled a palm-sized lead weight out of a bag, attached it to a line and began to cast it out across the ground, as if he were plumbing the depths of the sea from the side of a great ship. With each swing of the weight the man seemed to measure out the depth of a water pot. It was the physical re-enactment of the flag, a community gathered around its leader, delving deep into the reservoir of family history. I came away with one thought: history is important here in a way I had not previously understood possible. It was an active, dynamic, electric thing; it animated everything. For this trip, almost two decades after my first visit, I am keen to understand more about that poetry of history, by exploring more of this enthralling country.

Ghana is a fascinating country. The Akan people who make up the bulk of the country's population began to tame the thick area of forest that once covered the majority of this region three hundred years ago. The Akan are made up of a number of polities dominated by the Asante and the Fante. The tropical rainforest of West Africa was a very harsh place to live and work. Even today, nature remains incredibly invasive and aggressive here. Despite the conditions a complex and sophisticated kingdom developed that dominated a large region of coastal West Africa for two centuries. It was a polity that developed into a highly centralized kingdom that through the force of will of its leaders became an empire connected to an international economy built on gold and slavery. It seemed to come into being with an agenda, to rise out of an inhospitable environment – an instigator. Armed with little more than an idea, it carved out its place in the world with determination, establishing an unassailable position in the forest in the eighteenth century. It left an indelible mark on Ghana and remains a vital part of millions of Africans' lives around the world: the kingdom of Asante.

Asante grew into a powerful kingdom in an astonishingly short space of time. Yet it did not appear from nowhere. Asante was the culmination of important events and developments; it was the result of a unique psyche that had evolved over centuries. The Asante kingdom's power lay in its ability to exploit ancient traditions and beliefs which held the kingdom together in such a sophisticated way that even colonization could not fully stamp it out. I have always thought that what made this kingdom special, what drove its birth, growth and survival when it really counted, was its very special relationship to history and narrative. So in Ghana, even today, history is much more than facts and dates.

I begin my journey on one of the green manicured quadrants that mark out the pristine white campus of the University of Ghana, Legon. This is one of the great universities of West Africa. It was founded just after the Second World War and still has that sense of confidence and optimism that pervaded so many African intellectual circles then. Its students have gone on to run many of Ghana's ministries and industries; intellectuals who have worked within or around Legon have also been some of the bravest and most staunch critics of Ghanaian government when it was really needed. And thankfully its students still believe they will change the world. Perhaps the current generation will. It is the perfect setting to test out my romantic notion of the oral history that remains special and important to Ghanaians.

I have arranged to meet a group of history students preparing to graduate under Professor Addo Fenning. Fenning has been on the brink of leaving academia since he was refused a request to retire fifteen years ago. Over the last forty years he has developed an almost unrivalled reputation for his understanding of indigenous history and law. Which is why the history faculty at Legon have simply refused to let him go. I am keen to get a sense of what he and his students think is special about Ghana's relationship with history.

We gather under a tree on one of the lawns of the women's

college. It is lunchtime and the campus is buzzing. Even though Ghana's economy is booming and practical degrees, which support the burgeoning new industries, are popular, subjects such as history remain oversubscribed. With hundreds of students enrolling every year, the history department at Legon is bursting with energy and ideas. So I joined one of Professor Fenning's classes sitting in the shade of one of the huge old acacias that sit on the deep green, newly mown lawns.

Fenning explains how the traditional Asante kings (or Asantehene) were legitimized by history; without history their courts could not have functioned, their authority could not have been exercised, and because history linked people to land, inheritance systems would not have worked. His words provoke a lively debate. Rather than blindly agreeing, the students surprise me by nuancing the professor's words, arguing that although traditional history is important, today international written histories must be seen as the benchmark against which traditional oral history must be judged. They feel that the fragility of traditional history has left it vulnerable, obviously unscientific and weakened. They are keen on the idea of corroborative evidence from verifiable sources, on the deployment of vigorous method. Oral history becomes particularly important when other mechanisms for retaining history are thin on the ground. For this group of students with libraries of books upon which to depend, there are other priorities. Although no one says it, the natural outcome of their thinking is an acceptance of the changing attitude to oral history and perhaps by extension the traditions that they support. For these students, oral history should be treated not just as a source but as a fluid piece of material culture, sharing the kind of relationship with written history that painting does with photography. While there is unequivocal support for the idea of the importance of poetic narrative, they argue that knowing why these histories were venerated by the Asante is perhaps more important.

I leave inspired, agreeing that understanding why oral history and material culture were passionately supported by the Asante is key to knowing how exactly the kingdom of Asante came about, and what held it together.

So while I am at Legon, with that last idea ringing in my ears I drop in on the archaeology department. Visually it is a faculty that feels of another era – old buildings that hold a trove of expertise, shaded by ancient creaking trees. For anyone interested in beautiful old things, it is a treat. However, the methodologies and thinking deployed here are up to date. Archaeologists from the University of Ghana have managed to find a number of objects that have shed light on the dark centuries before the Asante kingdom emerged and perhaps give clues as to why the Asante thrived.

Over twenty years Dr Benjamin Kenkpeyeng has led a series of digs in an attempt to unearth clues about the Asante's forebears and their culture. His sites have yielded a range of clay finds, some of which have been radiocarbon-dated to the ninth century – in the context of the wider archaeology, this suggests a previously unknown culture that was active from the sixth to the eighteenth centuries. Perhaps these works are clues about the progenitors of the Asante, or offer clues about the world that they challenged. In 2010 he made some important discoveries in the north of the country.

From within an old printer box, Benjamin produces dozens of palm-sized red clay figures: fish and crocodiles, women with wings and men on horseback. Some are broken, revealing unrefined gritty clay that has been squeezed into shape with speed and efficiency – but every figure is exquisitely finished with ochre slips and ornate detail. The design and iconography suggest a complex culture that must have traded and had weaving technologies. From the details it is obvious that these were people who valued jewellery and body adornment. Benjamin explains that 'the clay figures were used by forest people in religious rituals – possibly shrines of worship or burial rituals. They depict animals and humans and their interlocking design makes them unusual and intriguing.' I am fascinated to follow the line of questioning opened up by the students, not just to suck out the histories they depict but to try to learn what they were used for. Benjamin tells me that they were probably laid in some form of shrine, and that

Clay figure on horseback. (Gus Casely-Hayford)

they were used in magic. He points to small holes in the surfaces which have been filled with some sort of resin, perhaps a substance that would have been used to activate a magical process. They are not overtly beautiful, but they have that quality of great age and care that makes you want to get close to them.

In all, Benjamin and his colleagues found eighty clay figurines that date back to a period shrouded by mystery around 1,500 years ago. Benjamin is cautious about a direct connection to the early Asante, but he is prepared to say that complex and rich cultures obviously lived in the region for hundreds of years before the Asante. His work shows that the people who made them were using sophisticated techniques. They also suggest that people have been living in the central Ghanaian forest for thousands of years. But we unfortunately still do not know very much about them. What is clear is that by the end of the sixteenth century most of the ethnic groups constituting the modern Ghanaian population – the Ga, the Asante and Fante, etc. – had settled in their present locations. Archaeology found on the coastal plain suggests that this area has been inhabited since the early Bronze Age six thousand years ago, but these early cultures, based on fishing in the extensive lagoons and rivers, left few clues about their way of life. The area around Asante and to the north of the forested region where these figures were found is known to have been inhabited as early as four to six thousand years ago. What these people's lives were like is unclear. In the forests of Ghana many of the objects were likely to have been used by these ancient people; baskets and cloth have not survived because of the corrosive nature of the climate and the soil. They were probably hunter-gatherers who existed in quite fragile communities. Through trade, and advances in agricultural technologies over hundreds of years, things changed. The people who crafted Benjamin's clay figures were part of complex economies by comparison.

Interestingly, Asante oral history suggests that the original population entered this region as early as the tenth century AD. These migrations can be corroborated as there was substantial population movement driven by the instability of some of the great kingdoms

Asante

An Asafo flag depicting an important person or 'big-man', sometimes referred to as an *Obaatan*, which means a deep, still water-vessel from which the whole community could seek

Above: This 1819 illustration depicts the first day of the Asante Yam custom. It shows the scale and the cosmopolitan nature of the royal court, and the importance and central focus of drums.

Right: The royal drums are core to the running of the court; they are used at most formal engagements, and are capable of complex and subtle communication.

Below right: Gold weights depict a wide variety of venerated aspects of Asante life. Here a male figure armed with the traditional hooked sticks beats an Asante drum.

Below: Twins are thought to be lucky in Akan society, and, perhaps auspiciously, twin brothers lead the Asante royal drum ensemble.

Bottom: Drums remain important, taking their place at the heart of most traditional ceremonies.

Above and top right: Gold being poured from a furnace at the Asante goldfields; the Asantehene adorned with a tiny selection of the crown jewels.

Below right and below: A spider's web, an important symbol from Asante mythology, and a fitting flourish at the top of a linguist's staff; the spider was seen, like the Kente craftsmen, to be weaving strands together to create something both protective and beautiful.

Right and below: The crown jewels, crafted in the highest-quality gold; a tiny golden ornamental stool, probably made to give to the Secretary of State for the Colonies at the time of the Empire Exhibition of 1924.

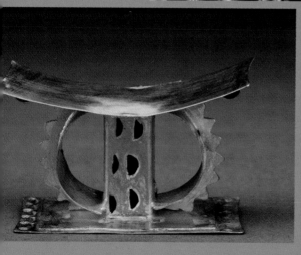

Almoravid and Almohad

Top: The Aghmat *hammam*'s thousand-year-old bathhouse gives a sense of the lifestyle of the Almoravid elite. The latest hydro-engineering technologies from all over the Mediterranean were used to build temples to their precious resource, water.

Middle: The Qubbat Barudiyyin, a luxurious bathhouse built in 1117 by an indulgent Almoravid dynasty in a final extravagant flourish of construction.

Right: The fortress of Ait Ben Haddou, constructed using the same rammed-earth technologies used by Almoravids in the twelfth century.

Top and middle: At Tinmel the Almohad built a fortified mosque in the mountains, which was protected by its obscure location and the complete loyalty of their local followers. Within you get a sense of the ambition of the burgeoning, confident dynasty. It is both heavily over-engineered and sumptuously ornate.

Bottom: The Fez tanneries, one of the earliest production lines, were one of the Almohad empire's jewels.

If you get the chance . . .

of western Sudan. The new immigrants brought with them traditions of pottery and gold work. How exactly the makers of Benjamin's clay objects fit into that history is unclear, but these migrants into the forested region were people with well-developed crafts and trading relations, and their aesthetic traditions suggest some knowledge of cultures to the north. The clay figurines Benjamin showed me resemble ceramic sculptures still made on the bend of the Niger. It seems feasible that as the great empires of Mali and Sudan collapsed, waves of migration brought these traditions and people southward, and with them came cloth, jewellery, new transcontinental trade routes and even horses – a rich foundation upon which the Asante could clear the forest and establish themselves.

I want to see the forests for myself. So the next morning I begin the long drive to Ghana's central region, to a place powerfully linked to Asante origination: Asantemanso. As I negotiate the crazed morning traffic I am not feeling that usual sense of pre-trip optimism. Trying to understand the origins of the kingdom of Asante is not easy. Much of what can be said about pre-Asante Ghana is conjecture based on joining the dots between a handful of works of pioneering men like Benjamin Kenkpeyeng. The climate, the environment and the location of the kingdom have each played roles in obscuring that early history from archaeology. It remains hugely challenging for archaeologists to find and excavate ancient sites in the thick, aggressive vegetation that thrives in Ghana's heat and humidity. At its peak, Asante extended beyond the borders of modern-day Ghana into Côte d'Ivoire. The kingdom emerged in a formidably hot region just six degrees north of the equator, an area of dense tropical rainforest that stretches across West Africa. Despite the work of men like Benjamin, historians and archaeologists simply cannot say exactly where the ancestors of Asante came from. But some oral history describes their origins, and that particular legend begins at Asantemanso – the sacred forest.

I am soon out of Accra and in the countryside. The road I'm following is one of a number that link central Ghana with the coast, following the original trade routes created by the early Asante. Ghana is not really a country of big vistas, but there are always fascinating things to see on the roadsides: tenacious hawkers, groups of perfectly groomed children on their way to school, overpacked minibuses of commuters shaking and vibrating their way from town to town. And as the forests close in, the scale of vegetation grows. The mobile phone masts are replaced by giant teaks and silk cottons, and workers emerge from the undergrowth to salute you. Gradually a different range of goods appears at the verges and kerbsides: machetes, palm wines, the occasional pangolin. It is only as you drive the road from the coast to Asante that it becomes apparent what a massive job clearing the forest and cutting roads through this region must have been for the Asante. The vegetation grows voraciously up, around and through any man-made structure, reclaiming hard-won land and returning it to forest. The formidable force of the environment is continuously working to wrench control of the world from human hands. The ambition and sheer will displayed by the Asante in waging a campaign to tame this environment is impressive in itself.

According to oral history my destination, Asantemanso, is the home of the Asante people. In fact it is more than their home, it is their place of origin, their genealogical fountainhead. It is the place from where they began in the fifteenth century to percolate out to tame the forest, before moving north to found Kwaman, which would become their capital, Kumase.

By the time I get to the town of Bekwai, where the sacred grove lies, in the late afternoon a ceremony to celebrate the founding of the Asante people has begun. The Queen Mother is leading a procession of about a hundred people down the main road, away from the town towards the sacred grove of Asantemanso. I run and catch up with the back of the group where two powerful men carry substantial *atumpan* drums laid horizontally on their heads that are being played by drummers who follow. Each drum is carved from a solid piece of unseasoned wood into a hollow, tapered, ornately finished tube of yellow wood that is capped with a skin membrane. The drumbeats create a slow walking rhythm for the procession, allowing me to negotiate my way quickly beyond the drummers and groups of old men who bring up the rear. I work my way into a cluster of women dressed in black and white cloth; among them a young woman carries a traditional Ghanaian stool on her head. As we pass a shrine by the road the stool is bundled down and the Queen Mother sits on it, watching as old men pour libations and glasses of venomous-tasting schnapps.

When we reach the sacred grove at Asantemanso, a space beneath the huge buttresses of some ancient silk cotton trees, the sun has already dropped low, casting long monochrome shadows. The men gather around the queen and a goat is sacrificed and its blood poured into seven clay dishes. According to oral tradition, Asantemanso is the place where the ancestors of the Asante came up from a hole in the ground; the seven dishes represent the seven first clans of the kingdom. The Asante people have a powerful sense of belonging here. Archaeology carried out at Asantemanso in the 1980s found some pottery suggesting habitation going back to the tenth century, but they did not find any holes in the ground from where the first Asante could have 'come'. A literal reading of this kind of oral history is never useful; perhaps considering why those beliefs were held is more pertinent. The reason that belief in the legend remains so strong is because it gave, and continues to offer, people a sense of permanence, a feeling of true locatedness in a very uncertain and constantly changing environment. Little survived here unless it was stone or metal, so rooting your history in the ground may have been the best way to create that sense of belonging. It doesn't need to be literally true to have power, it is the narrative that matters.

Before I leave, the Queen Mother beckons me over and pours some palm wine into a cupped waxed leaf for me. It fizzes aggressively with fermentation, but tastes sweet on the tongue.

That evening I reflect on the day and wonder if there is also another meaning in the legend. Around six hundred years ago people began to settle in the forest and they needed a steady supply of food. In order to grow food they needed to clear the forest. Perhaps the legend of coming-from-the-ground remembers the enormous effort made by the earliest inhabitants. Clearing vast amounts of rainforest is easy today. This area is now the centre of Ghana's sustainable timber industry, and it's easy to see why this has become an important part of the country's economy. In the fifteenth century, things were very different.

The next morning I meet historian Dr Wilhelmina Donkoh, an expert in the early societies that developed before the kingdom of Asante emerged. It is monstrously humid so we find shade beyond the Bekwai schoolhouse. Wilhelmina explains that settled communities could only grow where there was a supply of food, so clearing the forest was a vital precondition; until then there was only foraging and hunter-gathering. Once the forest was cleared, agriculture became possible.

The task in hand was almost beyond belief. Researchers have calculated that it would have taken one man around five hundred days just to clear a hectare of forest; and to feed a family he would need six hectares because the soil is so thin the crops would have to be regularly rotated. Working in temperatures often in the mid thirties with 90 per cent plus humidity, it must have been a hugely demanding endeavour. Wilhelmina explains that there were not enough people living locally to achieve this formidable task alone, even with a growing population, so a vast amount of slave labour was imported. In the first instance the form of slavery implemented was not like the transatlantic slavery that would follow. There was no monetary system so slaves were not bought or sold. Slaves were usually captured during wars and over time they could become integrated or married into the families with whom they resided, or in some instances regain their freedom through loyal service. This kind of slavery could be appalling, and degrading for the exploited, but one of its positive by-products was the rapid development of young societies. In an environment that was politically and socially unstable, where individuals owned very little, the protection someone might gain from being seen as part of an organized group had advantages. Some have said that the use of slaves in pre-Asante times can be seen as people finding ways and means of developing in very challenging circumstances. It was a social engineering device to seed rapid expansion. It was not an unusual practice; many societies in Africa and elsewhere used labour in this way. It was a means to an end.

The speed with which slave labour changed these societies was profound. As it was the fuel of rapid expansion, labour inevitably acquired a high value. The demand for it must have been overwhelming, drawing people both voluntarily and forcibly from across the region. And when traditional sources ran dry, new supply routes and more ruthless models for labour were sought. Thus a true slave trade was born. Gradually, slavery was transformed into an increasingly commercial and monetized activity as the numbers of slaves captured as a result of conflict were increasingly supplemented by others acquired through trade. By the early sixteenth century the supply of these traded slaves followed the established mercantile and migration routes, some coming from further north, traded by Muslim merchants who were connected to the trans-Saharan trade routes. Other slaves came from the southern coastal region, where they had been traded by Portuguese merchants who had acquired them from African merchants further east along the coast. This was before the time of established written records so how many slaves came into this area, and when, is not known, but historians believe that many tens of thousands were put to work clearing the forest.

The kinds of pioneering small farms that gradually turned inhospitable forest into productive agricultural land that could feed thousands still exist. Hundreds of years later the same system of mixed communal farming provides food for the majority of rural Ghana. After speaking to Wilhelmina, I want to get more of a sense of the nature of the work involved in clearing the forest. After the previous evening I sense that I may be welcome at the Queen Mother's house, and that she may be able to point me towards a farm.

She is delighted to see me and knows of just the farm for me to see.

Although Nana has been the Queen Mother of Bekwai for

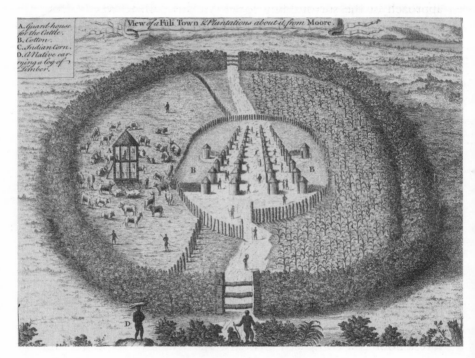

Eighteenth-century slave plantation.

thirty years, she has always maintained a farm. Her tennis-court-sized patch of land lies on the edge of a once commercial palm-nut farm. Between the trees she grows a range of crops from coco-yam to cassava and produces yields that allow her not only to feed her family but many of her court too. It is not a beautiful place, it is scrubby; it lies some distance from the nearest water source and she wages a constant battle against the inexorable approach of the surrounding forest. In this climate weeds grow into a matted, thorny, near impenetrable barrier within weeks, so keeping the greenery at bay is a battle no one can afford to lose. Now fifty, Nana works with the other men and women of her generation as a united front against the forest – but hacking back thick, dense, thorny undergrowth that is home to a myriad of biting and stinging insects is back-breaking work, often carried out in extreme heat.

As I leave the people of Bekwai working on their small farm, a few words of my conversation with Wilhelmina come back to me: 'This battle with nature, and with the climate, became a defining feature of these societies. That human beings could live here at all, let alone construct a sophisticated agricultural society, was seen as an enormous achievement.'

Up on the border with Côte d'Ivoire there remain some dense semi-deciduous primary forests like those that once covered the whole Asante region. Gargantuan silk cottons compete for canopy space with stately ancient mahogany and ebony. The forest floor is a compactly matted thicket of thorny bushes and creepers beneath which countless insects scuttle through the red soil. Temperatures and humidity only add to the challenge. It is not a place where most humans would feel at home, but even before the Akan began clearing the forests people made a life here hunting and gathering. Visiting today to watch the lumbermen at work only reinforces the respect I feel for those pioneers who broke and tamed large areas of this forest. It is a place where insects, animals and vegetation compete with an insane frenzy, consuming every piece of land, every glint of light, and turning on anyone brave enough to take them on.

The experience of clearing the forest was a formative one for these people. It shaped their identity in two important respects: firstly, there was a sense of great pride that this manual effort against the might of the forest had been successful; and secondly, once a niche had been carved out of nature, there was an imperative to produce as much as possible. These cultures respected abundance, plenty and fruitfulness, which resulted in an important mindset that has lasted for centuries. Abundance is a much greater marker of status than birth in Akan society, and has been since those days of forest clearance. Abundance was the result of hard work, much of it carried out by slaves. But none of that could have happened without a commodity the Akan were able to exchange to get those slaves in the first place: gold.

The next day I am back on the road, on my way to Obuasi, home to one of the biggest gold mines in Ghana. No one knows exactly when gold was first discovered by the Akan people, but it's thought that they were mining it around the same time as they began clearing the forest, during the fifteenth century. Back then, gold deposits were found near the surface; so much gold has been mined here since then that miners now have to travel 1,600 metres underground. Every year 2 million tons of ore and 700,000 tons of waste are drawn up from the mines at Obuasi. The mining and extraction of ore here is supported by a network of miles of tunnels, shafts and subterranean roads big enough for a fleet of trucks. Even as mines go, this is engineering on a formidable scale. It is not the most productive mine, but every day a gold bar the equivalent of £1 million in value is poured from its furnaces. Gold is an important part of Ghana's economy. It was vitally important to the people who first mined it.

In many ways gold is the key to understanding Asante. Without gold they could not have acquired additional slaves, and without those slaves they could not have cleared the forest and transformed themselves from a nomadic fragile culture into a settled agricultural community. Gold was also the Akan's link to the outside world. The Akan were connected to the economies of the

Mediterranean through the Saharan trade routes. They also exchanged gold with the Portuguese, who were trading in Asia and elsewhere in Africa. The particular genius of the Akan was to recognize the potential of these markets and profit from them. Whoever controlled the gold production was able to procure slaves; whoever procured and controlled slaves could mine for more gold, and clear more forest for agriculture. The handful of societies with the resources to develop in this way, by grasping the political authority, attracted more settlers and traders. This is how the Akan states began as throughout the forest region small communities became estates consolidated in political alliances and wars and growing into larger societies.

I have negotiated a rare invitation to see the final stages of gold refinement at the mine. It is a privilege, though I have never fully appreciated the aesthetic lure of gold. It is unquestionably beautiful, but its power to drive rational people to do extreme things has always puzzled me. The history of this region can be explained through this substance; slavery, the empowerment of empires and the taming of the forest, all driven by a yellow metal that was of very little practical use in a place where survival was a day-to-day battle.

Two squat cast-iron pillar-box-shaped furnaces sit at the end of a dark studio. Above the low, earth-rumbling howl of the giant gas burners comes the sound of chemistry – a fizzing. The extremities of the furnace glow a ruby red, but the mouth is a gaping, spitting froth of white molten metal. It's as if the ore is shrieking a desperate birth-cry. After twenty minutes the whole structure begins to tip forward and a pencil-thin neon-bright flow of molten gold spills over the brim of the furnace and down into a mould. After a few moments the ingots are dropped into baths of water to cool, already glistening. Gold has been made with only a subtle variation on this technique for thousands of years, and it is a process that remains atavistically attractive.

Once the ingots have cooled I am allowed to handle them. Their surface is mottled and pitted, but they seem to glow from within. Each has the footprint of an A4-size piece of paper and is about 5 centimetres thick, but they have an impossible weight for their scale. Perhaps for the first time I begin to see the metal's inherent attraction. In an environment where everything could be eaten, corroded or consumed, this substance retained a purity, an untainted quality, that must have seemed precious, miraculous.

These early societies varied in size and power, but they all grew from the same foundations: the forest and this magical substance gold. Both were central to the Akan people's experience. The Akan entrepreneurs who became rich on accumulated gold, slaves, land and people were known as *berempong*, which literally means 'big man'. They were wealthy in a way that had not been possible before; they possessed an array of new ways of showing that wealth. But as large families grew into established polities, symbols of wealth became symbols of authority. These proto-kingdoms developed a unique symbol of authority, one that has descended through the generations – the stool.

On the side of a dusty road in a suburb of Kumase called Awia is a collection of studios where these traditional stools are still carved. Stool-carving techniques have remained unchanged for centuries. It is the perfect place to meet one of Ghana's most eminent historians, Professor Kwame Ahrin, an academic and an Asante chief. He's also an expert on the history of Asante stools. We sit among the sawdust and carvers and watch the crafting of these spectacular stools from single pieces of unseasoned wood. With no more than adzes and axes they can fashion a finished stool within hours. 'Wood was not just a resource,' Professor Ahrin explains, 'it had symbolic value, and gold had symbolic value as well. It wasn't simply about economics. Wealth and power were connected.' Stools were the perfect symbol for the new Asante nation. They suggested a rootedness to a particular place, they were symbols around which families could rally; they were more than furniture, they were a symbol of continuity. He describes how new stools were blackened and brought to life, to become the focus of a family's lineage. The 'big men' held the major stool in the early Akan states; smaller families had smaller stools and were subordinate to the head stool. It was simultaneously the object that was sat upon and the symbol of political power.

In the 1600s the forest region was covered in a patchwork of Akan states, each one focused around a stool whose owner was probably the most powerful person in the area. The most powerful of these states was Denkyira. It controlled some of the richest gold mines of the forest. To avoid conflict, neighbouring states would placate Denkyira by sending gold, and the chiefs would offer their offspring to serve at Denkyira's court. For the Asante who arrived in the region, trying to build alliances and inculcate a deep sense of belonging in their new fragile kingdom was essential to their survival. They moved into a region where there was a powerful cause around which to build a confederation: most of the other ethnic groups shared their dislike of the Denkyira. Many people were opposed to the tributes Denkyira demanded and the perversely aggressive style of leadership they adopted to corral and scare their neighbours into submission. The seemingly unassailable Denkyira were running a regime of terror, forcing their neighbours to pay these huge tributes and punishing them severely if they did not oblige.

One young audacious soldier decided to take action. In 1701, Osei Tutu, king of the Asante, united five states in an alliance against Denkyira. It was not too difficult to rally the neighbouring peoples. Denkyira's defenders said all their opponents had in common was a shared dislike of the Denkyira. For Osei Tutu, that was precisely the point. The new alliance even called themselves the Asantefo – 'the because-of-war people'. And from the very beginning the Asante were devastatingly impressive on the battlefield, creating discrete military wings out of their new allies and building formidable formations. Even with their history of barbaric ruthlessness, the Denkyira were no match for the young Turks.

The Asante realized that the vacuum created by the fall of the Denkyira could lead to a sustained period of regional instability unless they acted quickly. They moved with ruthless efficiency to put in place the constituent elements of a new state and completely dismantle what it replaced. Osei Tutu made it a law that any member of groups that had fought with the Asante and built the confederation had to relinquish their histories; anyone relating their pre-confederation history would be punished, by death. Osei Tutu knew that history could unite people, but it also had the power to divide. So a new oral history began with the founding of the confederation and everything before it was forced to wither and die. Osei Tutu refocused his disparate peoples' attentions on things that united them – the tradition of stools and new myths of origin.

Anyinam, then a small and unremarkable village, found a new and important role in Asante culture as the birthplace of the first king of the Asante kingdom. Today Anyinam remains sacred to the Asante and it is clear that it became special within Osei Tutu's lifetime and has remained in a kind of temporal stasis ever since. All the sites within Anyinam where each incident of his birth story unfolded became places of celebration and pilgrimage. The warren of single-storey adobe houses where his pregnant mother sought refuge remains carefully conserved. The Ohin – the village chief – showed me through the buildings where Osei Tutu's mother was given shelter after the birth, simple, traditional one-storey structures that face inwards on to courtyards. Cooking, sleeping, living, shrine maintenance and prayer were communal. Whether or not Osei Tutu took anything from this place is not known, but the communal form of architecture, the impossibility of non-participation, is obvious here.

As I say my goodbyes and prepare to leave, the Ohin grabs my arm. I follow him and his court through a back door, out across an area of bush and through a gate. We stand in the half-light beneath a thick canopy of cathedral-like silk cottons, rows of their flying buttress roots leading the eye along the edge of a wide path. This, the Ohin tells me, is as close as someone outside the royal family can get to the shrine that commemorates Osei Tutu's birth. 'He was more than a man, he was our messiah, brave, intelligent, someone who through almost force of will forged this country.

He built a culture, it did not evolve; it was made by a great man.'

The kingdom of Asante established a new capital, Kumase. Today it is Ghana's second city, home to nearly two million people, a sprawling engine of commercial activity. It was here that Osei Tutu faced perhaps his biggest challenge – how to keep his new union together. To achieve this, he deployed his full strategic imagination and turned to mythology.

In the centre of Kumase is an intriguing statue. It isn't a statue to Osei Tutu, the man who founded the Asante kingdom, but his adviser, Okomfo Anokye, Osei Tutu's loyal priest. The statue depicts the seminal moment in the founding of the mythology of Asante: Okomfo Anokye's summoning of the legendary Golden Stool of Asante from the heavens. According to tradition, the Golden Stool was the spirit of the Asante kingdom. It was an ornately carved low stool made from solid gold. When Okomfo Anokye brought it down from the sky it settled gently on Osei Tutu's knees – demonstrating to the gathered crowd that he was the unquestioned authority. Osei Tutu wanted to make a division between the state and its kings, the Asantehene. The Asante union could not be his deification, it had to seem like something bigger than individual personalities; it had to be about instituting a state, founding a culture, and the Golden Stool, not the king, would be its symbol.

Historians are not even certain that Okomfo Anokye ever existed. The fact that there is a statue to a mythical event rather than to an actual king is a measure of how much investment the Asante make in the mythology that surrounds the history. Myths used to rationalize events or as symbols are not unique to Asante, but the unique environment of the Akan forest means that the relationship between fact and myth, and the role of narrative, is even more critical to culture than in ancient Rome or at King Arthur's court. With the Asante, fact and myth were mixed to create a powerful blend that made sense to its people. This goes to the heart of the storytelling tradition that is such a vital part of Asante. The Golden Stool, and the kingdom, was the culmination of many centuries of cultural development. It brings together many elements; the gold of the forest is represented, the stool is the accepted symbol of authority. The fact that it is 'other-worldly' gives it a permanence that is so important in a culture that battles to survive in a tropical rainforest zone. Nothing lasts very long here, even kings, but if the institution of the Golden Stool contains the spirit of the Asante nation, the kingdom may go on for ever. Okomfo Anokye was Merlin to Osei Tutu's King Arthur. He gave Osei Tutu the spiritual power to complement his military power. After the Golden Stool anointed Osei Tutu as Asantehene, the king of Asante, the stools belonging to other chiefs were ceremoniously buried or destroyed. Only one stool was important now.

The kingdom of Asante was ambitious. Its military success over Denkyira was just the beginning. In the first half of the eighteenth century the armies of Asante conducted almost continuous wars of expansion and consolidation. The kingdom established its dominance over a vast area, pushing beyond the boundaries of present-day Ghana. It became essential for the burgeoning Asante kingdom to find symbols to rally around, and drums were a critical part of that campaign. Drum language pre-dated the Asante kingdom, but the new state used it to great effect.

In central Kumase, outside the studio of the Asante master, I meet the Asantehene's drummers. They arrived in a minibus carrying their instruments: two large *frontomfrom* drums, each the size of a small man, were unloaded first, then a pair of smaller hip-high *atumpan*, a *dundun* that could fit under an arm, and lastly two bells. When both the drums and the drummers are dressed the performance begins. The *atumpan* and *frontomfrom* take the lead. These are the principal talking drums of the Asante people of Ghana and are played upright, usually in pairs, by master drum-mers using hooked drumsticks. Each drum, though paired, plays an individual range of tones: one is male and the other female, a deep resonant drum and a tighter brighter one. When played in an ensemble, the *atumpan* introduces each drum phrase, and is responded to by the massive *frontomfrom*. This group, the king's drummers, revolves around twin-brother master drummers who

Traditional talking drums, circa *1923.*

play the *atumpan* and *frontomfrom*, exploiting their natural closeness and mutual understanding to create a rich, deep, complex sound with unrivalled precision. Twins and pairs are thought to be special in Akan society, where the idea of symmetry and balance is especially important. State drums are played in pairs, the male drum sitting on the right, the female on the left, almost touching, but not quite.

Drumming holds great significance for the Asante; drummers are known as Odomakoma Kyerema ('God the Creator's Drummers'). They play every day before the king and a libation is poured to the drums. It is said that this evokes the spirits of the forest trees, the mighty elephant, and the deities of the earth and sky, all of whom are summoned to bless the drum, and its message. The drummers who play these state drums are seen as both privileged and important. Years ago a drummer who faltered or who played a wrong note was liable to be fined; in the distant past they may even have had an ear cut off. There's no risk of that today. In any case, every stroke is delivered with masterful accuracy.

To the right of the twins an older man plays West Africa's most popular drum, the *dundun*. British musicologists sometimes call it the hourglass drum, because of its shape – it's designed to slip under the arm and around the player's abdomen. The *dundun*'s tonal range is produced by leather strings that are tied to a leather membrane; a skilled drummer can tighten the membrane by squeezing the strings under his arm. There are many types of *dundun*. The most important, like the one being played today, is known as Lya-Ilu ('mother of drums'), which can produce an octave in the hands of a strong drummer.

These drums are all known for their ability to communicate messages. The *dundun*, *atumpan* and *frontomfrom* are all perfectly suited to the complex languages, like Twi, spoken by the Asante, in which many words are distinguished only by their tones. Twi is, like many African languages, holophrastic: whole phrases or combinations of ideas can be expressed in a single sound, so it is often difficult to understand a word out of context. In the process of translating spoken phrases into drum languages, small gongs are used to break up the consonants, making discrete words more obvious. Small gongs or pieces of metal are sometimes attached to the male drum to create a harsh, discordant note that suggests the consonant. Across Africa there are dozens of different gongs and rattles; the *ogene* (the metal gong), *ogene nkpinabo* (the double metal gong), *ogene nne na nwa* (the mother and child gong), *alo* (the small metal gong), *ogene nkpi-ito* (the triple gong) and *ogene nkpi-ino* (the quadruple gong) are but a few of an enormous and varied family. But today the king's drummers use two simple bells.

I have heard this configuration of drums played in many parts of the world and I was expecting something special from the king's drummers, but what they deliver is completely mesmeric – wave after wave of complex configurations of beats all held together by a simple repetition of three deliberate tones, the resonance wrapping us all in a blanket of hypnotic sound.

With the sound of drums still ringing in my ears, I join James, the royal drum-maker, in his studio to find out how these instruments are made. Like many Ghanaian craftsmen's workshops, it is an unfinished breeze-block shell. Its long frontage is broken by latticed panels of rusted iron rods; it does not give up any clues to the wizardry that goes on inside. Visiting in the late afternoon when the evening light casts long golden shadows through the wood-dust-heavy air is like visiting an alchemist's studio. There is magic in the air. I sit and watch James for almost an hour as he fashions the body of a waist-height *atumpan* with nothing more than an adze, working a rough, uneven hunk of wood into a perfectly even and elegant form.

'I learned this skill from my grandfather, and he from his father,' he tells me. 'Every drum has a personality. I have to find each drum within the wood – the sound is buried in the wood.' As he speaks he shaves palm-sized slices off the surface of the wood with amazing precision. 'Once we have found the drum we attach the skin and finish it. Drums are so important to us, they can tell our stories in special ways.'

Lubricated by gold and facilitated through slave labour, the Asante had built a complex, successful culture in a challenging environment, and now, through rallying cultural totems like drums, they sought to expand it and bring to bear a greater cohesion.

The next morning I begin the long drive to the coast. The arrival of Europeans at the end of the fifteenth century turned small coastal fishing towns into major trading emporia. Within decades of that initial European contact minor trade routes from the coast to the Asante interior had become major commercial highways. Gold, ivory and Islamic ideology travelled coastward, passing bales of European cloth, weaponry and Christianity wending its way north towards the Asante hinterland. The fulcrum of this activity was my destination, Cape Coast Castle.

The accumulation of wealth that had been part of the psyche of the Akan people for centuries was no different on a large scale. Warfare was profitable. Over the first few decades of its existence the kingdom of Asante expanded at an astounding rate and the state coffers were filled with tribute and taxation. The wars of expansion also resulted in the accumulation of vast numbers of slaves from the states it conquered – more than it could possibly need. Now, those slaves were no longer just useful labourers, they were valuable export commodities.

When the British took over Cape Coast Castle in the middle of the seventeenth century they saw it as a good base for expanding their slave trading ambitions. The region's gold deposits and rich trading opportunities had attracted a host of European powers, including the Portuguese and the Dutch. This fort was the headquarters of British colonial rule in this part of West Africa. Walking around Cape Coast Castle today, even long after slavery was outlawed, it remains a tainted place. Its setting is unquestionably beautiful. Sea-ravaged eighteenth-century traders' houses nestle along the coastline looking out over dozens of fishing boats, and the castle itself, a white, deep-walled, crenellated edifice, is impressive. But the horror of what went on here is still more than evident in the architecture: the dank, pitch-dark, brick-lined slave dungeons, pits that housed hundreds of people in the most degrading and filthy conditions, lead to 'the gate of no return', the doorway through which millions of slaves passed on their way to a life of captivity and drudgery in the New World.

I have come to meet Professor Adu-Boahene from Cape Coast University, an authority on slavery. He has spent years researching the lives of some of the big slave dealers and traders who worked as middlemen between the British and the Asante. We sit on one of the castle terraces looking out across the city and the coastline at a view that has remained remarkably unchanged for hundreds of years. Out to sea, mountain ranges of frothing breakers challenge fleets of fearless hand-crafted fishing boats that trail brightly coloured flags and bunting in their wake. While the past seems very present, it remains difficult on such a beautiful day to imagine the events that went on here. However, Professor Adu-Boahene is a master at conjuring up images of the past.

The Asante captured men in battle, sometimes thousands of them, and put them to work clearing the forest for arable farming, helping to build wealth to fund further wars of expansion. It was degrading and tough work, but at least in the early period it was generally accepted that slaves, or their children, could be integrated into families and thus regain their freedom. It was impossible for the children of a slave to gain high office, but in all other areas of life they could reintegrate and enjoy the freedoms experienced by free-born Asante. Beyond being a very lucrative model, it was a way of reaching out imperially across the region, forcing those they defeated to be fully inculcated in Asante thinking. The opening of the transtlantic trade turned slavery into a highly lucrative industry in which people were little more than goods. The fantastic amounts of money generated created the latitude for those involved to turn a blind eye to the obviously horrific nature of the industry. They were different times, perhaps governed by very different moral parameters, but even as it unfolded many of those involved felt tarnished by slavery – economically, culturally, morally. Its legacy has left a permanent shadow across this place and this history. For anyone who studies the history, for the thousands of African Americans who continue to visit Cape Coast Castle every year, and for those for whom it is a lingering ghost that stalks their genealogy, transatlantic slavery remains a monumental moral abhorrence that is painful to navigate and impossible to explain adequately.

By the early eighteenth century the territory south of the Asante kingdom was under European control and had become known as the Gold Coast. Gold was, though, just one element of the colonial economy. The original European traders on the Gold Coast, the Portuguese, had brought African slaves from trading posts further east and exchanged them at their forts for gold; they also provided the weapons that allowed Asante's rapid expansion in the early 1700s. By the end of the eighteenth century Asante's influence stretched from the coast many hundreds of miles into the interior. The power of the kingdom meant that more states accepted its dominance and joined the Asante confederation, often without a fight. At its peak, the kingdom of Asante was made up of dozens of different Akan states. For the wealth and success it bestowed on everyone who fell under their influence and complied with Asante vision, they wanted payback.

It was said that just as all roads of the ancient world led to Rome, so the roads of Asante radiated out from Kumase like spokes from the hub of a wheel, sucking power, taxes and influence into the vital central organ, and functioning as a singular source of executive control. The Asante kingdom's network of roads rivalled many European countries' of the same period. The so-called Great Roads had been military pathways used to expand the kingdom; they were now arteries of trade and tribute flowing into Kumase as well as tentacles reaching to the outer limits of the kingdom. The secondary, tributary towns and villages remained healthy, but in times of famine or hardship the balance could shift: the supporting towns and institutions could leach power and resources from the centre, becoming periodically very needy or enormously influential as an obdurate blocking force. When combined, these subsidiary towns were a formidable challenge for even the most effective Asantehene. The best Asante administrations learned to balance and negotiate their favour with forensic care, ensuring whenever possible the wealth and sustainability of both the greater empire and its various parts, propagating and nurturing ultimate loyalty to the Asante state via its subsidiary stools. The Asantehenes sent trusted men to live in the outlying states. These officials conveyed the latest missives from the palace in Kumase, and they also made sure everyone was behaving themselves. Even in times of feast the empire existed in a highly strung symbiotic tension; stress applied to almost any part of the spider's web could be felt across the whole of Asante. However, the states weren't held together simply by force, they retained their own identities. Somehow, the Asante had to find a way of pulling their kingdom together almost without anyone noticing they were doing it.

The Asante kingdom was nothing if not clever. Rather than see the diversity of its possessions as a disadvantage, it used it for its own ends. Communities surrounding Kumase had developed particular skills or crafts. Places such as Bonwire may not have been militarily powerful but they came to play an increasingly crucial role in binding the kingdom together. The Asante had already utilized pre-Asante crafts such as stool-making and drumming to pull the state together; now they began to look at new ways to co-opt the discrete crafts of the nations they had conquered into the national narrative.

Among the many Asante stories that were created during this period is one of two friends who went hunting in a forest and found a spider making its web; they stood and watched the spider weaving diligently for two days. When they returned home they copied what they had seen and wove the first length of kente. The veracity of this might now be hard to prove; it is also said that the mobile looms on which kente is woven crossed the Sahara with early traders, and the word kente is derived from the Twi word *kenten*, which means 'basket'. However, it does reinforce the idea that the Asante were keen to assert their sense of identity through a range of iconic objects, kente being perhaps the most obvious. What is clear is that the technologies and traditions that made kente the state cloth were conceived at the time when Asante came into being. The earliest kente cloths were made from cottons that were traded with Asante's neighbours, but with the arrival of Europeans on the coast so came access to Italian, Indian and North African silks. Silk could not only produce lighter cloth, the colours it was able to hold were far more intense and luminous. Unravelling trade cloth to recycle the thread was the main early source of raw materials to create early kente, until places like Bonwire were established and the economies of scale meant that new specialist trade routes began to feed the demand.

Bonwire is a slightly ramshackle town that is slowly being eaten up by the inexorable growth of Kumase. It is the place where the royal kentes are woven. There are now dozens of weavers and merchants who make their living making and selling kente. Most weavers work within tight parameters, replicating old cloths. They use their thin looms to weave the panels of patterns of bright colours and geometries and then add weft work woven into every available block of plain weave, to build texture and contrast. The cloths are known as much for their associated proverbs and names as for their design, and even more funda-mental than their formal title the cloth colours conveyed meaning: gold signified royalty, wealth and high status; blue, peacefulness, harmony and love; while green could be nature, growth and spiritual renewal.

The Cultural Centre is a cooperative where young weavers create and sell their cloths. It is a long barn-shaped building that buzzes with the sound of wooden looms being pushed as hard as their rickety frames can go. Along the building's edges hang hundreds of examples of their work, new rayon-bright kente alongside the deeper more regal colours of old silk cloths. It is here that the labour-intensive nature of kente weaving becomes plain. It can take months to weave a cloth, each panel pains-takingly individually crafted before being sewn together. Some designs are enormously complex, only made by a handful of master-craftsmen; these designs are held secret, and a few reserved for the king alone. Each pattern contains a meaning or a phrase or proverb that can be read by those who understand it. These proverbs often relate to the nation, to the unity of the people, and the essence that binds them together.

It is thought that weaving was commonplace in the forest from at least the sixteenth century, when trans-Saharan traders brought silks and other material to the Akan. The meanings stitched into kente cloth are directly connected to the Akan culture of narrative and storytelling. There are over three hundred patterns, each with its own name and meaning. The act of weaving is tied to traditional myths and ceremonies. What's so fascinating about these is that so many of the meanings reinforce the same central idea: the kingdom and the basis of its strength and power. They aren't just narratives about the history of Bonwire or of Asante. Kente cloth became a symbol of the kingdom itself. The over-whelming and explicit message in kente cloth, and the way narrow strips of material are stitched together to make the toga-style dress, is that it is greater than the sum of its parts. The Asantehene made sure that he wore Bonwire's kente cloth, underlining its royal significance. He used the pottery from another village, the wood carving from another, the stools and the drums from others as well. The power at the centre pulled in all the different crafts and customs of the villages and states and declared that each was a vital contribution to the kingdom.

It was a brilliant and effective strategy. The state used long-held traditions, took them for itself, and dictated its own version of what they meant. The people of the kingdom saw themselves reflected at the centre of power. But the kingdom was not just governed by ingeniously making everyone feel included. While there was support and consent, there was also highly overt control. I have come to meet the Asantehene's bodyguard, a retinue of gun and sword bearers who remain even today the first and last line of defence should the king ever be threatened. From a strong room they produce some of the important material history around which the Asante people have always rallied. This is the royal armoury. The weapons in here belonged to a number of Asantehenes who reigned during the eighteenth and nineteenth centuries. They were both a means of maintaining control and a powerful status symbol.

First they bring out guns, gold-hilted flintlock rifles commissioned by each of the Asantehenes. They allow me to touch and hold Osei Tutu's gun. It is heavy in the hand with a gold powder keg and carved embossing on its hilt. These weapons would have been imported from the European powers on the coast and paid for with gold and slaves. The Asante had no ideological objection to the inventions of European outsiders. They recognized European firearms as a vital way to consolidate their power. I am given permission to pull back the trigger. It is stiff and heavy, but I work it back into a cocked position, look down its barrel and pull the trigger.

One after another guns are produced, each beautiful, each commissioned by a different Asantehene. Their changing technologies tell the story of gun making, their solid gold customizations give an intimate picture of the personality of each king. I pick up another Asantehene's gun, Mensa Bonsu's huge thick cannon of a firearm with bold gold additions. I struggle to cock it, but cannot. This is as close as I will ever get to this man – history books can only take you so far. I now know how strong his thumbs must have been, how stocky his frame and how refined his taste in gold work. It is a lovely moment.

Then they bring out the swords, which I am not allowed to touch or unsheathe. Their gold scabbards are as beautiful as any object I have ever been in the presence of. Every one has a name and a whole body of supporting history. A bunch of palm-nuts clustered around a heart, an ants' nest, a long cobra, every one crafted from a solid buttery gold with unbridled care. These objects were more than weapons. Force, or the threat of force, was not the only way the state exerted control. The Asante kingdom was very sophisticated in how it displayed power. So the most sophisticated of all its bureaucracy was the treasury. It gathered the taxes of the kingdom. Taxation, like these more tangible symbols of power, was a vital way of centralizing political control in the state.

I meet Mary Owusu, another slavery expert from Cape Coast University. We sit in the reception room of the old Asantehene's palace, an invasion of butterflies fluttering about our heads. I am keen to understand what the empire was like at its peak. Mary has brought two books with her. Bowdich and Dupuis, two British pioneers who worked with the British government in the early nineteenth century to establish a trading relationship, produced some wonderful illustrated texts that paint a detailed picture of the Asante empire. Mary opens the books, folds out sumptuous illustrated pages and begins to describe the early Asante kingdom.

Most advanced societies had a system of taxation, but the Asante were different. The Asante were concerned not just with generating revenue, but controlling wealth. No Asante citizens were allowed to accumulate individual wealth. Wealth was power, and no one was allowed to be powerful without the state's say-so. Asante culture had been hacked and forged out of nature. No one was allowed to forget that the role of the Asantehene was to preserve the wealth of the kingdom, and therefore the kingdom itself. Gold was not simply a resource, it symbolized the kingdom. Showing it off, displaying power, was expected of the Asantehene. It was a demonstration of the kingdom's economic might and the status quo that enabled their ongoing success. By giving gold this heightened symbolic importance within the iconography of the monarch, the state had appropriated an aspect of ancient culture and tradition.

It is here that gold's value is plain. It was not just that gold was beautiful, or simply that it had an economic value, it also had an emotive cultural value. It crossed the boundaries between environment and economics. It was a natural substance that had come, as a result of much hard work, out of the forest. It represented the Akan people, and the Asante state was quick to make it the symbol of the kingdom. Not just in the Golden Stool, but in everything; the court was adorned in every imaginable way with gold. It demonstrated that Asante was not just commercially astute, it was powerful too.

For more than a century the status quo continued and the accumulation of wealth by the state was accepted by its people. In the nineteenth century things changed and West Africa's strongest kingdom was rocked to its foundations. Asante had become rich and powerful in part because of the trade in slaves, so when that trade was outlawed the economy floundered, falling into a severe recession and leaving the state's control over the Asante weakened. Asante merchants began trading other things with the European powers on the coast, and with traders from across the Sahara. Everything bought had to be paid for in gold. Suddenly, gold started flowing out of the kingdom at a great rate. Not only that, Asante subjects were increasingly coming into contact with people from beyond the kingdom who were making money for themselves. They identified lucrative new trading opportunities that conflicted with the demands of the Asante authorities. The Asante crown had exercised a near monopoly on trade; suddenly a mercantile class, people of lower status within the Asante kingdom, were grasping the opportunity to make money by trading with the Europeans. Many of them migrated, most to the south, embracing the capitalist and libertarian values of the European settlers. The effective monetizing of trade for a broad swathe of the Asante populace had a profound effect. Individuals began hoarding gold. There were no banks, so they buried it to avoid paying tax. It was a direct challenge to the authority of the Asantehene and the centralized power structure of the Asante kingdom.

The abolition of slavery was initially ignored then resisted by the Asante, but eventually they were forced to bow to the inevitable and begin to consider and build a new economic model. By then the burgeoning expectations of the Asante population and the size of the state had become an impediment to swift and efficient socio-economic change. The Asante tried to develop alternative coastal export routes. If Cape Coast was denied them as an outlet, they would try neighbouring Elmina, which was then under the control of the more amenable Dutch. This was only a short-lived solution; a consolidation of the British presence on the coast meant that Elmina fairly soon became part of the British protectorate, in 1872, cutting off once and for all viable Asante trading access to the coast. The Asante also had to deal with the demographic after-effects on their communities of decades of transatlantic slavery. The permanent export of so much labour had denuded the region of a significant proportion of its manpower, and with less income to attract and to pay for a legitimate labour force or to conduct new wars of expansion, the Asante found themselves under extreme stress. This happened while the Asante were in the midst of resource-sapping local wars and internal disputes. Once upon a time the Asante could have sold prisoners of war on the coast to replenish the state treasury, but with no coastal outlet, prisoners had become a logistical encumbrance. Without slavery, a vital anchoring thread of the Asante empire infrastructure was broken; the whole web, the whole complex Asante kingdom, rapidly unravelled.

The pressure on the Asantehene, Kofi Karikari, intensified and he began to make increasingly irrational decisions in his search for a firm footing, even attacking the coastal town of Elmina in frustration and taking a number of Europeans prisoner. On 4 February 1874 a British expeditionary force led by Garnet Wolseley marched into Kumase in retaliation. Armed with Gatling guns, the huge force made up of British and West African soldiers was unstoppable. As the British forces approached the Prah river 100 kilometres from Kumase, the Asantehene sent a delegation to open new negotiations. It was by then far too little much too late. The British ransacked the palace of the Asantehene and burned the city to the ground, taking a large portion of the crown jewels as reparations. As the British left a smashed and smoking Kumase in their wake, they carried with them gold beads and other worked jewellery as part of a massive indemnity charged to the Asante of 50,000 ounces of gold. On return to Britain, some of the gold was auctioned by the royal jewellers, Garrards, to provide pensions for the British wounded and their next of kin. The Victoria and Albert Museum subsequently acquired some of the Asante court regalia, in June 1874. Among the items bought by the museum were a pair of silver anklets and a number of beaten-gold pieces that were probably used to decorate state stools or swords. I have often wondered what the British royal jewellers thought of the work of the Asante royal jewellers – different continents, different contexts, but in many ways quite similar.

The complete humiliation of the Asante gave the British the opportunity to declare the region south of Asante theirs, and the Gold Coast colony was born. In the aftermath Kofi Karikari was destooled, throwing the state into a period of considerable instability. This was a highly significant moment. It was the first time in the history of the kingdom that an army had invaded Asante and 'won'. From the earliest days of the confederation the Asante had always won. The model for Asante was based on ideas of expansion and victory; the loss of the slave trade, the war, Kumase and the Asantehene seemed unreal. Within the Asante, the authority of the Asantehene and the power of the government were seriously undermined. As the supply of gold started to dwindle, a succession of Asantehenes responded in the only way they could: they introduced heavier taxation. Mensa Bonsu, who followed Kofi Karikari, tried to reverse the tide by being overtly authoritarian, indiscriminately seizing assets as well as gold dust and taking the wives of his subjects, if he liked the look of them, and executing the husbands if they objected. The wealthy, young and mobile began to leave the kingdom in significant numbers, taking their vital assets and manpower with them, leaving the state less able than ever to fight its corner or rally support.

As the state imploded there was increased dissent and rebellions began to break out against the court. An isolated Mensa Bonsu was deposed in 1883, and a destructive dispute followed over who should take possession and control of the Golden Stool. The Asante kingdom descended into brutal civil war. The violence only ended in 1888, when the factions agreed to a new Asantehene, Agyemang Prempe. He was only sixteen, but compared to his immediate predecessors Prempe I was a truly exceptional Asantehene. The young king's reign was beset by difficulties from the outset, but he knew his first and foremost task was to reunite the kingdom. He fought a courageous campaign among the Asante aristocracy and mercantile elite to rebuild the forward momentum of his forefathers while fighting a rearguard action against Britain's creeping efforts to bring his kingdom under its protectorate.

To restore power and faith in the kingdom, Prempe turned to the powerful symbol and myth that had been the key to uniting the early people, the Golden Stool. He reminded people that the spirit of the kingdom was contained within the Golden Stool. He used all the imagery and traditions of the kingdom to assure people that they were stronger together than apart. It was in many people's interests that the kingdom regained its power and wealth.

But Prempe was up against the rather different interests of another powerful empire. When Prempe was asked by the British to accept a protectorate over his state, he rejected it outright, arguing that the governor had misjudged the situation. He retorted passionately, 'My kingdom of Asante will never commit itself to any such policy of protection. Asante must remain independent as of old, and at the same time be friends with all white men.' The British had enjoyed the instability of the civil war to build their own protectorate and secure their coastal assets, but now that Prempe began to look as if he might be able to reunite Asante and return it to a viable footing, the British acted decisively.

In 1896 they returned to Kumase – but this time there was no violence. As the scramble for Africa raged, the British were in competition with other European imperial powers and were determined to incorporate the gold-rich Asante into the Gold Coast colony. When the British arrived, Prempe thought it was to talk trade, but he was very wrong. He was captured and exiled, along with his court and members of the ruling elite. The sovereign kingdom of Asante seemed to have come to an end. The British took possession of its territory; its people were now subject to colonial rule. There was one thing that the British had

Asantehene Agyeman Prempe I.

failed to acquire: the Golden Stool. The British sought it without success, but eventually the Asante gave it to them – a fake one; they buried the real one. By keeping the real stool, the power of the Asante throne was seen to have lived on. And at least in their hearts, the Asante felt they had never capitulated.

Ironically, in 1924 the British reinstated Prempe with greatly limited powers as Kumasehene, king of the metropolitan area of Kumase. Even the colonial regime had come to realize the benefit of having a unifying personality in Asante around whom its people could gather. The British offered to build a new palace, but the stool family refused the offer, rallying round and collecting funds to build a new house from their own coffers.

Today that old palace is a museum that sits at the back of the modern grand mansion that houses Osei Tutu II, the present Asantehene. The old building captures a moment of quaint, dignified pain. The museum galleries reveal their history: they are domestic in a heart-warming way, but with every turn something reminds the visitor of the scale of Asante history, something on which the early residents of this humble house must have constantly reflected. The gold weights, the photographs and the thrones are evidence that this was never an ordinary home. Asante culture is not like so many other lost kingdoms I have visited; even in those dark, difficult days of the kingdom's collapse it remained defiant. Much of the important stool paraphernalia was kept intact and hidden away, out of British hands, and is still used today. A large body of that priceless material is quietly stored in the museum among the waxworks and fading photographs.

As I descend the stairs to leave, I notice a small room near the stairwell with its door open. Inside the state treasurer is preparing the Asantehene's gold jewellery for a festival. I stand at the door and watch as from a fading suitcase dozens of pieces of jewellery are decanted on to the table: outsized bangles with scenes from Asante mythology, gold rings, thick-chained necklaces, all dazzling in a sumptuous buttery gold. Although they represent only a small portion of the royal collection, which must be priceless, these items nevertheless convey a powerful message about the state. Every piece of jewellery has a distinctive iconography; it has a story to tell. These were a confident self-assured people who knew how to let others know that. The Asante reinforced their message of confidence through every area of their history and material culture, and they did it with such style.

I step out into the sun to join the people of Kumase. The Akwaside, when the important Kumase chiefs gather at the palace with their stool families and dignitaries, remains the focus of the annual calendar. The festivals offer the Asantehene the opportunity to see his extended family and court and for his most loyal subjects to show him their love by offering him gifts. After quite a long and demanding trip during which I have been lucky enough to gain access and some insight into many of the components of the material culture of the Asante stool regalia, ending it at an Akwaside where they will be in plain sight is highly appropriate.

I wait among the early arrivals and ponder my journey. For a son of Ghanaian soil this has been an affecting odyssey; at each stage I have asked questions and have learned something new about the stool. Most importantly, I have discovered that the Asante kingdom was never lost. Even in its bleakest hour when the British thought they had broken and humiliated the Asante, the great project Osei Tutu had put in train three hundred years earlier remained a rallying point; the drums, the gold, the guns, the cloth, the Golden Stool were still as loved as they ever were, and that was because the key craft of storytelling, of keeping history alive, was as important then as it is today. However tenacious or well armed the British were, they could not challenge or break that tradition.

The first of the chiefs arrives with his retinue under outsized appliqué-adorned umbrellas, wearing primary-coloured embroidered cloth that sings in the sunlight. Led by a drummer, they process through the gathering crowds on the parade ground and find their place. Immediately another paramount chief and his family appear, attempting to outdo the first, playing leopardskin-coloured calabash drums and *dunduns*. They place their flat, lacquered, sandalled feet with considered deliberation to the beat of the *dundun*, their golden kentes sparkling on their dark skins. The Gyaasewahene, the state general, enters with his men armed with the old Asantehene's guns, all wearing black waxed cloth and dubbin-black belts and crowned with tight lacquered black helmets. They would be a formidable sight to behold on a battle-field. Each chief is adorned with extravagant amounts of gold, rings embellished with deep relief, sunset-yellow golden bangles pulled five at a time up forearms, gold necklaces hung with amulets. Each group carries their family stool. Group by group they fill the square, chiefs from across Kumase, each coming to celebrate their differences and the unity they find under the Asantehene.

Then one of the cloth weavers recognizes me from Bonwire. He tugs my arm and I am pulled through the crowds, tripping and stumbling deep into the bowels of the palace. We pass through gate after gate, past more and more important dignitaries, each preparing to greet the king. We're running against the flow, and the passages get thinner and more crowded, but we force our way through whispered conversations and past large expanses of cool creamy skin, my nose buried deep in kente and my arms getting bruised against the corners of stools. Then we turn a corner and there, facing me, is the king. He does not blink. The momentum of the day has begun, he gives me a fleeting look, almost smiles, and is whisked past me up on to a palanquin and back along the corridor at head height and away into the sunlight. We are carried with the flow of the procession and spat out on to the parade ground where the afternoon has erupted into a cacophony of drumming. Hundreds of people hold up their palms, with their first two fingers raised – the Asante greeting to their king.

It is an uplifting sight. The Asante utilized force, gold and slavery to forge one of the most sophisticated kingdoms West Africa has ever seen. They built their kingdom in a recalcitrant environment by confederating a number of groups and then using a range of new symbols and material culture traditions to bind them into a society. The arrival of a substantial British presence in the region changed the regional political and economic balance, challenging the viability of the Asante kingdom. But even at its lowest ebb, when the Asante royal family were exiled, the state maintained a relevance and the Asantehene continued to be loved.

I squeeze into a space quite close to the Asantehene's throne and watch as for much of the afternoon chiefs slip out momentarily from under their umbrellas and are ushered forward to speak to him. It is painfully hot but beneath the layers of umbrellas there is some respite. Behind us a drummer begins to play a very simple beat, each strike slow and deliberate on a tiny *dundun*. Then the early evening explodes into drumbeats, what seems like dozens of drummers weaving subtle modifications around the tune. A single drummer deviates with a fiery barrage of fast, tighter beats and is joined by the whole drum battery, bassy *frontomfrom* drums quickening their beat with every strike. When the tempo can't quicken any more a group of drummers drops slightly out of tempo, and then another group peels away. More and more complex passages of beats diffuse one into another. The ground quakes with drumbeats, every drummer across the breadth of the parade ground beating every drum, every adjustment of tempo a flirtation with the original beat, every beat tight, arriving almost before it was there, lingering long after it should have gone.

As the sun begins to wilt, I gather my things to leave. The great and the good are heading home and the crowds are beginning to thin, but even as the last golden shafts of daylight crumble beneath the treeline, the drumming goes on.

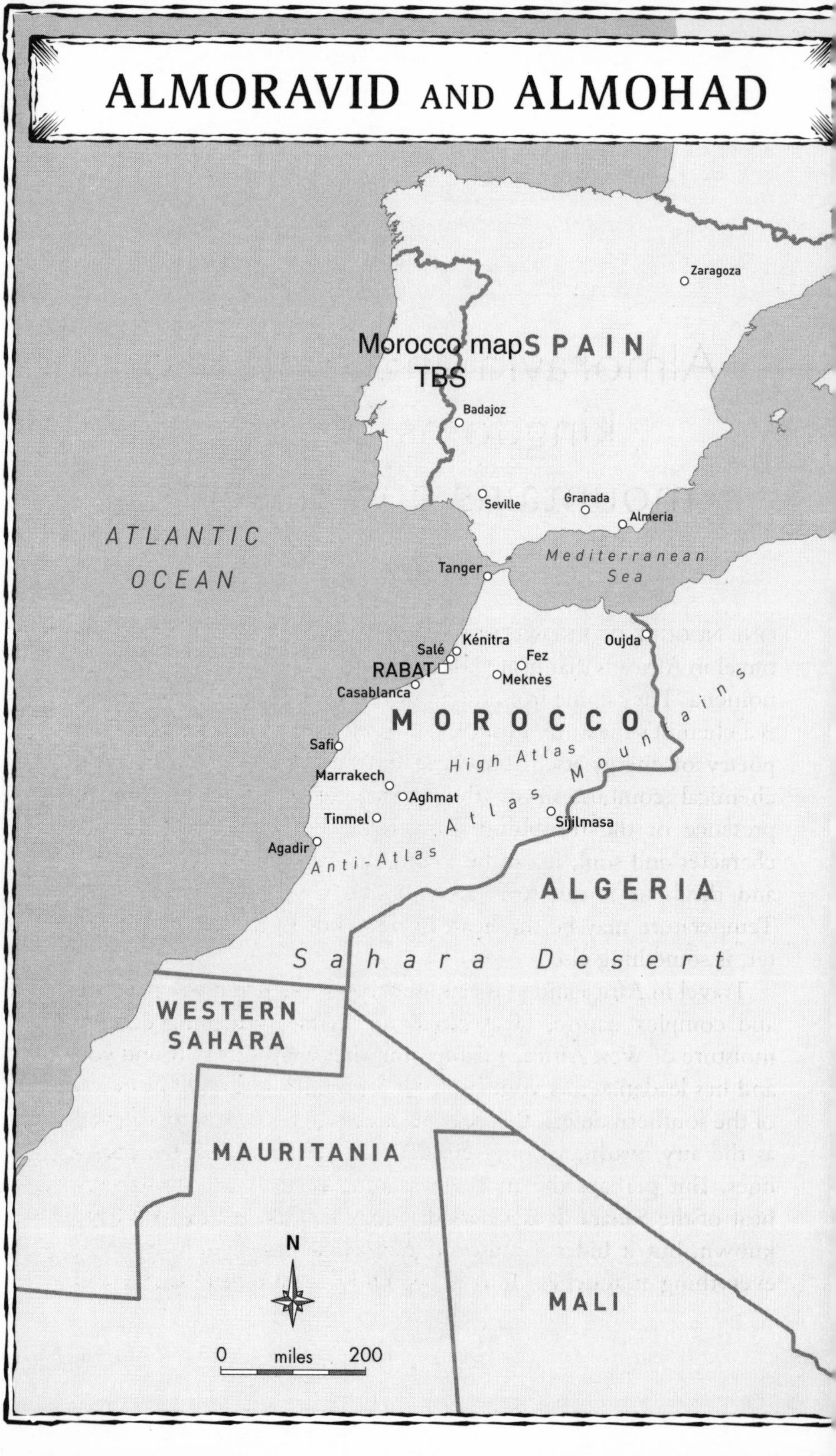
ALMORAVID AND ALMOHAD
Zaragoza
Morocco map
TBS
SPAIN
Badajoz
Seville
Granada
Almeria
ATLANTIC
OCEAN
Mediterranean
Sea
Tanger
Kénitra
Salé
Oujda
Fez
RABAT
Meknès
Casablanca
MOROCCO
Safi
High Atlas
Marrakech
Aghmat
Atlas Mountains
Tinmel
Sijilmasa
Agadir
Anti-Atlas
ALGERIA
Sahara Desert
WESTERN
SAHARA
MAURITANIA
N
MALI
0 miles 200

Almoravid and Almohad: kingdoms of the mountains and deserts

ONE NUGGET OF KNOWLEDGE I HAVE ACQUIRED AFTER YEARS OF travel in Africa is that heat and temperature are very different phenomena. They come from different realms of reality. Temperature is a chemist's measure. Heat, by contrast, is the complex and fluid poetry of energy itself. Heat can be the crackle at the heart of chemical combustion or the ghostly glow of recent human presence or the throbbing warmth of the sun itself. Heat has character and soul; it can be loving and comforting, it can tease and thrill, or it can turn on you like a psychotic constrictor. Temperature may be the heart of heat, but its nature, its character, is something else.

Travel in Africa and you can quickly experience heat's perverse and complex nature. Heat can come as the deadening doughy moisture of West Africa, a damp quilt that wraps itself around you and lies leaden across your back, or as the desiccating blow-torch of the southern deserts that sears its presence on your skin, or even as the airy, warm, wooing embrace of the Indian Ocean coastlines. But perhaps the most devastating is the languorous, silky heat of the Sahara. It is a heat that may feel like a heat you have known, but it hides a caustic toxicity that blisters and dries out everything it touches. It is a beguiling breath that dances and shimmers across the surface of your skin, eroding the fabric of your constitution with lacerating, leaching embraces until it becomes you, and you become heat.

Knowing that, strangers have traditionally avoided the Sahara. But it has bred a fascination as an immutable, unnavigable barrier, a place where little can survive and through which few pass. To the Romans and the Phoenicians the Sahara was an impenetrable area only a cursed few with almost supernatural knowledge could traverse. For the trading elites of the great ancient West African empires the desert was an unnegotiable sea of sand that only those with an almost innate understanding could survive. For thousands of years the Berber were almost uniquely its native guardians, building their lives in one of the hottest, least hospitable places on earth, trading and escorting merchants across a near fluid landscape that could disappear in a storm. The Berber built a culture by working trade routes that were dangerous, tough and demanding. The great fourteenth-century Islamic philosopher Ibn Khaldun wrote that when Ifriqish, son of Qays, first encountered these strange people with their unusual tongue, he remarked 'What a *barbara* you have', referring to the deep warbling intonations of the Berber language. And so they became known as Berber. They were a people who never quite threw off that aura of danger and otherness, of their one-ness with the environment, of their almost supernatural ability to rise up out of the sands and melt back into the heat haze. Over hundreds of years their habitat, their lifestyle, became inextricably linked with a wildness; even their name gave rise to the Latin word *barbarus*, or 'barbarian'. These were a people who seemed to have the sand, the very untamed nature of the landscape, running through their veins. On this journey I want to trace the history of the Almoravid and the Almohad, the two Berber dynasties that left the deserts and mountains and founded new Islamic cities that became the centre of vast empires and defined swathes of North Africa for centuries.

The slur that first defined the Berber may have been tolerated, and then accepted, but it was always inaccurate and somewhat cruel. The Sahara was not always a region of sand; during various periods over the last five thousand years it has been more temperate, differing very little in climate to the Mediterranean. The ancestors of the Berber may have had pastoral cultures on huge arable plains that were long ago consumed by the sand. As the desert grew and the fertile lands dried up and died, the Berber, the native population, were forced into smaller and more remote groups to survive. As the desertification of North Africa isolated these communities and drove them into more fragile and nomadic traditions, they continued to share dialects of a lost common language, and a way of life, maintaining a love and respect for the desert and a unique willingness to work within its limitations.

Today the Sahara has one of the most unforgiving climates in the world. It is a massive region of unproductive rock, scrub and sand the size of western Europe. To visitors like myself it may feel lifeless and barren, but for centuries it has been home to the Berber. It was from this seeming wasteland that the Berber launched a campaign to transform the north-west corner of Africa into a commercial and military empire that stretched from the West African Atlantic coast into southern Europe. They may once have been dismissed as barbarians, but the history of the Berber reveals something quite different. They built up a succession of kingdoms that were enormously successful. During the ages of the great Almoravid and Almohad dynasties they enjoyed an almost unrivalled dominance over the region. They left a legacy of great architecture and innovative engineering; they built a seat of learning that rivalled anywhere else in the Mediterranean region. Theirs was a commercial enterprise on an unprecedented intra-regional scale. But these were kingdoms riven by conflict. Over the course of three hundred years, epic battles were fought for trade routes and territory, but mostly for the hearts and minds of the Berber people. Great military campaigns instigated the rise and fall of the Almoravid and the Almohad. They were cultures driven by powerful forces – money and Islam, factors that made them increasingly ambitious. It is a sad irony that perhaps the most profound legacy of these mighty dynasties was the ultimate loss of Berber identity. On this journey I want to find out how a divided, disparate group of 'barbarian' nomads built a hugely influential kingdom armed with little more than determination. I also want to see how the constituent causal elements that came together to create this empire ultimately unravelled and brought about its downfall.

Arriving in Marrakesh at dusk is like arriving in the city by time machine. It remains a monarchy today, but very different from the one established by the Berber almost a thousand years ago. In so many ways, contemporary Morocco feels very different to the African continent that I know. The influence of Mediterranean and Arab culture is everywhere, in the fashion of the young people, the architecture, even in the language. There is a long history of this region looking north and east. So much of its story is dominated by the influence of foreign interlopers and imperialists from the Romans to the Phoenicians to the Arabs, and in more recent times the French, that it is easy to forget that the beginnings and the heart of these cultures are distinctly African.

Surrounded by the buzz and bustle of a modern city, it is hard to imagine what Morocco was like in the eleventh century before the Berber kingdom was established. The Berber are a people who have left no grand genealogies or oral history or texts that record their origins. So we must suck clues from what is left. Marrakesh is a modern city full of trendy iPhone-brandishing young people dressed in the international uniform of jeans and trainers. But as dusk settles the modern laid-back city gives in to its past. Below the tower of the Koutoubia Mosque the city lets its mask fall, as it has for a thousand years. The market rises like a medieval spectre to control the night – snake charmers, pyrotechnic magicians, cooked spiced sausages, young men on street corners playing small ceramic drums, fresh crisp vegetables glistening with condensation like jewels, banks of dried nuts and fruits, men shouting, women gathering, children running. The smells, the noise . . . the atmosphere crackles with possibility. Beyond hosting a market, the central square is a place where people have always come to gather. Buzzing mopeds flit through the crowds as friends rush to hug friends, watch the tricksters, jugglers and magicians, or simply to talk and exchange news. News about the latest thinking and fashions from across the Sahara, from Egypt and the Arabian Peninsula, from southern Europe, would once have been funnelled into this central square in Marrakesh. But this place was not just a sponge for existing ideas, it was where old ideas were contested and new thinking was forged. It was where great thinkers came to be among peers.

I am meeting Professor Mohamed Knidri, a native and a lover of the city who discovered a fascination with its history through his first love, chemistry. Mohamed tells me that there is a long tradition of Berber chemists that goes back as far as the discipline itself. We meet on the edge of the old souk. As we walk he tells me that the ancestors of the people, the ancient Berber, were the men who gave the world alchemy – 'al-chemistry'. Like many of his ancestors, Professor Knidri has spent his life trying to understand the metaphysics that underpin the mechanics of the natural world. In the Middle Ages Berber intellectuals combined religion and science with poetry and epistemological studies to create an all-encompassing philosophy of humanity. Like the scientists who today utilize the Hadron Collider in their search for the God particle, they sought out something divine in atoms and cells. It was a generation of Berber who wanted to challenge orthodoxy by searching out the essence of spiritual truth with the hope of finding a simple, perfect mathematical proposition there, a divine axiom that they could harness and which would explain everything. Looking at the faces of the people shopping in the market, I think that perhaps in essence it is a quest that links Berber over millennia. These people of the desert have always craved cultural ways to reflect and work in sympathy with their native environment. They intuited, and had learned in the hardest way possible, that despite the ferocity of their environment this was a place that could support life, if you understood and respected its rules, if you knew how to harness its potential. For great thinkers and nomadic traders alike there was a simple set of truths that underpinned the viability of life.

Though by no means frozen in a heritage aspic, the old city is almost unaltered from its eleventh-century majesty. We meander through dusty alleyways conceived in a period when deliveries were made by camel and horse, but which now sing with the constant whine of mopeds. We walk beneath reed-woven awnings that keep the streets cool and dapple the paving slabs with the last switches of sunlight, just as they always have. Hawkers, traders and barrow-boys jostle to fill each vacant patch of path, and sun-dried fruit, flavoured almonds and freshly butchered chicken are thrust in front of us as we walk. It is a magical backdrop against which to listen to Mohamed describing how Islam first reached this region in the seventh century from Arabia.

Islam took hold because of its compatibility with Berber beliefs; the two traditions had a fundamental shared understanding of justice and morality. However, while the Berber were pious, most converts had little knowledge of the laws of Islam; they practised a variety of localized versions of the religion. The Arab invaders named the region 'Maghreb', which meant 'of the setting sun' or 'of the West'. This was the Wild West, the very unorthodox edge of the Islamic world. It was a region that encompassed Morocco, Libya, Western Sahara, Algeria, Tunisia and Mauritania – a vast swathe of territories that were the traditional home of the Berber.

For four centuries this process continued as more and more Berber converted to Islam. By the eleventh century Islam had begun to spread down into the Sahara to impact the desert Berber and their trading partners. For the Berber this was a very different kind of trade relationship. They were used to their role as interlopers, as the cultural interface between communities separated by the desert. But the very word 'Islam' is derived from an Arabic word that means 'submission'. To become a believer, to become part of this new world, was not just to take on new customs and thinking, it was also to relinquish something fundamentally Berber.

The new converts were insular or isolated in their discrete pockets with their particular accommodations of Islam, and that situation may have lasted indefinitely had it not been for a single charismatic Berber, a man better travelled than most Berber –

Abd Allah Ibn Yasin. His travels to the great centres of Islamic teaching had left Ibn Yasin an evangelist for a devout legalistic interpretation of the Qur'an. He was determined to edify his fellow Berber, to raise them from their isolation and ignorance. Ibn Yasin wanted to instruct them in what he knew from his travels to be the true Islam. He had converted to Sunnism, a branch of Islam that adheres to the very specific living habits and thinking of Muhammad. Its followers had extended the tenets of the Qur'an to create guidance in every area of life, addressing people's intimate, domestic details, major questions of law, and also the way in which men and women related. It was more than a set of beliefs, it was a way of life.

It may have been a process that began with the conversion of individuals in small communities, but it built into a series of events that transformed north-western Africa fundamentally. Ibn Yasin carved out a foothold among his own people, the nomadic camel drivers from Western Sahara. Geography had always been the most immutable barrier to ideas. He knew from his travels that on the northern edge of the Sahara and beyond the Atlas Mountains lived really hardy and insular Berber who needed religious clarification. In 1054 he gathered his supporters and made his way north to save his brothers. He began his campaign in Sijilmasa, on the northern edge of the Sahara.

As I drive down into Sijilmasa purple clouds begin to tumble off the tops of the distant Atlas Mountains and roll down across the plains towards the town. It begins to rain – an extremely rare thing here. In fact it has not rained here for more than ten years. The first few drops bring people out of their houses on to the streets, but then the clouds disgorge a torrent on to the town. The roads quickly become rust-brown pools of soup-thick water. What started as curiosity quickly becomes wariness as the roads transform into fast-moving watercourses. I join a convoy of slow-moving cars edging through the flowing mud into the city.

According to the chronicles of the period, by the time Ibn Yasin arrived in Sijilmasa he had gathered an army of thirty thousand Berber Muslims. Ibn Yasin and his increasing number of followers drawn from across the Sahara region called themselves Almoravid, from a saying meaning 'those who are bound together in the cause of God'. It was a rapidly growing movement of a variety of different Berber peoples, many of whom had previously shared very little but their ethnicity. But as the Almoravid they were a single group, single-mindedly determined to bind all the Berber to their cause, to bring them under the mantle of their new movement. Ibn Yasin, their leader, their visionary, had a mission: jihad. Today the word has negative or problematic connotations for many non-Muslims, but jihad as perpetuated by Ibn Yasin in the eleventh century was a radical breath of fresh air. It was aimed at their fellow Muslims, it was not designed to be directed at non-believers. It was a struggle to uphold a true understanding of Islam and therefore it was a way of honing, refining, belief. For these Sunni Almoravid it was not an option, it was a fundamental duty. Like most religious duties, it meant sacrifice. The very word jihad means 'struggle', or 'striving'. It is a concept that is entirely logical in Islam. In order to live a moral life it is necessary to follow the teachings of the Qur'an and to encourage others to do so. Jihad may have eventually come to mean Holy War, but for the Almoravid – who had a particularly strict understanding of Islam, a Malachite interpretation – it meant living according to a very particular application of the Qur'an.

This new approach relied upon the learned input of an elite group of expert theologians, or *faqihs*, who advised the Almoravid on how to live well in this rapidly changing world, and to do so according to Islam. The *faqihs* were wise men and advocates, interpreters and arbitrators, who redefined common law through a prism of divinity. The result was a collection of Malachite rules that defined Almoravid society called the Risala. Every area of life came under the influence of religion, every action had a broader religious context. While the general tenets of Islam were not onerous to accommodate, for many traditional Berber these new ways of thinking must have meant significant change and sacrifice.

Sijilmasa was the first city to feel the brunt of the Almoravid application of Malachite law. The Almoravid executed the elite and influential of the city, destroyed musical instruments and burned down any shops that sold wine. Anything associated with the excesses and indulgences of the previous regime was rejected. But the Almoravid were not simply imposing their will on a resistant population. This was in part a people's revolution.

Driving into Sijilmasa on the edge of the desert in the rain is a curious thing. Many of the traditional buildings in Sijilmasa are constructed from mud bricks are rendered with quick-to-crumble adobe finishes. The concerns of people who live here are rarely about flooding. Sijilmasa is traditionally famous for its water management. It does not just sit on the edge of the desert, at the end of a trade route, but in the middle of a vast oasis. When Ibn Yasin came here he was in part attracted by a highly successful economy that supported thousands of people in a region surrounded by desert. But the city was also attractive because it thrived on the benefits of some advanced irrigation technologies. Some of Sijilmasa's water management thinking had been refined over millennia by Saharan cultures, but some of the knowledge had travelled along the trade routes from places such as Iran and Iraq.

The people of Sijilmasa augmented the flow of water from local springs, building a long and narrow city on a rocky mound bounded by two rivers. In a place where it might not rain for years, geography simply was not enough to make complex agriculture sustainable. Without irrigation specialists the spring water would simply have stagnated on the surface or evaporated, leaving layers of acrid salts on the sand and rendering the already poor soil barren. The engineers of Sijilmasa turned the waters from subterranean springs into an organized irrigation system that fed verdant arable land that could sustain substantial numbers of people. They developed lined underground channels, called *kheterra*, which funnelled and dispersed the water over miles to where it was needed. They then carried the spent water and sewage away from the city and built the infrastructure to support another ancient kind of alchemy: the production of valuable soil from sand. Fertile soil was carefully created by mixing the by-products from harvests with already composted materials to slowly build beds for future crops. Gradually, over many decades, after generations of forensic tendering, a fragile agricultural ecology was created. It was an environment that only remained sustainable so long as there was a continued investment in complex, labour-intensive irrigation technologies. Dates, grains and vegetables were grown at Sijilmasa, crops that could support livestock and thousands of people.

Founded in the eighth century, Sijilmasa, the jewel in the Western Sahara, attracted people from far and wide. The town was a powerful magnet for trade; caravans of up to a hundred camels, each carrying more than a man's weight in merchandise, would regularly pass through. Over the last fifteen years archaeological digs have revealed huge walls which surrounded the city and much of the oasis as well. This made Sijilmasa strategically vital on the trade routes running south to north. It was one of a chain of oases cities that ran south and south-east from the High Atlas Mountains that ended in Massa near Agadir. These ancient Berber trade routes linked the northern lip of the Sahara with merchants and goods that had come from the gold-rich kingdoms of West Africa. Sijilmasa attracted books and horses from the Middle East and ceramics from Asia; indeed, goods and expertise passed through this desert conduit from far and wide. It was the hub of exchange that linked Ethiopia to Andalusia. Cottons came from Egypt and were turned into garments, gold from the ancient kingdom of Ghana was minted into coins that were exported to the Gulf, dried fruits and nuts came from the Maghreb and were distributed across West Africa on a spider's web of desert trade highways. The hybrid communities that came together in these exchange hubs were enormously successful. They became hotbeds of radical thought and technological innovation, drawing influence from across the Sahara, the Middle East and southern Europe.

While Sijilmasa was unquestionably successful as a place of exchange, and Ibn Yasin recognized its value and potential, he was frustrated by the lax version of Islam it seemed to tolerate. But his mission wasn't solely driven by religious ideology, it had political relevance too. The local population of Sijilmasa, a city fuelled by entrepreneurial freedom, were frustrated by the stultifyingly aggressive tax policies of their rulers. The Almoravid argued that no taxes should be levied that were not mentioned in the Qur'an, or supported by *faqihs*. In the eyes of the people of Sijilmasa, the Almoravid not only had more legitimacy to govern than their current leaders, they also offered the population direct economic benefits. The Almoravid made the incumbent leaders look shoddy and old-fashioned, and not only on religious grounds: the financial freedoms they offered could only enhance the economic attraction of Sijilmasa, the oasis jewel that offered vital supply lines in the valley of Tafilelt. So the Almoravid swept into power in Sijilmasa not just because of their numbers and their military might but because they had a popular mandate and an unquestioned moral authority.

It has been estimated that the city had a population of around fifty thousand in the eleventh century – a good number to add to the Almoravid cause. With Sijilmasa under their influence, an important part of the gold trade route was under the Almoravid's control. News of this new power would have percolated up and down the trade routes. There had always been change and political instability in the region, but this was something quite different. Before Sijilmasa, the Almoravid had strategic imagination, moral authority and military might; now they also had the perfect base from which to continue their expansion and create an empire.

Today, the layer of archaeology that tells the story of Ibn Yasin's Sijilmasa is buried deep under thick accretions of sand and mud. The town was built on a gravel bank between two rivers, and the ancient building materials used were the very earth and stones that still surround the area. Archaeology and geophysical surveying are tough here. The nature of the construction techniques means that even within the Almoravid's own time the town was being constantly eroded and rebuilt. Sijilmasa was almost like a sand-castle. Perhaps some residue of Ibn Yasin's Sijilmasa lies beneath seventeenth-century ruins out on the edge of the modern city. It may be the case that there is a little of those early structures remaining in a form that can be read by archaeologists, but it is highly unlikely. Much of the layer of archaeology that would have helped to tell the story was used as building aggregate by successive generations of builders, or its friable nature has meant that it is now simply part of the general site.

What is clear, particularly after rain, is that there is a huge amount of Almoravid period material simply sitting on the ground or in the inner aggregate layer of the disintegrating walls of the seventeenth-century site. There are shards of unglazed pottery similar to those found on the bend of the Niger, flecks of glazed Middle Eastern ceramic that may be tile fragments from the Sijilmasa Mosque, and thousands of pieces of local pottery. These scattered fragments of evidence reinforce the written history: Sijilmasa was a focal point of a complex trading network, with a rich culture.

The road north from Sijilmasa opens up on to vast scrubby plains bounded on the distant horizon by mountains. For hour after hour of driving the spectacular vistas alter little. The only visible intervention by man is perhaps the Berber's most profound technological advance, the *kheterra*. The subterranean canals they dug to carry water from the streams, springs and mountains down the gently cambered landscapes to the fields and centres of population are impressive enough, but to aid water replenishment, easy access and maintenance they also built mounds every 20 metres for mile after mile of watercourse. There are hundreds of these mounds, each one 3 or 4 metres high, standing like soldiers out to the otherwise blank and barren horizon. Every mound is hollow, concealing deep holes that descend as far as the natural springs, carrying cool fresh water to where it is needed. If, like Rome and Victorian London, empires can be judged by their water management technologies, then for its day this was as sophisticated as anything else on the continent.

With the taking of Sijilmasa, Ibn Yasin's Almoravid jihad had gained a powerful, almost unstoppable momentum. It was unlike anything anyone had seen before and those who stood in its way had few military answers to its sheer weight of numbers. Victory at Sijilmasa simply made Ibn Yasin's followers more ambitious. They wanted to take their brand of Islam to every Berber, to unite them all as an unassailable force, but that meant tackling a huge natural obstacle: the Atlas Mountains.

The High Atlas Mountains extend 1,500 miles across Morocco, Libya and Algeria, forming a natural divide between the desert and the more fertile plains that lie between the mountains and the Mediterranean Sea. They were a formidable challenge in the medieval period; snow-capped all year round, and with peaks of more than 13,000 feet, they must have seemed impregnable. Ibn Yasin must have realized that even though he had so far been unmatched, this was a challenge of a different order. Beyond the natural hardships, he faced another kind of barrier. In a land often described as lawless and dangerous by outsiders, the Atlas were bandit country.

Nearly a thousand years ago, when Ibn Yasin and his army began their forays up the precipitous mountain passes that cross the High Atlas, they were entering hostile, difficult territory. They were desert warriors; the mountains and everything beyond was a completely alien world to them. But they were driven by a desire to capture a jewel every bit as strategically valuable as Sijilmasa. After an arduous trek across the mountains in 1058, they took possession of the beautiful and wealthy city of Aghmat, which nestled in a valley on the north side of the mountains. They named Aghmat the capital of their growing empire, and the city became the new base for Ibn Yasin and his army and their expansionist plans.

Modern-day Aghmat is beguiling, just a sleepy village surrounded by farms, but it hides a secret. Until fifteen years ago, no one knew where ancient Aghmat was. It was assumed to have disappeared centuries ago. But a visiting amateur archaeologist overheard a young boy talking about an area with strange geographical formations, weird undulations that did not seem natural. On seeing the site she was immediately convinced that it was ancient Aghmat. She persuaded a team of archaeologists to investigate, and beneath layers of sand accreted over a thousand years they uncovered the remains of the lost city. That was not the only surprise: the archaeology revealed a spectacular bathhouse, or *hammam*.

The *hammam* at Aghmat does not appear particularly impressive from a distance. After years of archaeology, and after the removal of many tons of soil to reveal its roofline, the bathhouse looks a little like three long-abandoned sheds or a row of air-raid shelters. The squat, barrel-shaped frames of the structures and the surface of mortar and large stones are plain and utilitarian in appearance. However, as you descend the stairs into the site, the herringbone red-brick floors of the entrance and the brick base of a fountain begin to reveal something more exciting. Inside, beneath the barrelled rooftop, are a series of three bathing suites. When standing within them, the rolling repetition of arches and the perfectly incised doorways that cut between the rooms bring the suites to life. These were spaces that were once decorated in painted plasters and tiles through which hot and cold water would have run – and remember, this was a desert city. Aghmat was obviously a place of wealth and influence. This was not just a bathhouse, but a temple to that precious resource, water.

We get some insight into the wealth of the population from accounts of the early years of the Almoravid occupation of Aghmat. Ibn Yasin's army was led by the dynamic Abu Bakr Ibn Umar, general of the Almoravid. Abu Bakr was a different sort of military tactician to many Almoravid. He might have seemed on the surface to be as strict in his adherence to Islam as his caliph, but he combined this with diplomatic stealth. As he began his campaign to win the city, one of the offensive manoeuvres he made was falling in love. Abu Bakr became consumed by, and eventually married, one of Aghmat's most influential citizens, the wealthy widow of the former ruler Zaynab an-Nafzawiyyat. According to the oral history, Zaynab led Abu Bakr to a secret subterranean repository full of gold and told her lover that everything he saw was at his disposal. Perhaps he was dazzled by the gold, perhaps he saw the strategic benefit of marrying into Aghmat aristocracy, perhaps she saw the advantages of being allied to the new regime, but maybe the romantic version of the history is accurate and they simply fell for each other's charms. Whatever the case, what is clear is that the union helped to secure not only the city but also the hearts and minds of its residents. Aghmat, a city of almost vital strategic importance, enhanced the wealth and influence of the ambitious Almoravid regime. Once it had fallen, the Almoravid turned it into an unrivalled citadel with palaces, gardens, markets and, of course, a bathhouse.

Aghmat was the Almoravid's first real taste of metropolitan life. But the city was too small for this ambitious expanding dynasty, and for a people who knew and loved the desert it was in the wrong place. Surrounded by mountains and hills on three sides, it was considered not to be in a good defensive position for the Almoravid, who had a tradition of fighting in the open. They needed a new capital city with strategic benefits Aghmat could not deliver. So after little more than a decade the Almoravid sought a new home.

It took a while to find a suitable site for their new capital. As a once nomadic desert people they shunned the need to be close to arable land, existing trade routes, or on the bank of a large river. These people had sand running through their veins and they wanted to be where they felt most comfortable. The Almoravid selected an open piece of land with plenty of room to expand about 25 kilometres from the foothills of the Atlas Mountains. They pitched their tents and called their city Marrakesh, from the Berber 'Land of God'. For the very first time the centre of power was not on the coastal plain facing the Mediterranean but in the traditional heartland of the Berber. They were also creating a city from scratch; for once they would not be interlopers and invaders. The foundation of the new city in 1070 represented the point at which a group of nomadic traders threw off their wandering traditions and became a rooted imperial force to be reckoned with.

The Almoravid's project of expansion was beginning to take on the shape of a kingdom. At its centre was a new capital city with all the trading might of Sijilmasa and the sophistication of

Aghmat. People were drawn to Marrakesh for the Almoravid's practical and spiritual protection and in return they paid taxes, but they also offered their loyalty. From its foundation the city was run on strict Malachite lines and an increasing number of *faqihs* made sure that everything was done in strict adherence to Islamic law. As the new city grew voraciously out of the desert, so in turn did the Almoravid's ambition to continue to expand. The city provided them with all the wealth and security they needed to take their jihad and their way of life to the rest of North-west Africa. Marrakesh was to be a trading, religious and intellectual hub unlike anything else. After the death of Ibn Yasin in 1059, a new caliph, Yusuf Ibn Tashfin, took on the job of leading the next phase of the expansion and continued where Ibn Yasin had left off, making an even greater impact. He turned what was an ambitious fledgling kingdom into a burgeoning empire.

Today, this period of Marrakesh's initial growth is still evident to anyone who visits in the vast labyrinthine market that sits inside the gargantuan city walls, the indulgent diversity of goods that have been sucked from sources across North Africa and beyond, the variety of ethnicities of the stall holders and the use of Arabic, the unifying language of the region. When Ibn Tashfin became the caliph, it must have felt like the centre of the world. As I reach the limits of the old city at the edge of the market I come upon an ancient gate set in the huge city wall. It is one of the few surviving Almoravid gates. It is very simple and somewhat modest for a dynasty of merchants who controlled trade on a previously almost inconceivable scale. It sits about 8 metres high, a classic ogee with a pinched-apex brick arch. It was deliberately created to be plain to suggest respect and modesty, but like so much Berber culture it hides a complexity within its seeming simplicity. It is an arch made from two sets of curves that twist in opposite directions, one concave and one convex, meeting in a point. The balance of opposing energies brought together into a sharp apex is very pleasant on the eye. For the desert Berber who entered the new city through this gate, many of whom followed forms of animist religion and were used to the classical silhouette of the

Jem 'el Fna gate, Marrakesh. (Gus Casely-Hayford)

Roman arch and the adobe arches of Western Sahara, this must have been radical to behold. Ibn Tashfin wanted to send out an uncompromising message to everyone who entered the city: this is an empire on the move, think of us as barbarians at your peril.

As Ibn Tashfin and the Almoravid's influence grew, so his city grew, and with it his trading power and, crucially, his army. Over the course of his forty-year reign the Almoravid army doubled its size. As a result they took over the area that is today Morocco and Algeria. It had taken a mere twenty-six years to advance from their first incursion out of the desert, with the taking of Sijilmasa, to the point where they controlled a considerable amount of North-west Africa.

Then, for the very first time, the voracious shark that the Almoravid dynasty had become, a kingdom that almost had to expand to meet the expectations of its population, met a more formidable obstacle: servicing its own ambition. When the small Muslim city-states of the Iberian Peninsula began to come under pressure from the Christian kings of northern Spain, they called on the Almoravid for assistance. To deny Muslim brothers, especially ones of such strategic importance, was intolerable for a kingdom that had been founded on a belief in jihad and the constant drive to expand. And so an already stretched Yusuf Ibn Tashfin began a campaign of support, successfully quelling a number of attacks. However, rather than becoming more independent, their Iberian Muslim brothers became even more reliant on Ibn Tashfin and the requests for help did not diminish.

Eventually, Ibn Tashfin grew exasperated and bored with the indolent Iberian Muslims' constant requests. He disliked their lax dedication to Islam and their continual moaning. So he led a grand invasion of the Iberian Peninsula and took Seville, Badajoz, Almeria and Granada one by one, releasing the population from the huge tax burdens levied on them by the indulgent emirs. Other than Zaragoza, he seized the whole region. When he had brought it to heel he gave himself the title Amir al-Muslimin, Commander of the Muslims. It was the last successful invasion of a European territory by an African power. Never before had so much Muslim territory been brought together under a single man in one kingdom, united politically and spiritually. It was the strategic culmination of the programme begun in Sijilmasa. The Almoravid Marrakesh was now the capital of a vast kingdom that reached from the Sahara to Spain and east to Algeria. And it was the so-called barbarians of the desert that had created it.

It was a golden moment, and the Almoravid reinvested in Marrakesh to make it a capital worthy of their new empire. But in 1106 the great leader died and the massive responsibility of ruling the Almoravid kingdom passed to Ibn Tashfin's twenty-year-old son Ali Ibn Yusuf. He was a devout Muslim, just like his father, but he was not a child of the desert. He loved Marrakesh, its sophistication and its refinements. So under Ali Ibn Yusuf a very different era began.

The young caliph came into a treasury brimming with gold and silver and he worked very hard to spend the resources he'd inherited, projecting his cosmopolitan tastes on to the city around him. His father had led an army that had devised new military technologies, he'd pioneered a fashion for carrying two swords, for warfare waged with daggers and javelins. Ali, by contrast, was not a warmonger and wanted to turn Marrakesh into a learned capital, drawing on influences from throughout the kingdom, especially Andalusia, to win the battle of ideas. It was the final relinquishing of Almoravid nomadic traditions, a re-casting of the once fluid warring culture into stone. Gardens centred around fountains, reminiscent of oases, were built, and mosques with a series of translucent carved screens like permanent tents. The once portable fabrics were re-rendered in stone; the transient world of the migratory Berber was reanimated in wood and coloured glasses. Everything that was once portable was fixed, everything that was once unpolished manufactured, finished and refined.

Until comparatively recently it was thought that no buildings were left that could show us what Ali's grand vision might have looked like. Then in 1952, during renovations of outbuildings of the nearby Ben Yusuf Mosque, the Qubbat Barudiyyin, a grand bathhouse built in 1117 as part of a palace complex now long

THE LOST KINGDOMS OF AFRICA

gone, was found right in the centre of the city. The bath kiosk, once buried, now stands proud. Its squat rectangular base sits several metres below the level of the adjacent buildings. It is only when you climb inside that it reveals its wonders. Its base is dominated by a bath, a shallow 4-metre-long rectangle. It is very simple and elegant. Above it is sumptuous stone carving that stretches up on to the inner surface of the dome. Layers of complex, ornate, crushed fabric carving follow the surface of the dome up to the apex. Beneath the dome is a rim of text that has sadly now eroded away, but only decades ago when the site was first excavated it was said to have been legible, proclaiming the name of its proud builder Ali Ibn Yusuf. This bathhouse was the way the new caliph sought respect, not on the battlefield. This was not simply an indulgence. The bath below the spectacular dome was once used for ablutions before prayer and it relied on the revolutionary hydraulics of *kheterra*, and also had a system of toilets and showers, and drinking water on tap.

Perhaps there were powerful reasons why Ali wanted his name inscribed into the building's surface. This exquisite architectural statement in the palace grounds showed just how far the Almoravid had come from their days as desert camel drivers bent on Holy War. This kind of architecture was a clear break from the more utilitarian architecture of the reign of his father, when the Almoravid were driven by a much more austere aesthetic. It is a celebration of the caliph's religious dedication while also being something of a folly.

There were critics who felt that under Ali the Almoravid lost their ambition and their integrity. While Ali was busy creating a more beautiful capital, the Almoravid kingdom was beginning to unravel. There was a weakness at the empire's heart and it had not gone unnoticed by their many enemies and rivals.

It was in Spain, Ali's pride and joy, that the cracks first began to appear. In 1118, while they were still putting the finishing touches to the Qubbat Barudiyyin bathhouse, Zaragoza, the single state his father had failed to defeat, was lost to the Christians. It would be the first of many losses as the cities of the Spanish emirs fell during a period of catastrophic change. They were overstretched, and suddenly the vast empire ceased to seem like a well of economic potential, but instead became a bubbling cauldron of plots and problems. The Almoravid's most serious challenge, however, came from much closer to home, from the mountains.

The next morning, I begin the long trip out to the High Atlas region. It is a beautiful drive along an ancient road that slowly rises up from the plains as the hills become mountains. A thousand years ago this part of the gold trade route carrying the precious metal from West Africa over the mountains towards the coast would have been a dangerous, lawless place, difficult to manage. The slopes and crags provided perfect ambush opportunities for thieves interested in what merchants might be carrying. The people who lived in this region turned their villages into fortresses, or *qusur*. The *qasr* (singular of *qusur*) at Ait Ben Haddou is still partly in use. It is one of hundreds that cling to the mountain passes of the High Atlas, the perfect place to stop and have a break from driving.

Like the buildings of Sijilmasa, Ait Ben Haddou was constructed from mud-rammed frames placed one on top of another. Like castles of ice they are constantly melting, wind and rain whittling battlements and friezes into stumps. There was an acceptance that you could never beat the desert wind, that you could only find ways to complement it by crafting your home from the desert sand. These buildings were never designed to defy time and the elements, unlike the great bathhouses at Aghmat and Marrakesh. They followed the ethos of the traditional desert Berber who never recorded their history; they simply let narrative fade and fail. They were meant to reflect time, to be in a constant state of flux and repair. They will never allow their inhabitants to forget the fragility of their presence, the inexorable flow of time, the irresistible power of the desert.

Sadly, no Almoravid *qasr* from the twelfth century remains, but Ait Ben Haddou, like Sijilmasa, was created using the same construction techniques that allowed for robust multi-storey structures that could flex and give. These were complete towns

Mud-rammed frame building at the top of Ait Ben Haddou. (Gus Casely-Hayford)

within fortifications; there are areas where animals were kept, shops, defensive towers and vented bakeries. Wandering from area to area, I begin to gain an understanding of how they balanced the need for light against the desire for the spaces to be comfortable and well ventilated. There was always a tension between a desire to keep interiors cool by blocking out the sun and the desire to allow in light. In the high towers, where some of the original painted stucco remains, you get a sense of how they might have found that balance. These white rooms are refreshingly cool, the walls radiating cold air and light into the space. Such design traditions made these earth-constructed spaces fresh and very comfortable.

As I descend the stairs from the ramparts to leave, I hear an old Berber woman singing. She is singing to keep time as she weaves carpets with her daughters using traditional techniques. I stop and watch as single lengths of yellow wool are pulled across a frame, in and out of vertical lengths of string, each one left in the perfect position for the composition before being pushed home with a comb. Then lengths of blue wool are knotted one by one across the frame to form the pattern. It is amazingly labour-intensive work, but gradually, over months, rugs are constructed. It is a craft that has been practised almost unchanged for a thousand years, like pottery and henna decoration. They give a sense of what traditional Berber life might have been like.

The sound of her song is still with me as I continue my drive up through the hills to the mountains. As the incline steepens I spot the distant snowy peaks of the High Atlas looming between the clouds. The Almoravid never fully controlled the hills and mountains of the High Atlas. They were ill at ease in mountainous terrain, and they were either evaded or ambushed whenever they tried to root out trouble. I am on my way to Tinmel, one of the most impressive and impregnable of the mountain fortresses that the Berber built. The name is derived from the Berber word for 'white', and as you ascend the serpentine mountain passes it is clear why. Even in the midst of summer the mountains remain snow-capped and the lower reaches of the High Atlas, where

Tinmel perches, remain startlingly chilled. In the days of the Almoravid, these roads, then paths, were almost impassable for strangers. The villages that bank the road could only be approached on horseback along broken, precipitous guarded paths that made an invasion inconceivable. Up here in their mountain lair, echoing the early days of the Almoravid, a small fundamentalist branch of Islam laid the groundwork for their gradual domination of this whole region.

The leader of this revolution was Mohammad Ibn Tumart. Ibn Tumart was not a child of the desert, like the Almoravid, he was a mountain Berber. Like the founder of the Almoravid, Ibn Yasin, he too had spent a decade studying the fundamental tenets of Islam in the universities and madrasahs of the Middle East. But Ibn Tumart believed that he had interpreted Islam with greater rigour than the Almoravid down on the plains. Ibn Tumart had, in effect, been looking down from his mountain stronghold at Tinmel on the Almoravid administration and he could see what they had done right and what they had done wrong. Ibn Tumart and his followers believed that the Almoravid had lost their way. They had become like the emirs of Spain – indulgent, corrupt and weak. They had allowed the interpretations of the *faqih*s too much influence rather than relying on the Qur'an as their true guide. Ibn Tumart became known in Marrakesh for his uncompromising interpretation of the Qur'an. His lectures were notorious for their fiery rhetoric; he even unsaddled the caliph's sister for not wearing a veil.

Up in the mountains, Ibn Tumart's followers built a mosque. The mosque at Tinmel was not like other mosques in Berber territory. To get to it you have to navigate some of the most precipitous roads of the High Atlas, negotiate paths that curl along the edges of rivers and down around the rims of deep gorges. It is a striking landscape. The air is crystal clear and soft mists pour off the mountainsides down into isolated valleys. Women, bent double with the weight of crop-filled baskets, climb the hillsides. It is a place that seems to relish its inaccessibility. The mosque sits on a promontory protected by mountains behind. It is easy to miss if you are looking for a mosque because from the outside it looks like a fort, minimally decorated and heavily fortified.

Ibn Tumart wanted radical and sweeping changes. He proposed the division of the sexes, the banning of music and the abandonment of luxury and excess. The irony that these were ideas strangely reminiscent of the early ideology of the Almoravid was not lost on Ibn Tumart; hypocrisy was also on his list. With the failing, overstretched Almoravid regime in Marrakesh looking increasingly weak and Ibn Tumart's popularity mounting, it seemed only a question of when the old firebrand would attack. But in 1128, fate intervened: Ibn Tumart died in his mountain lair at Tinmel. His legacy was the basis of a new popular movement, and his death did not slow its growth. The new movement became known as the Almohad, which meant 'people who believed in one God'.

The great mosque at Tinmel was built twenty years after Ibn Tumart's death as a commemoration of the new movement, and the coming regime. What is strange about the mosque is what greets you within. The building may be almost completely roofless, but its remaining arches and supports still tell a fascinating story. The entrance and prayer area still have their original stucco, the remains of a complex ceiling that compares to the Qubbat Barudiyyin bathhouse in Marrakesh. If Ibn Tumart and his followers really were offended by the excesses of the previous regime, it is not clear here. Deep rococo swirls twist and ascend into the dome. The building's interior decoration is rich and beautiful; this is not a minimal, fundamentalist fortress. One has to conjecture that this might be a metaphor for their approach to politics: externally devout and minimal but perhaps hiding something else within. Was this really a drive for economic dominance justified through religious ideology? What Ibn Tumart had done, even posthumously, was to hit the Almoravid where it hurt most, by undermining them intellectually.

In the late afternoon, before the evening mists completely consume the serpentine roads of the High Atlas, I begin my descent to the plains and Marrakesh. News has just begun to filter through of a bomb that has been detonated in the central square, in the very place where I began my journey, and where I hope to be staying this evening. It is very strange that the same issues of interpretation of scripture and political ideology still have such resonance here. Nine hundred years before me an army of Almohad came down from the hills along this same road and began laying siege to the cities held by the Almoravid, because they believed that the other regime's application of the Qur'an was wrong. Armed with that belief, just like the bombers today, they believed they were invincible.

The Almoravid were already overstretched and fighting on multiple fronts. Their campaigns in Spain against an equally zealous Christian opposition were unravelling, their tax revenues were diminishing as citizens in towns and cities across the empire began to sense a weakened leadership, and their caliph, though a devout Muslim, was not a natural military tactician. The kingdom began to suffer multi-organ failure as the institutions they had once relied on began to come under extreme pressure. Policies the Almoravid were once able to implement unchallenged began to attract opposition. For many, the Almoravid remained foreigners from the desert who could not act decisively without consulting their *faqihs*, and now that they looked weak people began to question their right to rule. But it was their tax policies that may have really tipped the balance. The Almoravid had swept to power arguing that they would only support taxes that were sanctioned in the Qur'an. As the empire expanded and the cost of administration and wars of conquest increased, Ali had felt forced to raise taxes. These were so loathed that he had to employ Spanish tax collectors because no local would have dared to do such unpopular work. He might in his defence have been able justifiably to point to foreign wars and the maintenance of the empire's sophisticated infrastructure, but many of his people saw him as spoiled and indulgent.

The Almohad laid siege to Marrakesh just as the Almoravid had once laid siege to Sijilmasa. Here in the Almoravid heartland the residents did not welcome the invaders; they knew their leaders were not perfect but they feared the alternative. The people of Marrakesh built a range of substantial city walls in direct response to the Almohad threat. It is a sad irony that a culture based on freedom, nomadic traditions and tents should in its most desperate moment rely on huge walls. Their ancient Berber beliefs that walls imprisoned rather than protected proved accurate: they became embattled and then trapped within the city. The caliph's golden city became a gilded cage. It still took twenty years of skirmishing and systematic attrition before the will of the city broke.

When the Almohad finally entered the city of Marrakesh in 1147 the Almoravid's reign was over. A dynasty that had led the Berber from desert nomads to a kingdom that ruled an area of Africa and southern Europe of enormous strategic and commercial importance was gone, almost unmourned. Now, like the rulers before them, the Almohad used Marrakesh as a base for an imperial expansion even more ambitious than that of their predecessors. The Almohad seized the neighbouring lands of Ifriqiya, the former Roman province that stretched across Libya. In Spain they took back all their old possessions in Andalusia, and Valencia and Catalonia. They did not want to make the same mistake as the Almoravid so they invested significant personnel and political attention on Spain. Andalusia was so important that Seville became Almohad's second capital. The Almohad wanted to show rivals and allies alike that they were not to be trifled with, that they were a ruthless, formidable fighting force much more ambitious than the Almoravid.

They also wanted to show that they were not barbarians. They wanted their allies, their trading partners and their supporters to know that the new dynasty might reject excess, but they were every bit as sophisticated as their predecessors. In 1185, Sultan Ya'qub al-Mansur built his own gate in the now even more fortified walls of Marrakesh. Driving back into an unnervingly still Marrakesh late in the evening, it suddenly strikes me how well fortified the city has always been. Today, after the bomb, the city is flooded with police, but this was historically an even more contested and troubled place than it is today. The walls the Almohad built were almost 30 feet thick and up to 40 feet high, designed to leave no one in any doubt about the impregnability of the new regime. The new gate, by comparison, the Gate of Guinea, was decorated in floral patterns that surrounded a shell. It was highly ornate, a gate of which the indulgent Ali, the last of the Almoravid, would have been proud. Like their predecessors, the Almohad were being pulled in opposing directions: they wanted both to impress and to show piety.

It was at the Koutoubia Mosque, the great Almoravid mosque and symbol of its piety, that the new regime made this most apparent. It provided the Almohad with the perfect way to demonstrate their intellectual superiority. They demolished the old mosque and constructed a new one on the same site, claiming that after consulting their advisers they'd discovered that the old mosque had not been built facing Mecca. It is clear just by comparing the still standing foundations of the old mosque with the walls of the new one that the alignment was never definitive. The orientation of a mosque was an issue that would have been discussed and ruminated over by intellectuals. There could have been no objective definitive answer, and that is demonstrated by the fact that the difference in the placing of the two buildings is barely perceptible. The decision to demolish the old mosque was probably driven as much by contemporary politics as anything else. It may well have been a new regime flexing its muscles, defining the new era through new buildings, confident exhibitions of their ambition.

The exterior of the mosque is somewhat plain, perhaps as may be expected. But recently, up at the top of the minaret, researchers have found images of boats clandestinely carved into the inner walls. This is intriguing; mosques do not usually carry images. It is known that the Almohad brought skilled craftsmen from across their empire to build their new city. One has to wonder if these ancient graffiti artists were craftsmen from coastal cultures hankering after home; or perhaps it was a metaphor for the Berber as the desert sailors. Maybe it simply reflects court gossip.

The Almohad had almost exhausted lands to conquer and had begun to look westward. Many of the grand projects they invested in were on the coast, looking out towards the ocean. While they were in part driven to better the Almoravid, that was also somewhat prosaic. The Almohad sought a kind of immortality that could only come about by redefining the age, by reinvigorating every intellectual discipline. They wanted to glorify God, to develop the commercial viability of the empire, to keep their allies happy, but since coming down from the High Atlas they had begun to think about how they were seen and how they might be remembered. In the twelfth century the 'Abd al-Mu'min, the first Almohad emir, built the Gardens of Agdal, one of many ornamental lakes that doubled as reservoirs for the city waterworks. They were so much more than a reservoir; the Gardens of Agdal are a poetic interpretation of Berber history, a meditation on the past using the constituent parts of the oases: water, palms, olive trees, fruit trees – Berber history re-cast as art. Everything was conceived to remind us of where the Berber came from. There are horticultural rooms of olive trees and long vistas of orchards interrupted by ornamental lakes and the inescapable tinkle of an irrigation system supplied by *kheterra* but which in the hands of a gifted designer have become something even more magical. Perhaps the Almohad realized, like the Almoravid before them, that impressive visual statements could win hearts and minds too. Or maybe the puritans had begun to soften a little.

I spend a morning in the garden listening to the very distant sound of police sirens. After everything that is unfolding in the city beyond its walls, the Gardens of Agdal is the perfect sanctuary, an oasis of tranquillity. At the end of the fourteenth century the Muslim philosopher Ibn Khaldun wrote that the state the Berber created was like a garden. He argued that government turned like a wheel: there was no justice without the monarch, no monarch without the army, no army without taxes, no taxes without the wealth of the people, and no wealth without justice. Ibn Khaldun's metaphor is particularly poignant in the faded grandeur of the Gardens of Agdal. Once the gardens would have been immaculate, used only by an elite few; today I find the place in a somewhat ramshackle state. After years of neglect it has acquired a layer of romantic decrepitude. Rogue flowers, perhaps from previous planting plans, interrupt flower borders, wild patches of guerrilla mint, sage and daisy disrupt the views; crumbling walls have become Zimmer frames for aged climbing plants, semi-derelict buildings refuges for fugitive seeds. Just like the old Berber buildings that melted away into their landscape, so this garden is gradually, at its edges, beginning to soften a little. Even though it is quite a formal garden, it seems comfortable with this dishevelment. During the time of the Almohad it always had the mountains as a backdrop, it always used water and the plants of the oases as its palette, never allowing its users to forget where they came from.

As the decades passed so the Almohad empire seemed to gain confidence and ambition. They knew they could not rest on their laurels like their predecessors. Their future security relied upon wealth created by low taxation and vigorous trade between the many parts of the great empire. That wealth began with reinvestment in a string of highly productive cities. I leave Marrakesh behind and head for Fez, one of those cities of the Almohad empire, still a centre for trade. Fez remains probably the most complete medieval city centre in the world. Some parts of it have barely changed in the last nine hundred years. Here, Almohad merchants traded sugarcane and cotton, gold, copper and pottery. Positioned between the Mediterranean and the Sahara, Fez was perfectly situated to thrive. The city's inhabitants did not just trade goods, they made things too. At the height of the Almohad kingdom, Fez boasted 372 mills, 9,082 shops, 47 soap factories and 188 potters' workshops. The Almohad had built upon the Almoravid trading base, becoming a formidable maritime trading force. Goods that were made here were traded from Venice to Catalonia. And artisans from Andalusia and elsewhere came to settle, bringing yet more skills with them.

One of the great Almohad industries was leather production. The tanneries of Fez are still used today. They remain almost unchanged, still operating much as they would have done at the time of the Almohad. You can smell the detritus of the process long before you reach the old tannery on the edge of the Medina. As you cross over the Binlamdoune river that barrels at high velocity along the edge of the building, your nostrils, throat and lungs begin to fill with an acrid fug. It is not a deeply offensive smell, it is the earthy, bitter scent of composting offal, with a secondary aroma, a ureic tang that seems to get ever stronger until it leaves a bromic acid-like taste in your mouth, long before you have even entered the site.

The entrance is a low thick door through which the fresh skins of sheep, goats and cows are delivered. Beyond the entrance is a medieval world. Standing in the tight, confined porch is a sinewy man dressed in nothing but short trousers that long ago ceased to be fabric and have transmogrified into what seems to be a polished shellac. He is using a long sharp knife to strip the wool from a sheepskin. With each movement down the skin long slithers of matted hair and fat fall off the creamy leather on to the floor. The floor, the wall, everything is covered in a thick film of greasy fat. I squeeze past two barrels the size of family cars that rotate on rickety frames, and past the rinsing and drying of shaved, cleaned skins, into the site.

Though ancient, the site is designed like a modern factory, and beyond the barrels the next stages of a hyper-efficient assembly line begin to unfold. In an area the size of a football pitch the hides are soaked in lined concrete basins, each one deep enough for a man to stand upright. Perhaps forty of the basins are full of a limey solution. Here the hides are soaked for two weeks to soften them, then they are moved on to vats of a gloopy bile-coloured solution of guano for a week, before finally being placed into one of a number of baths of coloured dye to be finished.

The site was designed by medieval tanners and is not made to be easily negotiated by the newcomer; channels where one might intuitively walk are thick with a slurry of the natural by-products of this fairly unpleasant process, which flows through the site out into the Binlamdoune. I step over a number of severed animal limbs and disembodied heads that are fermenting in a festering soup of rancid offal. It would be more unpleasant, but there is a high concentration of caustic lime running down the channels; lime has its own acrid smell, but it overpowers the stench of the copious amounts of rotting waste. I quickly realize that the only way to cross the area efficiently is by walking along the tops of the thinly rendered greasy walls between the vats. All around the tanners work, stirring vats, wringing the skins and watching me. They are tough. Even to stumble here might be nasty, and to fall into a vat could prove very painful on the ego. But with the help of the tanner I manage to weave myself along the 10-centimetre-wide walls. The lime and guano are highly alkaline so they work very effectively to reduce the slippery greases, but it is still nerve-racking.

The men go about their task with complete confidence, carrying armfuls of hides from vat to vat, working the surface of the hides to make them more malleable. It is deeply fascinating to watch. This is one of the earliest examples of a production line. All the processes deployed today are as they were in the Almohad period; the lime and the guano are natural and abundant, and the dyes are made from ingredients like poppies and herbs that would have been used for hundreds, perhaps thousands of years. It gives a clue to what this Almohad hive of industry must have been like: a medieval metropolis that deployed the most sophisticated technologies and production methods, that imported goods and expertise from right across the Mediterranean and North Africa, and here combined and finished them in startling ways, ready for export. Perhaps more than anything else the Almohad were experts in refining ideas and making the very notion of invention theirs. That was most in evidence in their schools.

In the centre of the medina, far from the smell of the tanneries, is an old madrasah, an Islamic school. It was established in AD 859, well before any of the colleges at Oxford and Cambridge. The Almohad University of Fez attracted thinkers and scholars from around the Mediterranean world. This is the institution where many of the greatest thinkers of the Middle Ages gathered, writing books and developing ideas that went on to define the age. There are aspects of the university building, such as the huge arched entrance and the carved and painted beamed ceilings, that give clues to its age and complex history. Yet, like so much Moroccan heritage, the library has been used, loved and organically adapted over the years. Although a madrasah has been on this site for centuries, the building feels almost modern.

The space is mosque-like – high ceilings and rows of neat desks. As I enter, I can see a pile of books waiting for me on one of the many oak-coloured tables. Navigating down between the desks, it is not difficult to imagine the great thinkers of the Almohad age working here. Men like Moses Maimonides, regarded as one of the most respected Jewish philosophers of the past two thousand years, spent time working in this library. He was attracted to this place because of the quality of the thinking; the library was a magnet for western European ideas, for thinking from the Middle East, both of which merged here with indigenous intellectual traditions. Maimonides worked alongside the great Averroës – Muhammad Ibn Rushd, the Berber intellectual giant. Averroës was both an originator of new thinking and a commentator on the philosophies of ancient Greece and contemporary Europe. St Thomas Aquinas wrote admiringly of his seminal work on Aristotle, calling him a profound philosopher. It is one of Averroës' great texts on Aristotle that I am here to see.

Opening a book that is a thousand years old is a very special experience. The yellowed pages of handwritten Arabic are worm-eaten and foxed, but the words are still legible. Averroës battled constantly with ideas of epistemological and ontological truth. Like his nomadic Berber forefathers he was plagued by the idea of the fragility of knowledge, and he spent a considerable amount of time investigating what underpins truth. He shared Plato's thought that we only have a partial insight into the bigger truths. It was to Aristotle and his metaphysics that he turned for most of his answers, crafting some of the most innovative thinking of his age. Sitting beside the Averroës volume is a work commissioned by Ibn Tumart, the mountain Berber who inspired the Almohad movement, a man who took care to preach in eloquent Berber. But it is also, like the Averroës volume, written in Arabic. This kingdom that started in the desert was clearly no longer looking at its southern Berber roots, but north towards Europe and east to Mecca.

Everything the Almohad did was in part to challenge how they were once seen. The University at Fez, like so much else, consciously communicated the fact that this was not a cultural backwater but a place with significant intellectual gravitas. Al-Mansur, who ruled at the peak of the Almohad empire, was not warlike or an indulgent connoisseur like his Almoravid predecessors. He was deeply interested in ideas, particularly philosophy. He seemed at home when surrounded by a coterie of the most respected thinkers. He even maintained the era's greatest contemporary intellectual, Averroës, at his court. But that must be placed in context: Al-Mansur and his regime still constructed considerably more mosques and forts than libraries, palaces and gardens. Their acceptance of new ideas sat on a hair-trigger; al-Mansur at one point imprisoned Averroës and burned his books, and demonstrated little tolerance of Jews. Like the Almoravid before them, the Almohad were deeply conflicted.

Just as the Almoravid had chosen a site and built Marrakesh, their new capital, from the ground up, so the Almohad caliph Ya'qub al-Mansur chose to build Rabat as his capital. It might have sat on one of the corners of his empire, but it held opportunities unlike any other. As European ocean-based trade became an increasing threat to their once secure desert trade routes, the Almohad were forced to consider the ocean. In the late twelfth century, as the graffiti artists of the Koutoubia Mosque had predicted, the caliph turned his attention to opportunities across the sea. But building their new city in Rabat was not just about opening up new trade routes, it was also, crucially, a chance to take their brand of Islam further afield.

As when the Almoravid first arrived in Sijilmasa, the Almohad began Rabat by building the fortifications for the old town, constructing large ramparts and gates. Then in 1195 they began something to eclipse the greatest Almoravid and Almohad achievements thus far, a new mosque. The gargantuan, unfinished Hasan Mosque is an indication of what can happen when the wheel that Ibn Khaldun described falters and stops turning. This mosque would have been the largest of its kind in the Muslim west, big enough to hold an entire army. Consisting of three hundred columns and a hundred pillars, it would have had a roof that covered the equivalent of two football pitches. But it was never completed.

Standing among the unfinished columns is quite affecting. It is a poignant memorial to a failing dynasty. The ambition is obvious. The Hasan Mosque is on a scale as impressive as the great Roman architecture of North Africa or the buildings of Mecca. It spoke to Almohad heritage, and to God, and it was as permanent a statement as could be made. Monumental columns stride out across the enormous site, dwarfing the human frame, and at one end the thick, squat base of the unfinished minaret adds to a feeling of incompleteness. Almost a carbon copy of the minaret in Marrakesh, this was like one of the markers showing the full extent of Almohad territory. There is also one very like this in Algeria, and another in the Giralda in Seville. However, unlike this one they were all completed and became symbols of regional success.

The reason why there is no top on the Hasan minaret and no roof on the prayer hall is because in the year 1199, only four years after work started here, Ya'qub al-Mansur died. With him went the confidence that had bred economic growth and military expansion. It was the beginning of the end for the Almohad dynasty. The unfinished mosque sent a message across the empire to their rivals, their enemies, and most profoundly their own people, a message of vulnerability. As with the Almoravid dynasty before them, there was no fighter to carry on the good fight. The monarch, one of the crucial components in Ibn Khaldun's wheel, had gone and the wheel simply stopped turning. Al-Mansur's death initiated a period of rapid decline. The Almohad gradually lost more and more territory in Andalusia and their sovereignty started to unravel at home as increasingly hedonistic young caliphs tried to fill the shoes of al-Mansur. No African power would ever control a piece of Europe again. The gradual loss of Spain coincided with increasingly intense Arab rebellions in the Maghreb. By the middle of the thirteenth century the Almohad abandoned Spain to Christian conquest and lost control of Tunisia and Algeria. As tax revenues collapsed the straitened Almohad army atrophied, rendering the failing empire ungovernable; everywhere power leached away. Eventually the collapse of vital systems began to undermine the regime's legitimacy to rule. In 1269 the Marinid ejected the Almohad from Marrakesh and it was over.

For a hundred years the Marinid tried to re-create the glory of the Almohad empire but by the fifteenth century the age of Berber dynasties was well and truly at an end. Arab influence increased across the region until Berber identity was all but extinguished. The Berber, once a nomadic people, had built one of the most impressive African empires ever seen. It stretched across much of North-west Africa into southern Europe, attracting some of the most influential minds and sophisticated technologies, and at its heart was belief. But for both the Almoravid and the Almohad the ideological compromises required to build their empires sowed the seeds of their demise. Eventually the Arabs became the most powerful force on the Moroccan plains, and no ruler could hold authority without their support. Ironically, the same religious zeal that had enabled the African Berber to create an Islamic empire eventually ensured that it was an Arab dynasty, which claimed direct descent from Muhammad, that remained in power over the kingdom the Berber had created. That dynasty was the Alawi – and they have weathered the Arab Spring and are still in power today.

A Final Brief Thought . . .

WHEN I BEGAN THIS SERIES OF JOURNEYS I REALLY WAS NOT SURE what I would find. Looking back now over the many tens of thousands of miles travelled, the adventures I had and the scrapes and challenges I navigated, I am left with a composite memory of warm welcomes, inspiring and impassioned experts, and the love and pride of the traditional custodians of Africa's past.

I wanted to pursue the history of lost kingdoms, but I was very keen that these journeys would not just uncover stories of Africa's past. I wanted to capture some of the latest archaeology and absorb the most insightful thinking on African history, but I wanted to do so while immersing myself in contemporary Africa. How that would fit together as a series of coherent journeys was unclear at the outset. After almost two years of travelling, driving from the High Atlas to the Sahara, from the Great Lakes of central Africa to the golden beaches of the Swahili coast, from the adobe mosques of West Africa to the mega-city that is Lagos, from Great Zimbabwe to the battlefields of the Zulu wars, I have been left deeply affected by my experiences. My suspicion that it was possible to pursue a kind of cultural archaeology by pulling at the threads of contemporary life has proved at least partially correct.

Africa may not have Europe's archives or South-east Asia's breadth of surviving ancient material culture, but it has developed its own mechanisms for capturing history and celebrating its past. I found that a substantial amount of the story of the continent can be partially mapped through surviving traditions, skills and customs.

And, thankfully, there continues to be a near pan-continental acceptance that investment in the maintenance of these indigenous customs is, at least theoretically, a good thing. The reality is that some of this surviving culture is vulnerable to the pressures of contemporary life, to political manipulation and poor resourcing. But oral histories and the material culture of the distant past remain sufficiently in evidence to make deep and fulfilling historical investigation possible for most travellers.

In my pursuit of the material culture and these oral histories, I seemed to spend a lot of my late afternoons sitting out under the branches of silk cotton trees listening to many wonderful people recounting their histories. Perhaps the most memorable was Irene Odetei, a formidable ex-Legon professor who is one of those powerful Ghanaian women who seem scared of nothing, and of no one. She has been an ally of the truth throughout her life, contributing to the post-colonial reconstruction of the official Asante history while simultaneously, like many women, becoming a custodian of an unofficial people's history. We sat out on the lawns of the Asantehene's palace as the sun was beginning to turn a late-afternoon gold, luring clouds of fat dusty moths up into the branches of a giant silk cotton tree. It was a perfect setting to listen to oral testimony. I was keen to understand the last days of Asante's independent rule, and she was keen for me to understand the people's story.

Irene's favoured history was not the received history of kings and gold. She retold the history through the parallel trajectory of women, through Yaa Asantewaa, the Asante Queen Mother who through strategic political marriages built the platform to secure the Golden Stool for her son, and who in the face of British encroachments led an active campaign of rejuvenation and reunification of the Asante. At least in part, Yaa Asantewaa's early successes came about because she knew how to harness the power of storytelling, the power of conversation in marketplaces, the power of gossip among farmers, the power of tales between fishermen, the power of women who hold court around hearths. It is an African world that continues to be important even in the face

The Queen Mother of Asante, early twentieth century.

of contemporary change, and it is a network that preserves important elements of the continent's history. It reminded me of something that the Queen Mother of Bekwai, one of the old generation of Asante dignitaries, said to me: 'It is the women of Asante who hold our story together, who bind families and build communities. It is strong women who encourage men to be as great as they can be, who nurture children, who keep the farms, who hold the lineage and the family together.' As she said the words, she was bristling with passion.

Looking for Lost Kingdoms in Africa, I became fascinated by the sexual and social politics beneath the history, and the way in which there always has been a rich seam of historical narrative curated and preserved by ordinary people. And that seems to remain true. The history does not just reside in universities and books, there is a vein of thriving, living oral history that is vital to telling the complex story of the contemporary continent. That people's story continues to be loved and relevant, not just because it reflects the history of fascinating personalities, but also because many of the same conditions, issues, scenarios and motivations that triggered major events in ancient times seem to resonate today. The battle for resources that drove the politics of ancient Sudan continues; the doctrinal ructions that destabilized the big Moroccan kingdoms still resonate; the inter-ethnic struggles that fuelled the development of eighteenth-century South Africa and the tension between regional ethnic sociology and broader pan-regional politics in West Africa still endure. These narratives continue to act as an adhesive that binds societies together, as forces that underpin identity, and as a medium that holds the narrative continuum. That is best seen in the thriving traditions for recording and preserving history. So for contemporary South Africa, Sudan, Morocco, Zimbabwe and Uganda these histories of Lost Kingdoms remain as loved and incendiary for many of the internet generation as they were for their forefathers.

I began with a hypothesis that some of the continent's history remains out there in the African ambience, and I have enjoyed every moment of interrogating that thought. If you get the opportunity, I would recommend that you experiment yourself. Travelling in Africa can be tough, it can be challenging, but it is enormously rewarding. New archaeological thinking continues to reveal what oral history has always celebrated: this is a continent with a rich, complex and diverse history that we could all benefit from knowing better. From the largest mud-brick buildings and the most ancient ceramics to the oldest forms of continuous Christian tradition, Africa is so much more than what conventional media chooses to tell us. From its earliest times, it has pushed boundaries of thinking and creativity to produce astounding things. Meeting the descendants of the people who made this history, watching them animate the past through their customs, seeing the material substantiation of this history recovered, and gaining an understanding of the rich context of its creation can be enormously uplifting. So if you get the chance . . .

Acknowledgements

I would like to thank the many and varied people who helped with and inspired this project, including the teams at the BBC, IWC, PFD and Transworld.

I would also like to thank all the wonderful people that I shared my journeys with, particularly those who contributed many of the photographs that illustrate the text. And I must not forget the seemingly bottomless well of humbling African expertise and encouragement that was so ceaselessly forthcoming at every stage of this project.

Thank you.

Picture Acknowledgements

The maps on pages vi, 14, 46, 78, 124, 160, 206, 240 and 284 are by Tom Coulson at Encompass Graphics.

Photo credits
Endpapers (hardback edition only), kente cloth: Adire African Textiles, London.

In the text
Watercolours by Gus Casley-Hayford: viii, 22, 61, 147, 183, 247, 301, 306; Werner Forman Archive: 36; George Rodger/Magnum Photos: 42; Getty Images: 50 (both), 54, 121; © Mary Evans Picture Library/Alamy: 73; Popperfoto/Getty Images: 88; © The Trustees of the British Museum: 108, 204, 209, 235; Mary Evans Picture Library: 113; De Agostini/Getty Images: 141; Library of Congress, Washington D.C.: 155; © The British Library/Heritage Images: 173 top; © Iziko Museum/Africa Media Online: 173 bottom; Stapleton Historical Collection/Heritage Images: 177; National Army Museum/Bridgeman Art Library: 200; © The Art Archive/Alamy: 222; © The British Library Board: 254; MS 455/3/106 © RAI: 263; © The Print Collector/Alamy: 278; Hulton-Deutsch Collection/Corbis: 323.

Colour sections
(Images are listed clockwise from top left.)

First section
Part of a tomb wall: © The Trustees of the British Museum.
Kerma and cow relief: Gus Casley-Hayford; desert hotel: Almudena Garcia Parrado; pyramids, Meroë: David Wilson; view from Jebel Barkal: Gus Casley-Hayford; dancers: Getty Images.
Ascent of Debra Damo: both Almudena Garcia Parrado; Debra Damo summit and illuminated manuscript, Honey Church: both Gus Casley-Hayford; priest with mead and congregation outside Honey Church: both Almudena Garcia Parrado; parishioners climbing: Gus Casley-Hayford.
Yeha and angels: both Gus Casley-Hayford; tabots, Aksum: Almudena Garcia Parrado;

priest holding crosses: Gus Casely-Hayford; Church of St George, Lalibella: Almudena Garcia Parrado.

Stele at Aksum and window, Lalibella: both Almudena Garcia Parrado; monkey-heads, Debra Damo, photo and watercolour: both Gus Casely-Hayford.

Second section
Football crowd entertainer: Peter Prada.

Drummers: Peter Prada; all remaining photos: Victoria Balfour.

Early-morning mist on the river and dhow: Ishbel Hall; Kilwa coins: © The Trustees of the British Museum; mosque at Kilwa, interior and exterior: © STR/Reuters/Corbis.

Zimbabwe, outer wall and cone-shaped tower: Christopher Scott/Getty Images; curved passage and doorway (bottom left): both Gus Casely-Hayford; doorway in wall: Christopher Scott/Getty Images.

Mapungubwe, aerial view: © Roger de la Harpe/Africa Imagery/Africa Media Online; gold figurines: both © Melita Moloney/Africa Media Online.

Third section
San rock painting: Gus Casely-Hayford.

Zulu soldiers: Gus Casely-Hayford; Battle of Isandlwana by Charles Edwin Fripp, c. 1885: Getty Images/courtesy of the Council, National Army Museum/The Bridgeman Art Library; Cetshwayo, King of the Zulus by Carl Rudolph Sohn, 1882: The Royal Collection © 2011 Her Majesty Queen Elizabeth II/The Bridgeman Art Library; site of the battle of Isandlwana: Gus Casely-Hayford.

Bandigara cliff, granaries: Gus Casely-Hayford; dancers: © Peter Adams/Corbis; mosque at Djenne: Gus Casely-Hayford; author and Kene on motorbike: Michael Simkins; Bandigara cliffs, general view: © Paule Seux/Hemis/Corbis.

Benin bronzes: all Gus Casely-Hayford.

Bronze head of an Oba: © Werner Forman/Corbis; textile: © The Trustees of the British Museum.

Fourth section
Asafo flag: Peter Adler collection.

'The First Day of the Yam Custom' from Mission from Cape Coast Castle to Ashantee by Thomas Bowditch, 1819: © Lambeth Palace Library/The Bridgeman Art Library; twin drummers and group with drummers: Victoria Balfour; gold weight: Henri Crouzet/Thanakra-Paris; royal drums: Gus Casely-Hayford.

Furnace: Victoria Balfour; Asantehene in procession and two views of Asante gold: all Peter Prada; miniature gold stool: Finch & Co.; linguist staff: image © The Metropolitan Museum of Art/Art Resource/Scala, Florence; kente weaving shop: Gus Casely-Hayford.

Aghmat *hammam* and Tinmel interior: Gus Casely-Hayford; Tinmel exterior: age footstock/Robert Harding; tanneries, Fez: Peter Prada; Ait ben Haddou and Qubbat Baudiyyin: both Gus Casely-Hayford.

View, journal and hat: Gus Casely-Hayford.

Index

Page numbers in *italics* denote an illustration

INDEX

Chelmsford, Lieutenant General Lord
198, 199
Christianity
and Buganda 117
and Ethiopia 10, 55–6, 66, 67, 71–2,
74
and Uganda 117–18
Chwezi 84, 85, 90, 91–3, 94, 95, 97,
122
Cisse, Amadou 225, 226–7, 228, 229,
230
clay figures (Ghana) 246–8, 247, 249
cloth 5–6
kente 269–71
kpokpo funeral 5
cobra 31
communication systems, in Africa 20–1
Congo 114–15
Conrad, Joseph
Heart of Darkness 208
Cultural Centre (Bonwire) 270

da Gama, Vasco 140
Dama ritual 219–20
Darfur 39
Debra Berhan Selassie church (Gondar)
62
Debra Damo church (Ethiopia) 68–71,
72
Deffufa (Kerma) 24–5, 27
Dembele, Adamo 214
Denkyira 259
Dennet, R. E. 21
desertification 287
dhows 129
diamond rush (South Africa) 194–6
Dimbleby, Jonathan 47
Dingane, king 188, 189–90, 191–2, 194
Diogenes 130
Djenné 227–31, 238
Dogon 216, 219–23, 233
blacksmithing 224–5
burial chambers 218
and Dama ritual 219–20
granary doors 221, 222
Dolo, Kene 215–16, 218, 220, 221, 223

Donkoh, Dr Wilhelmina 252
Doukki Gel (Kush) 24
drums/drumming 20–1
and Asante 262–5, 263, 280, 282
and Buganda 98–102
Duggan-Cronin 196
dundun (drum) 264, 280, 282
Dungu (god) 101
Durban 185

East African coast see Swahili coast
Egyptians 9, 17, 29
conquering of by Nubia 32–4, 45
invasion of Nubia 29, 31–2
Elmina 274, 275
Erythraean Sea 128, 129, 132, 133, 135
Eshowe 165
Ethiopia 9–10, 47–76
Aksum stelae 72–4, 73
alliance between Christians and
Muslims under Fasiladas 58
and Ark of the Covenant 10, 52, 56,
71
and battle of Adwa 49, 50, 51–2
cave churches 63–4
and Christianity 10, 55–6, 66, 67,
71–2, 74
Debra Damo church 68–71, 72
early human development 67
ending of Selassie's rule 48
famine 47
flag 48
founding by son of Solomon and
Sheba legend 52–3, 56, 76
Gondar castle 59–60, 61, 62, 70
honey wine of communion 64
and Judaism 56
and Kebra Nagast 52–3, 65, 66
Lalibela churches 65–6
links between Old Testament and
royal family 53, 60, 62, 76
map 46
and Portuguese 58–9
war with Italy 49–51
Ethiopian Church 55, 56, 58
Eureka (diamond) 194

334

ikwla 178
ilobola 171
Indian Ocean 128, 129, 130, 132, 136, 140
inkhata 189
Inneh, Ikponmwusa 237
Ireli (Mali) 219–23
ironworking 37, 225, 230
irrigation system, Sijilmasa 293–4
Isaacs, Nathaniel 186
Isandlhwana, battle of (1879) 198–9
Islam 229, 230, 232
  and Berbers 290
Island of Menouthis 130
Italy
  war with Ethiopia 49–51
Iyasu, emperor 62
izimpondo zankoma see horns of the
  buffalo formation

Jebel Barkal 29–34
  Amun Temple 30–1
  cobra carved into mountain 31, 33
  Taharka's temple 33–4
Jenné-jeno 225–8
jihad 292, 300
Judaism 56

Kabalega, king 109–10, 119, 120
Kabugozza, Omutaka 104
Kadugli 40
Kagula 102
Kambala (dance) 44–5
Kampala (Uganda) 97–9, 117
Kampala Stadium 80–2
Kamuhangire, Dr Ephraim 92
Karikari, Kofi 275, 276
Kathimuni, Ndlovu 188
Kebra Nagast ('The Glory of the Kings') 52–3, 65, 66
Kenkpeyeng, Dr Benjamin 246, 248, 249
kente cloth 269–70
Kerma (Nubai) 24–9
  and cattle 28–9
  Deffufa 24–5, 27

destruction of by desert 37
Eastern cemetery 27–8
extent of kingdom 27
and human sacrifice 28
pottery 25–6
Khartoum 15, 17, 21
kheterra 293, 296
Kibiro salt fields (Uganda) 95
Killie Campbell Library (Durban) 187
Kilwa Kisiwani 136–40, 154, 158
  Great Mosque of 139
Kimberley 194, 195, 196
Kimberley, Lord 195
Kitara 84, 85–6, 89, 91, 96, 122
Knidri, Professor Mohamed 289–90
Koutoubia Mosque (Marrakesh) 312
kpokpo funeral cloth 5
Kumase (Ghana) 250, 261, 268, 275, 279–80
KwaZulu-Natal 165, 168

Lalibela 64–5
Lalibela churches 65–7
Lalibela, emperor 64–6, 67
Last of the Nuba, The (film) 41
leather production (Fez) 314–16
leopard 223
Leopold II, king 114
Lhote, André 208
Limpopo river 148
Lion temple (Naga) 35
Livingston, David 114
lizard mask 220, 221
Lugard 119

McGregor Museum (Kimberley) 195
Maimonides, Moses 317
Malendela 167
Mali 213–31, 249
'Mama' 102–3
Mansa Musa, emperor 231
al-Mansur, Sultan Ya'qub 311, 318, 319
Manyikeni (Mozambique) 140–5, 153
Mapungubwe (South Africa) 145–52, 153
Marrakesh (Morocco) 288–90, 299–302,

ABOUT THE AUTHOR

Gus Casely-Hayford is a curator and cultural historian and is the former Executive Director of Arts Strategy for Arts Council England. He is currently a Research Associate at the University of London's School of African and Oriental Studies (SOAS). He has presented arts programmes for the BBC and Channel 4, including *The Miracle of British Art* in 2010. He is a member of Tate Britain's Council, a Trustee of the National Portrait Gallery and a Clore Fellow. Gus has lectured at the Royal College of Art, Sotheby's Institute of Art and Goldsmiths College, and gained a Ph.D. in African History from SOAS, London University. Gus presents *The Lost Kingdoms of Africa* for the BBC, now in its second series.